Mastering Efficiency: A Guide to Process Management in Operating Systems

Table of Content

Chapter 1: Introduction to Process Management

- Definition and importance of process management in operating systems.

- Explanation of crucial terms such as processes, threads, and multitasking.

- Historical context and the evolution of process management in operating systems.

- Differentiating between foreground and background processes.

- Exploring the life cycle of a process, including states like ready, running, and blocked.

- In-depth analysis of the PCB and its role in managing processes.

- Introduction to concepts of concurrency and parallelism in process management.

- Overview of IPC methods for processes to exchange data and information.

- Identifying common challenges such as deadlock and contention.

- Real-world examples demonstrating the impact of effective process management.

Chapter 2: The Fundamentals of Operating Systems

- Defining an operating system and its role in computer systems.

- Exploring the kernel, shell, and file system components.

- Overview of different types such as batch, time-sharing, and distributed systems.

- Breaking down the architecture into layers and modules.

- Understanding the structure of file systems and directories.

- Exploring command-line interfaces (CLI) and graphical user interfaces (GUI).

- The role of device drivers in communication between hardware and the operating system.

- Overview of security features such as authentication and authorization.

- Introduction to system calls and their importance in facilitating communication between applications and the operating system.

- Analyzing notable operating systems and their impact on the evolution of computing.

Chapter 3: Synchronization Techniques for Seamless Operations

- Defining synchronization and its significance in multi-process environments.
- Understanding race conditions and critical sections in concurrent processes.
- In-depth exploration of semaphores and mutexes as synchronization mechanisms.
- Analyzing the concept of deadlock and strategies for prevention.
- Exploring methods for controlling concurrent access to shared resources.
- Overview of synchronization models, including producer-consumer and reader-writer.
- Understanding synchronization challenges in multithreading environments.
- Challenges and strategies in synchronizing processes across distributed systems.
- Examining the performance implications of synchronization techniques.
- Real-world examples illustrating the impact of effective synchronization.

Chapter 4: Task Scheduling Strategies for Optimal Performance

- Defining task scheduling and its role in optimizing system performance.
- Exploring different scheduling algorithms such as FCFS, Round Robin, and Priority Scheduling.
- Understanding the concept of multilevel queue scheduling.
- Exploring real-time scheduling requirements and challenges.
- Scheduling challenges in multithreading environments.
- Importance of load balancing in distributed systems.
- The role of interrupts in task scheduling.
- Exploring dynamic scheduling techniques based on system workload.
- Challenges and strategies in scheduling tasks in cloud computing environments.
- Analyzing instances where effective task scheduling contributed to system efficiency.

Chapter 5: Memory Management in Operating Systems

- Defining memory management and its critical role in system performance.
- Understanding the concept of address spaces and memory segmentation.
- Exploring memory allocation techniques such as contiguous and non-contiguous allocation.
- Introduction to virtual memory and its importance in modern operating systems.
- In-depth analysis of page replacement algorithms like LRU and FIFO.
- The role of memory mapping in linking files to memory locations.
- Importance of memory protection in preventing unauthorized access.
- Challenges posed by fragmented memory and strategies for compaction.
- Synchronization challenges in managing memory for concurrent processes.

Chapter 6: I/O Management: Enhancing System Interactions

- Defining I/O management and its role in facilitating communication between the system and external devices.
- Overview of different I/O devices and their controllers.
- Understanding the role of device drivers in mediating communication between the operating system and hardware.
- The importance of I/O scheduling in optimizing data transfer between devices and the system.
- Exploring buffering mechanisms to enhance data transfer efficiency.
- Strategies for managing interrupts generated by I/O devices.
- The role of DMA in improving data transfer speed between devices and memory.
- Identifying common errors in I/O operations and strategies for error detection and recovery.
- Challenges and strategies in managing I/O in distributed and networked systems.
- Analyzing instances where effective I/O management contributed to enhanced system performance.

Chapter 7: Error Handling and Fault Tolerance

- Defining the importance of error handling in maintaining system stability.
- Identification and classification of common errors in operating systems.
- Exploring techniques for detecting errors in processes, memory, and I/O operations.
- Strategies for recovering from errors and restoring system functionality.
- The concept of fault tolerance and its significance in critical systems.
- Implementing redundancy through backup systems and data replication.
- Techniques for rolling back processes and recovering from system failures.
- Importance of maintaining error logs for diagnostic purposes.
- Methods for predicting potential errors before they occur.
- Analyzing historical instances where effective error handling and fault tolerance saved critical systems.

Chapter 8: Future Trends in Operating System Process Management

- Setting the stage for exploring emerging trends in operating system process management.
- Examining the role of AI in optimizing process management.
- The influence of blockchain technology on distributed process management.
- Evolving security measures to combat modern threats.
- Exploring the potential impact of quantum computing on process optimization.
- Strategies for designing energy-efficient operating systems.
- The rise of edge computing and its implications for process management.
- The integration of human-centric design principles in process management.
- Strategies for developing eco-friendly operating systems.
- Encouraging readers to stay informed and adapt to the evolving landscape of computing.

Introduction

Embarking on the immersive journey of "Mastering Efficiency: A Guide to Process Management in Operating Systems" opens a gateway to the dynamic realm of technology, where the optimization of processes within operating systems stands as a linchpin for seamless functionality. In this ever-evolving landscape, the significance of comprehending and refining these processes cannot be overstated. This comprehensive guide, crafted with precision and insight, extends its reach to both novices entering the domain and seasoned professionals seeking to deepen their understanding.

As we navigate the complexities of modern operating systems, the initial chapters serve as a foundational exploration, introducing the very essence of process management. Concepts such as multitasking, the life cycle of a process, and the intricacies of interprocess communication lay the groundwork for a thorough comprehension of the subject matter. Whether one is a newcomer seeking to grasp the basics or a seasoned professional looking to reinforce their foundational knowledge, these introductory chapters cater to diverse levels of expertise.

The subsequent sections delve into more advanced topics, offering a meticulous examination of the intricacies involved in process management. Memory management, a crucial facet in optimizing system performance, unfolds in detail, covering aspects such as virtual memory, paging, and segmentation. The guide then navigates into the terrain of file systems, exploring how data is organized, stored, and retrieved, providing invaluable insights for those engaged in designing and maintaining file structures.

Device management, an integral component in the orchestration of operating systems, is given due consideration, unraveling the complexities of device drivers, I/O operations, and interrupt handling. Security and protection mechanisms form yet another critical juncture, and the guide meticulously dissects topics such as access control, authentication, and encryption, illuminating pathways for fortifying the robustness of operating systems against potential threats.

User interface design, a facet often overlooked but crucial for user experience, is explored in depth, emphasizing the significance of creating intuitive and user-friendly interfaces. The landscape expands further with an exploration of distributed systems, real-time systems, and the design and implementation of operating systems, providing a holistic understanding of the broader ecosystem.

As the journey unfolds, the guide embraces practical applications, bridging theory with real-world scenarios. Concepts such as troubleshooting, performance optimization, and adapting to evolving technologies serve as invaluable tools for professionals seeking to implement their knowledge in practical settings. This bridge between theory and practice enhances the guide's relevance, ensuring its applicability in a rapidly evolving technological landscape.

In the ever-accelerating pace of technological advancements, staying abreast of current trends is imperative. Therefore, the guide concludes with a forward-looking perspective, touching upon emerging technologies, paradigms, and challenges within the realm of operating systems. This foresight equips both newcomers and seasoned practitioners with the tools to navigate the future landscape with adaptability and innovation.

In essence, "Mastering Efficiency: A Guide to Process Management in Operating Systems" is not merely a guide but a journey—an odyssey through the heart of technology, where efficiency is the compass guiding us through the ever-shifting landscapes of operating systems. With its comprehensive coverage, practical insights, and forward-looking approach, this guide becomes an indispensable companion for those who seek mastery in the dynamic and ever-evolving world of process management within operating systems.

Chapter 1: Introduction to Process Management

Definition and importance of process management in operating systems.

Process management in operating systems refers to the efficient control and coordination of tasks, or processes, within a computer system. It is a critical aspect of operating system design and functionality, playing a pivotal role in ensuring the smooth and concurrent execution of multiple applications. At its core, process management involves the creation, scheduling, synchronization, and termination of processes, contributing to the overall efficiency, responsiveness, and reliability of the operating system.

One of the fundamental aspects of process management is process creation. When a user initiates an application, the operating system creates a corresponding process, allocating the necessary resources and establishing a separate execution environment. This ensures that different tasks can run independently without interfering with each other. The ability to create and manage processes enables the operating system to support multitasking, allowing users to run multiple applications simultaneously.

Scheduling is another crucial aspect of process management, influencing the order and duration of process execution. The operating system employs scheduling algorithms to allocate CPU time to different processes, optimizing resource utilization and ensuring fairness. Effective scheduling contributes to improved system responsiveness, reduced latency, and enhanced overall performance. Real-time operating systems, in particular, rely heavily on precise scheduling to meet stringent timing requirements for tasks such as industrial control systems and robotics.

Synchronization and communication mechanisms are vital components of process management, facilitating cooperation and data exchange between concurrently executing processes. Operating systems employ various synchronization techniques, such as semaphores and mutexes, to manage access to shared resources and prevent conflicts. Effective synchronization ensures the integrity of data and coordination between processes, enhancing the reliability and correctness of the overall system.

Process termination is the final stage in process management, involving the release of allocated resources and the removal of terminated processes from the system. Proper termination mechanisms are essential to prevent resource leaks and ensure the efficient use of system resources. The operating system must manage the graceful termination of processes, handling any open files, releasing allocated memory, and updating relevant data structures.

Memory management is intricately linked to process management, as each process requires a designated space in the system's memory. The operating system must allocate and deallocate memory dynamically to accommodate varying process sizes and prevent conflicts. Efficient memory management contributes to system stability, preventing issues such as memory leaks or insufficient memory for critical processes.

Error handling and recovery mechanisms are crucial elements of process management, ensuring the robustness and fault tolerance of the operating system. When errors occur during process execution, the operating system must identify and handle them appropriately to prevent system crashes or data corruption. Effective error handling enhances the reliability of the system, minimizing downtime and providing a more resilient computing environment.

Security is a paramount concern in modern computing environments, and process management plays a key role in enforcing access controls and protecting sensitive information. Operating systems implement security measures at the process level, defining permissions and privileges to regulate access to resources. Process isolation is essential to prevent unauthorized access and ensure the integrity of user data, making process management a cornerstone of overall system security.

In a distributed computing environment, process management becomes even more complex as processes may run on multiple interconnected machines. Coordinating processes across a network requires sophisticated communication and synchronization mechanisms to maintain consistency and coherence. Distributed process management is crucial for achieving scalability and fault tolerance in large-scale systems.

In conclusion, process management is a foundational aspect of operating system design, influencing the efficiency, reliability, and security of computer systems. Through the creation, scheduling, synchronization, and termination of processes, the operating system orchestrates the execution of diverse tasks, enabling multitasking and ensuring a seamless user experience. Effective process management is essential for optimizing resource utilization, enhancing system responsiveness, and facilitating error handling and recovery. As computing environments continue to evolve, with the advent of technologies such as cloud computing and the Internet of Things, the importance of robust and adaptable process management becomes increasingly evident, shaping the foundation of modern operating systems.

Explanation of crucial terms such as processes, threads, and multitasking.

Processes, threads, and multitasking are fundamental concepts in the realm of computer science and operating systems, playing pivotal roles in shaping the way modern computing systems operate. A process, in the context of computing, can be viewed as an independent program in execution. It represents a dynamic entity with its own memory space, code, data, and system resources. Processes provide a level of isolation, allowing multiple applications to run concurrently without interfering with each other. The operating system, responsible for process management, oversees the creation, scheduling, synchronization, and termination of processes, ensuring efficient resource utilization and system responsiveness.

Within the broader context of processes, threads emerge as a finer-grained unit of execution. A thread represents the smallest unit of a process that can be scheduled by the operating system. Unlike processes, threads within the same process share the same memory space and resources, allowing for more lightweight communication and coordination between them. Threads enable parallelism within a process, enabling the execution of multiple tasks simultaneously. This concurrency at the thread level is particularly beneficial in scenarios where tasks can be decomposed into smaller, independent units that can be executed in parallel, improving overall system performance and responsiveness.

Multitasking, a concept closely related to processes, refers to the ability of an operating system to execute multiple tasks concurrently. It allows users to run several applications or processes simultaneously, providing the illusion that they are all executing at the same time. Multitasking is achieved through the rapid switching of the CPU's attention between different processes or threads, giving each a time slice for execution. This interleaved execution creates the perception of concurrent execution, even on systems with a single processor core. Multitasking is a cornerstone of modern computing environments, enabling users to perform a multitude of tasks seamlessly and efficiently.

In the context of multitasking, there are two primary types: pre-emptive multitasking and cooperative multitasking. Pre-emptive multitasking, prevalent in modern operating systems, involves the operating system forcibly interrupting and suspending the execution of a process or thread to allocate CPU time to another. This pre-emptive approach ensures fairness and responsiveness, preventing a single misbehaving process from monopolizing system resources. On the other hand, cooperative multitasking relies on processes or threads voluntarily yielding control to the operating system, requiring a higher degree of coordination among concurrently executing tasks. While cooperative multitasking can be more efficient in certain scenarios, it is also more prone to issues such as deadlock if not managed carefully.

The concept of processes, threads, and multitasking becomes particularly significant in addressing the challenges posed by the increasing complexity and diversity of modern computing environments. As computer systems evolve, incorporating multiple processors or cores, the effective utilization of parallelism becomes essential for achieving optimal performance. Threads, with their ability to execute concurrently within a process, provide a means to harness this parallelism and exploit the capabilities of multi-core architectures. This adaptability is crucial in scenarios ranging from scientific computing and data processing to multimedia applications, where the efficient handling of concurrent tasks is paramount.

Moreover, in the context of distributed computing and networked systems, the management of processes and threads takes on added complexity. The coordination and communication between processes running on different machines require sophisticated mechanisms to ensure consistency and reliability. Distributed systems leverage concepts such as remote procedure calls and message passing to facilitate communication between processes, enabling the seamless integration of computing resources across a network. This distributed nature further emphasizes the importance of effective process and thread management to achieve scalability, fault tolerance, and responsiveness in large-scale, interconnected computing environments.

In conclusion, processes, threads, and multitasking are foundational concepts in computer science and operating systems, shaping the landscape of modern computing. Processes represent independent units of execution, threads offer finer-grained concurrency within processes, and multitasking enables the concurrent execution of multiple tasks. The effective management of processes and threads is essential for achieving optimal system performance, responsiveness, and adaptability in the face of evolving computing paradigms. As technology continues to advance, the significance of these concepts persists, influencing the design and functionality of operating systems across a diverse range of computing environments.

Historical context and the evolution of process management in operating systems.

The historical evolution of process management in operating systems reflects the continual quest to enhance the efficiency, reliability, and functionality of computing systems. Early computing systems, characterized by a single-user environment and batch processing, lacked the need for sophisticated process management. The introduction of multiprogramming in the 1950s marked a significant milestone, allowing multiple programs to be loaded into the computer's memory concurrently. However, these early systems had limited support for process isolation and lacked the capability to execute multiple tasks simultaneously.

The advent of time-sharing systems in the 1960s brought about a paradigm shift in process management. Time-sharing allowed multiple users to interact with a computer simultaneously, with the operating system rapidly switching between different tasks. This development laid the foundation for the concept of multitasking, enabling the illusion of concurrent execution and significantly improving user interaction. The Compatible Time-Sharing System (CTSS) and later, the Multics project, played pivotal roles in advancing the capabilities of time-sharing operating systems, introducing features like dynamic process creation and interactive user interfaces.

The 1970s witnessed the emergence of microprocessors and the development of personal computers. With these advancements, the demand for more sophisticated process management capabilities grew. Operating systems like Unix, born at Bell Labs, became pioneers in process management, introducing the fork() system call for process creation and the concept of lightweight processes known as threads. Unix's modular design and emphasis on process isolation laid the groundwork for subsequent operating systems, influencing their approach to process management.

The late 1970s and 1980s saw the rise of personal computing, with operating systems like Microsoft's MS-DOS and Apple's Macintosh System Software becoming prevalent. While these early systems lacked robust multitasking support, they set the stage for the graphical user interfaces that would become integral to modern computing. The shift towards graphical environments in the 1990s, exemplified by Microsoft Windows and Apple's Mac OS, presented new challenges and opportunities for process management. These operating systems introduced preemptive multitasking, allowing for more seamless execution of graphical applications and improving system responsiveness.

The 1990s also witnessed the rise of networked computing and the Internet, leading to the development of distributed systems. Operating systems like Windows NT and Novell NetWare introduced features to manage processes across networked environments, enabling remote communication and coordination. The client-server model became prevalent, and process management extended beyond the confines of a single machine to encompass distributed computing scenarios.

The turn of the millennium marked a significant shift towards mobile computing and the proliferation of devices with diverse architectures. Operating systems for mobile platforms, such as Android and iOS, faced unique challenges in terms of resource constraints and power efficiency. Process management on these platforms evolved to optimize battery life, memory usage, and responsiveness, introducing techniques like background process prioritization and application sandboxing to enhance user experience and system stability.

In parallel, server-oriented operating systems underwent transformations to accommodate the demands of cloud computing. Virtualization technologies became widespread, allowing multiple virtual machines to run on a single physical server. This shift introduced new challenges and opportunities in process management, as hypervisors needed to efficiently allocate resources and ensure isolation between virtualized environments.

The 2010s witnessed the resurgence of interest in containerization, led by technologies like Docker. Containerization introduced a lightweight and portable approach to process management, encapsulating applications and their dependencies in isolated environments. This development revolutionized the deployment and scalability of applications, influencing modern operating systems and reshaping the landscape of cloud-native computing.

The evolution of process management has been closely tied to advancements in hardware architecture, user interface paradigms, and the changing demands of computing environments. Operating systems have continually adapted to meet the challenges posed by new technologies, from the early days of mainframes to the era of cloud computing and edge computing. Concepts such as process isolation, preemptive multitasking, and support for parallelism have become integral to the design and functionality of contemporary operating systems, reflecting the ongoing quest for optimal resource utilization, responsiveness, and adaptability in the ever-evolving world of computing.

Differentiating between foreground and background processes.

Foreground and background processes are fundamental concepts in operating systems, representing distinct states of execution that influence the user experience and system functionality. In the context of a computing environment, a foreground process refers to a task or application that actively engages the user and occupies the primary focus of the system. This can include applications with graphical user interfaces, command-line programs requiring user input, or any process that demands direct user interaction. Foreground processes typically run in the foreground of the user interface, and the operating system dedicates significant resources to ensure their responsiveness and smooth execution.

Conversely, background processes operate discreetly and independently of direct user interaction. These processes are designed to execute tasks without requiring immediate user input or attention. Background processes often perform system maintenance, handle automated tasks, or carry out operations that can run in the background without hindering the user's primary activities. Examples include system updates, file backups, or network services that operate continuously in the background to support various functionalities. Background processes are essential for maintaining the health and efficiency of the system but are intentionally designed to operate inconspicuously to avoid disrupting the user experience.

The differentiation between foreground and background processes becomes more pronounced in multitasking environments, where the operating system manages the concurrent execution of multiple processes. In such scenarios, users can interact with foreground processes while background processes continue to run concurrently. This capability enhances the overall user experience, allowing individuals to perform various tasks simultaneously without waiting for each operation to complete sequentially. Multitasking is a cornerstone of modern operating systems, enabling users to run multiple applications concurrently, switch between them seamlessly, and maintain a responsive computing environment.

Foreground processes typically have a higher priority in terms of resource allocation, ensuring that the user's immediate interactions receive prompt attention from the operating system. This prioritization is crucial for providing a responsive and interactive user interface. Background processes, on the other hand, often have lower priority to avoid impacting the performance of foreground tasks. Operating systems implement scheduling algorithms to allocate CPU time effectively, ensuring that both foreground and background processes can coexist without unduly compromising system responsiveness.

In graphical user interfaces (GUIs), foreground processes are often associated with the windows and applications actively in use, visible on the user's screen. Users can interact with these foreground applications, manipulating data, executing commands, or navigating through menus. The responsiveness of foreground processes is a key factor in delivering a positive user experience, and the operating system prioritizes their execution to maintain smooth interactions.

Background processes, while not directly visible to the user, contribute significantly to the overall health and functionality of the system. They may include tasks such as automatic updates, antivirus scans, or routine system maintenance. Background processes are designed to operate efficiently without requiring constant user oversight, enhancing the system's reliability and security. In server environments, background processes may include tasks like managing network services, handling file transfers, or monitoring system health.

Foreground and background processes also play crucial roles in the context of job control and terminal sessions. In a command-line interface (CLI), foreground processes are those actively running in the terminal, and they typically require user input. Background processes, on the other hand, can be started with an "&" symbol in the command, allowing them to execute independently while the user continues to interact with the terminal. This capability is particularly useful for running long-running tasks without tying up the terminal session.

The distinction between foreground and background processes becomes especially relevant in scenarios where system resources are limited. In resource-constrained environments, such as embedded systems or low-powered devices, effective management of foreground and background processes becomes crucial for optimizing performance. The operating system must strike a balance between prioritizing user interactions, maintaining system stability, and ensuring the execution of essential background tasks.

Moreover, the concept of foreground and background processes extends to the realm of mobile computing, where devices often operate with constrained resources and varied user interactions. Mobile operating systems manage foreground processes associated with active applications, allowing users to engage with their devices seamlessly. Background processes on mobile devices may include tasks like synchronization, push notifications, or location tracking, contributing to the overall functionality and convenience of mobile applications.

In conclusion, the differentiation between foreground and background processes is a foundational aspect of operating systems, influencing the user experience, system performance, and overall functionality. Foreground processes demand immediate user attention, often through graphical interfaces or command-line interactions, while background processes operate discreetly to perform automated or maintenance tasks. The effective management of foreground and background processes is essential for creating responsive, multitasking computing environments that cater to diverse user needs while ensuring the reliability and health of the underlying system.

Exploring the life cycle of a process, including states like ready, running, and blocked.

The life cycle of a process is a dynamic and intricate journey, encompassing various states and transitions as it moves through different phases of execution within an operating system. At its inception, a process is born during the creation phase. This phase involves the allocation of essential resources, such as memory space and initial values for registers, to enable the process to execute. The process then transitions into the ready state, eagerly awaiting its turn to be executed on the CPU. In the ready state, the process is prepared for execution, but it is not actively utilizing the CPU.

As the operating system's scheduler selects the process for execution, it enters the running state. This is the phase where the process's instructions are actively executed on the CPU. The running state is characterized by the process actively consuming CPU resources to perform its designated tasks. This phase continues until the process either voluntarily yields control, such as through an I/O operation or a system call, or until the scheduler decides to preempt the process to allow another to run. Voluntary relinquishing of control is common when a process requires input or output operations or when it needs to wait for a particular event to occur.

Upon relinquishing control, the process may transition to the blocked state. In the blocked state, the process is temporarily suspended, waiting for a specific event or resource to become available. This event could be the completion of an I/O operation, a response from a user, or the availability of a resource previously locked by another process. While in the blocked state, the process is not actively utilizing the CPU, allowing other processes in the ready state to be scheduled for execution.

When the awaited event occurs or the required resource becomes available, the process transitions back to the ready state, rejoining the pool of processes awaiting CPU execution. The operating system's scheduler then determines the next process to be executed, considering factors such as process priority, time-sharing algorithms, and system load. The selected process returns to the running state, resuming its execution on the CPU.

The life cycle of a process continues as it moves through these states, alternating between ready, running, and blocked, depending on the nature of its tasks and the occurrence of relevant events. This cyclical movement is known as process scheduling, a critical aspect of operating system management that aims to efficiently utilize system resources and maintain responsiveness.

Termination marks the conclusion of a process's life cycle. A process may terminate voluntarily, completing its tasks and releasing allocated resources, or involuntarily due to an error or system intervention. During termination, the operating system reclaims the resources allocated to the process, including memory space and other system resources. Cleanup tasks may include closing open files, releasing allocated memory, and updating process-related data structures.

Understanding the life cycle of a process is essential for efficient resource management and optimal system performance. Operating systems leverage various scheduling algorithms to determine the order in which processes are executed, taking into account factors such as priority, time constraints, and fairness. Real-time operating systems, which operate in environments with strict timing requirements, employ specialized scheduling techniques to ensure that critical tasks are executed within specified deadlines.

In a multiprocessing or multi-core environment, the life cycle of a process becomes even more intricate. Each processor or core can independently execute processes, allowing for true parallelism. The states of ready, running, and blocked are replicated across each processor, and coordination mechanisms are implemented to ensure synchronization and prevent conflicts between concurrently executing processes.

Moreover, the concept of threads introduces a finer level of granularity to the life cycle of a process. Threads within the same process share the same memory space but can execute independently. Each thread has its own program counter and register values, allowing for concurrent execution within the process. The life cycle of a thread mirrors that of a process, with transitions between ready, running, and blocked states, but within the context of the broader process life cycle.

In conclusion, the life cycle of a process is a dynamic journey, consisting of states like ready, running, and blocked, each with its own significance in the overall functioning of an operating system. The process transitions between these states based on events, resource availability, and the scheduling decisions of the operating system. Understanding the life cycle of a process is fundamental to effective process management, resource allocation, and the creation of responsive, multitasking computing environments.

In-depth analysis of the PCB and its role in managing processes.

The Process Control Block (PCB) is a fundamental data structure within operating systems, serving as a repository of information that encapsulates the essential details about a process and plays a central role in the management of processes. At its core, the PCB is a data structure maintained by the operating system for each active process, holding information necessary for the system to manage and control the process effectively. This information encompasses a wide array of details, including process state, program counter, register values, memory management information, and various accounting and scheduling parameters.

One of the primary roles of the PCB is to store the current state of a process. The state information indicates the phase of execution in which the process currently resides—whether it is in a ready state, actively running on the CPU, or waiting for an event to occur in a blocked state. This state information is crucial for the operating system's scheduler, allowing it to make informed decisions about which processes to run, suspend, or transition between states. The PCB acts as a snapshot of the process's execution context, facilitating context switching and enabling the resumption of a process from where it left off.

The program counter, a key component of the PCB, holds the address of the next instruction to be executed by the process. This information is essential for context switching, ensuring that when a process is resumed, it picks up execution from the correct point. Additionally, the PCB stores the values of various registers associated with the process, preserving the process's CPU state during context switches. The operating system relies on the information stored in the PCB to maintain the integrity of process execution and seamlessly switch between different processes.

Memory management details are another crucial aspect encapsulated within the PCB. This includes information about the process's memory allocation, such as the base and limit registers, which define the range of memory accessible to the process. The operating system utilizes this information to enforce memory protection and isolation between processes. When a process requires additional memory, the PCB is updated accordingly, ensuring that the process can dynamically allocate and deallocate memory during its execution.

The PCB also contains information about open files and I/O devices associated with the process. This includes file descriptors, pointers to open files, and information about the status of ongoing I/O operations. This information is vital for managing file access and ensuring proper synchronization when multiple processes interact with shared files or devices. The operating system relies on the PCB to maintain coherence in file access and prevent conflicts among concurrently executing processes.

Additionally, the PCB plays a crucial role in accounting and resource allocation. Information such as the process ID, parent process ID, user ID, and group ID is stored in the PCB, providing the operating system with the necessary data for tracking and managing processes. Accounting details, such as the amount of CPU time consumed by a process, are also maintained in the PCB. This information is valuable for performance monitoring, billing purposes in a cloud computing environment, and assessing the overall system workload.

The PCB is instrumental in the implementation of process scheduling algorithms. It contains priority levels, scheduling parameters, and information about the process's execution history. These details assist the scheduler in making informed decisions about which process to execute next, considering factors such as priority, deadlines, and fairness. The scheduler consults the PCBs of active processes to determine the most appropriate process to run, facilitating efficient and responsive multitasking in the operating system.

Moreover, the PCB is a key player in inter-process communication and synchronization. When processes need to communicate or coordinate with each other, they may employ mechanisms like message passing or shared memory. The PCB stores information related to inter-process communication, such as message queues, signals, and synchronization primitives. This information allows the operating system to manage communication and synchronization between processes, preventing data corruption and ensuring orderly interactions.

The PCB also plays a pivotal role in process termination. When a process completes its execution or is terminated prematurely, the operating system updates the PCB to reflect the termination status. This involves releasing allocated resources, closing open files, and updating accounting information. The termination details stored in the PCB allow the operating system to perform cleanup tasks and maintain the integrity of the system.

In a multi-threaded environment, where multiple threads within a process share the same address space, each thread has its own thread control block (TCB), a structure similar to the PCB. The TCB contains information specific to the thread, such as the thread ID, program counter, and register values. However, the TCB often shares certain information with the PCB, such as memory management details and file descriptors, to ensure consistency and coordination among threads within the same process.

In conclusion, the Process Control Block is a cornerstone of process management in operating systems, serving as a comprehensive repository of information about each active process. Its multifaceted role encompasses storing the process's execution context, managing memory, facilitating inter-process communication, supporting process scheduling, and enabling efficient resource allocation. The PCB is a linchpin in the seamless and organized execution of processes, contributing to the responsiveness, stability, and functionality of modern operating systems.

Introduction to concepts of concurrency and parallelism in process management.

Concurrency and parallelism are foundational concepts in the domain of process management, representing essential approaches to harnessing the power of modern computing systems for improved performance and efficiency. Concurrency refers to the execution of multiple tasks or processes seemingly simultaneously, allowing for overlapping periods of execution. It introduces the idea that processes can make progress independently and concurrently, enhancing the overall responsiveness of a system. Concurrency is a critical aspect of multitasking operating systems, enabling users to run multiple applications concurrently and switch between them seamlessly. It is achieved through mechanisms such as time-sharing, where the CPU rapidly switches between different processes, giving the illusion of simultaneous execution. Concurrency is particularly valuable in scenarios where tasks can be decomposed into smaller, independent units that can execute concurrently, optimizing resource utilization and reducing overall processing time.

Parallelism, on the other hand, involves the simultaneous execution of multiple tasks or processes to achieve faster and more efficient computation. Unlike concurrency, which primarily focuses on the overlapping of tasks in time, parallelism emphasizes the simultaneous execution of tasks in parallel. This concept is deeply tied to the hardware architecture of a system, leveraging multiple processors or cores to execute tasks concurrently. Parallelism is crucial for tackling computationally intensive problems, as it allows for the division of a task into smaller subtasks that can be executed simultaneously. This simultaneous execution significantly enhances the overall processing speed and computational capacity of a system, making it a fundamental principle in high-performance computing and scientific applications.

In the context of process management, concurrency and parallelism play pivotal roles in shaping the behavior and performance of operating systems. The concurrent execution of processes allows for efficient multitasking, enabling users to interact with multiple applications simultaneously without undue delays. Operating systems employ scheduling algorithms to manage the concurrency of processes, allocating CPU time to different tasks based on priority, time-sharing, and other factors. This approach ensures that processes can make progress in a seemingly simultaneous manner, providing a responsive and interactive user experience.

Parallelism, on the other hand, is closely associated with the hardware architecture of a system. Modern computer systems often feature multiple processors or cores, allowing for parallel execution of tasks. The operating system, through its process management capabilities, must effectively leverage this hardware parallelism to maximize performance. Parallel execution is particularly beneficial for tasks that can be divided into smaller, independent units of work, known as threads. Each thread can be executed in parallel on different processors or cores, significantly improving overall processing speed and throughput.

Threads, a key concept in concurrent and parallel computing, are independent units of execution within a process. They share the same address space, allowing for efficient communication and data sharing. Concurrent threads can run independently within a process, providing a finer level of granularity for achieving concurrency. Parallel threads, on the other hand, can be executed simultaneously on multiple processors or cores, exploiting the hardware parallelism inherent in modern systems. The management of threads involves coordination and synchronization mechanisms to ensure orderly execution and prevent conflicts when threads access shared resources.

Concurrency and parallelism are not mutually exclusive concepts; they often coexist and complement each other in modern computing environments. A multitasking operating system may leverage both concurrency and parallelism to provide an efficient and responsive user experience. For example, multiple processes running concurrently may internally use parallelism by employing threads for parallel execution of specific tasks. This combination of concurrency and parallelism allows for a more sophisticated and adaptable approach to process management.

The management of concurrent and parallel execution requires careful consideration of synchronization, coordination, and resource allocation. Operating systems must implement mechanisms to prevent conflicts when processes or threads access shared resources concurrently. Techniques such as mutual exclusion, semaphores, and locks are employed to ensure that only one process or thread accesses a critical section of code at a time, preventing data corruption and maintaining the integrity of the system. Effective synchronization is crucial for achieving the desired balance between concurrency and parallelism, avoiding issues such as race conditions and deadlocks.

Concurrency and parallelism become particularly significant in addressing the challenges posed by the increasing complexity and diversity of modern computing environments. With the advent of multi-core processors, graphics processing units (GPUs), and distributed computing architectures, the effective management of concurrent and parallel execution becomes essential. In cloud computing environments, where resources are distributed across multiple servers, the coordination of concurrent processes and the exploitation of parallelism are critical for scalability and efficient resource utilization.

The concepts of concurrency and parallelism are also prominent in the development of software applications. Programmers design and implement concurrent and parallel algorithms to optimize the performance of their applications, taking advantage of the capabilities offered by modern hardware. Parallel programming frameworks and libraries provide abstractions and tools to facilitate the development of parallel applications, allowing developers to harness the power of parallelism without delving into low-level details of hardware architecture.

In conclusion, concurrency and parallelism are fundamental concepts in process management, shaping the behavior and performance of operating systems in the face of evolving computing architectures and user expectations. Concurrency enables the simultaneous execution of multiple tasks, improving responsiveness and multitasking capabilities. Parallelism, rooted in hardware architecture, leverages the simultaneous execution of tasks on multiple processors or cores to achieve higher computational throughput. Operating systems must adeptly balance these concepts, employing synchronization mechanisms and resource allocation strategies to ensure the orderly and efficient execution of processes. As technology continues to advance, the effective management of concurrency and parallelism remains a critical aspect of designing and optimizing operating systems for diverse and complex computing environments.

Overview of IPC methods for processes to exchange data and information.

Interprocess communication (IPC) is a crucial aspect of modern operating systems, allowing processes to exchange data and information, collaborate, and synchronize their activities. Various IPC methods have been developed to facilitate communication between processes, each with its own strengths, use cases, and considerations. One of the fundamental IPC mechanisms is the use of shared memory. In shared memory IPC, multiple processes can map a portion of their address space to a common region in physical memory. This shared region allows processes to read and write data directly, enabling efficient and fast communication. However, shared memory requires careful synchronization mechanisms, such as semaphores or mutexes, to avoid conflicts and ensure data integrity when multiple processes access the shared region simultaneously.

Another widely used IPC method is message passing, which involves processes exchanging messages through the operating system. In this model, processes communicate by sending and receiving messages, often through system calls provided by the operating system. Message passing can be implemented using either a synchronous or asynchronous approach. In synchronous message passing, the sender and receiver must be ready to exchange messages simultaneously. In asynchronous message passing, a process can send a message without waiting for the recipient to receive it immediately, allowing for greater flexibility and concurrency. Message passing is versatile and can be implemented using various communication primitives, such as pipes, sockets, and interprocess communication (IPC) mechanisms like signals.

Pipes, a form of IPC, provide a unidirectional communication channel between two processes. One process writes data into the pipe, and another reads from it. Pipes are commonly used for communication between a parent process and its child process, allowing them to share data efficiently. Named pipes, or FIFOs, extend the concept of pipes to enable communication between unrelated processes. Pipes are especially useful for implementing producer-consumer patterns, where one process produces data, and another consumes it. While pipes are straightforward, they are limited to unidirectional communication, and for bidirectional communication, two pipes are needed.

Sockets, a mechanism commonly used in network communication, can also be employed for interprocess communication on the same machine. Socket-based IPC allows processes on the same or different machines to communicate using network protocols like TCP/IP or UDP/IP. Local sockets, or Unix domain sockets, provide a faster alternative for IPC on the same machine without the overhead associated with network communication. Sockets offer a flexible and widely adopted model for IPC, making them suitable for scenarios where processes need to communicate over a network or locally.

Another form of IPC is signals, which are software interrupts used by processes to notify each other about specific events. Processes can send signals to one another, allowing for asynchronous communication. Common signals include SIGINT for interrupt,

SIGSEGV for segmentation fault, and SIGTERM for termination. While signals are lightweight and efficient, they have limitations. For instance, they provide only a basic form of communication, often used for signaling events rather than exchanging data. Moreover, signals can be less reliable for data communication, as they are not designed for large or complex data transfers.

Named semaphores and message queues are advanced IPC mechanisms that provide more sophisticated synchronization and communication capabilities. Semaphores are used to control access to shared resources, acting as counters that multiple processes can increment or decrement. Named semaphores extend this concept to enable synchronization between unrelated processes, offering a powerful tool for coordinating activities. Message queues, on the other hand, allow processes to exchange messages with a queue-like structure. Processes can enqueue messages for other processes to consume asynchronously, providing a robust and efficient way to transfer data between processes.

Remote Procedure Calls (RPC) offer a high-level abstraction for IPC, allowing processes to invoke functions or procedures on a remote machine as if they were local. RPC mechanisms handle the communication details, making it seamless for processes to interact across different machines. This approach is widely used in distributed systems, where processes on separate machines need to collaborate. Technologies like XML-RPC, SOAP, and gRPC provide implementations of RPC for various use cases, allowing processes to communicate transparently over a network.

Memory-mapped files represent another IPC method that enables processes to share data by mapping a file into their address spaces. This mapping allows processes to read and write data directly from and to the file, offering a persistent and efficient means of IPC. Memory-mapped files are particularly useful for scenarios where large amounts of data need to be shared between processes, and the data can persist beyond the lifetime of the processes. This mechanism is often employed in database systems and other applications where efficient data sharing is critical.

The choice of IPC method depends on the specific requirements of the application, including the nature of data to be exchanged, performance considerations, and the relationship between communicating processes. Shared memory is suitable for scenarios where fast, low-level communication is essential, and processes can synchronize effectively. Message passing mechanisms, such as pipes and sockets, are versatile and can be applied to various communication patterns, providing flexibility in different scenarios. Advanced mechanisms like semaphores, message queues, and memory-mapped files offer more sophisticated synchronization and data exchange capabilities, making them suitable for complex applications with specific requirements.

In conclusion, interprocess communication is a fundamental aspect of operating systems, enabling processes to exchange data and information for collaborative and synchronized execution. The diverse range of IPC methods, including shared memory, message passing, pipes, sockets, signals, semaphores, message queues, RPC, and memory-mapped files, offers a rich toolkit for developers to choose from based on the specific needs of their applications. The careful selection and implementation of appropriate IPC mechanisms contribute to the design of efficient, scalable, and reliable systems that meet the demands of modern computing environments.

Identifying common challenges such as deadlock and contention.

In the realm of concurrent and parallel computing, identifying and mitigating challenges is essential to ensuring the reliability, performance, and stability of systems. Two common challenges that can arise in these environments are deadlock and contention. Deadlock is a state where two or more processes are unable to proceed because each is waiting for the other to release a resource, resulting in a circular waiting scenario. This situation can lead to a standstill in the execution of processes, causing a significant impact on the overall system's performance and responsiveness. Deadlocks can manifest in various scenarios, such as when processes contend for exclusive access to resources, like files or locks, and reach an impasse. Mitigating deadlocks often involves careful resource allocation, using mechanisms like locks, semaphores, or other synchronization primitives, along with algorithms like deadlock detection and resolution to identify and break deadlocks when they occur.

Contention, on the other hand, is a challenge arising from multiple processes or threads vying for shared resources concurrently. Contention can lead to performance degradation, as competing processes contend for access to critical sections of code, shared data structures, or other resources. This competition for resources may result in increased waiting times, reduced throughput, and diminished overall system efficiency. Effective strategies to address contention involve optimizing resource management, employing fine-grained locking mechanisms, and minimizing the time spent in critical sections. Techniques such as lock-free and wait-free algorithms aim to reduce contention by allowing processes to progress without having to wait for exclusive access to shared resources. Additionally, advanced synchronization mechanisms, like reader-writer locks, aim to strike a balance between read and write access, enhancing parallelism and mitigating contention.

Concurrency control challenges are particularly prevalent in database management systems, where multiple transactions may compete for access to shared data. Transaction contention occurs when two or more transactions attempt to access or modify the same data simultaneously. This contention can lead to performance bottlenecks, increased transaction latencies, and reduced overall system throughput. Concurrency control mechanisms, such as locking protocols (e.g., two-phase locking) or optimistic concurrency control (e.g., timestamp-based protocols), are employed to manage contention in database systems. These mechanisms aim to strike a balance between ensuring data consistency and allowing for concurrent execution of transactions.

In distributed systems, challenges related to contention and coordination are accentuated due to the nature of distributed computing environments. The lack of a shared clock and the presence of network delays introduce additional complexities. Distributed contention may arise when multiple nodes attempt to access a shared resource or coordinate their activities. Coordinating distributed transactions and maintaining consistency across distributed databases present inherent challenges, as achieving consensus among distributed nodes introduces the risk of increased contention and latency. Distributed locking mechanisms, consensus algorithms (e.g., Paxos or Raft), and techniques like sharding or partitioning are employed to address these challenges, striving to balance performance and consistency in distributed systems.

In multi-threaded programming, where multiple threads execute concurrently within a single process, contention poses a significant challenge. Threads often contend for access to shared data structures, leading to potential race conditions, data corruption, and performance bottlenecks. Careful synchronization mechanisms, such as locks, semaphores, or atomic operations, are employed to manage contention and ensure thread safety. However, overuse of locks or poor design choices can result in contention becoming a limiting factor, and strategies like lock-free programming, fine-grained locking, and thread-aware data structures are employed to alleviate these issues.

Parallel computing environments, whether in shared-memory or distributed systems, are susceptible to load imbalance, where the workload is unevenly distributed among processing units. Load imbalance can result in some processors being underutilized while others are overwhelmed, leading to suboptimal performance and inefficient resource utilization. Load balancing algorithms, dynamic task scheduling, and parallelization techniques are employed to address load imbalance, ensuring that the computational workload is evenly distributed across processing units. Additionally, adaptive load balancing mechanisms dynamically adjust the distribution of tasks based on the changing characteristics of the workload during execution.

In real-time systems, contention and timing constraints pose unique challenges. In scenarios where processes or threads contend for access to resources, timing predictability becomes crucial to meet real-time deadlines. Contention leading to unpredictable delays can jeopardize the correctness of real-time systems. Techniques such as priority-based scheduling, rate monotonic scheduling, and resource reservation mechanisms are employed to manage contention and guarantee timely execution of critical tasks in real-time systems. Ensuring determinism and minimizing contention-induced delays are paramount in such environments, where failure to meet deadlines can have severe consequences.

Furthermore, challenges related to contention and coordination extend to the field of cloud computing, where multiple virtualized instances may share underlying physical resources. Contention for shared resources, such as CPU, memory, or network bandwidth, can impact the performance of cloud-based applications. Cloud providers implement resource allocation policies, virtual machine (VM) placement strategies, and load balancing mechanisms to manage contention and ensure efficient utilization of cloud resources. Additionally, cloud-based distributed systems face challenges related to coordinating data consistency and managing contention across geographically dispersed data centers.

Addressing contention and deadlock challenges requires a holistic approach that encompasses careful system design, effective resource management, and the utilization of advanced synchronization and coordination mechanisms. Developers and system architects must consider the characteristics of the specific computing environment, the nature of the application workload, and the criticality of timing constraints. Balancing the trade-offs between performance, responsiveness, and resource utilization is essential to mitigating contention and deadlock challenges in diverse computing scenarios. As technology continues to evolve, the identification and resolution of these challenges remain crucial for the design and optimization of robust and efficient computing systems across a spectrum of applications and domains.

Real-world examples demonstrating the impact of effective process management.

Effective process management plays a pivotal role in the functioning of numerous systems and industries, impacting various aspects such as efficiency, resource utilization, and overall system responsiveness. In the realm of operating systems, the significance of process management becomes evident in scenarios where multiple tasks need to be executed concurrently. One notable real-world example is the contemporary desktop environment, where users run multiple applications simultaneously. An operating system with robust process management ensures that these applications coexist harmoniously, allowing users to seamlessly switch between tasks, providing a responsive and efficient user experience. The operating system's ability to schedule processes, allocate resources, and manage their lifecycles directly influences the responsiveness of applications, enabling users to work on diverse tasks concurrently without encountering delays or disruptions.

In the domain of server environments and data centers, effective process management is critical for optimizing resource utilization and ensuring the stability of services. Consider a cloud computing platform hosting a myriad of applications and services for multiple users. Through efficient process management, the cloud operating system allocates resources dynamically, ensuring that each application receives the necessary computing power, memory, and network bandwidth. This adaptive resource allocation allows the cloud platform to scale elastically, accommodating fluctuations in demand without compromising performance. The ability to handle diverse workloads concurrently, allocate resources judiciously, and manage the lifecycle of applications is essential for the success of cloud computing platforms, impacting industries ranging from e-commerce to data analytics.

Moreover, process management plays a fundamental role in the realm of embedded systems, where resource constraints and real-time requirements are prevalent. Consider the case of a smart home automation system where multiple devices, such as thermostats, security cameras, and lighting controls, operate concurrently. Effective process management ensures that these embedded systems can handle various tasks simultaneously without compromising their responsiveness or energy efficiency. For instance, the thermostat must continuously monitor temperature, the security camera needs to capture and process video feeds, and lighting controls must respond promptly to user inputs. Well-designed process management in embedded systems allows for the seamless execution of these tasks, providing users with a reliable and responsive smart home experience.

In the context of scientific computing, process management is crucial for parallelizing computations and optimizing performance in high-performance computing (HPC) environments. Computational simulations, weather forecasting, and molecular modeling are examples of applications that heavily rely on parallel processing. In a supercomputing facility, efficient process management ensures that complex simulations are divided into smaller tasks that can be executed concurrently on multiple processors or cores. This parallel execution dramatically reduces the time required for computations, allowing researchers and scientists to simulate and analyze intricate phenomena, from climate patterns to molecular interactions. Effective process management in HPC environments not only accelerates scientific discovery but also influences breakthroughs in diverse fields, including medicine, materials science, and environmental research.

In the financial industry, effective process management is instrumental in handling large-scale transactions, data processing, and risk analysis. Consider a scenario in an investment bank where trading platforms must process a high volume of transactions in real-time. Robust process management ensures that trades are executed promptly, market data is processed efficiently, and risk assessments are performed concurrently. The ability to manage multiple processes concurrently enables financial institutions to respond rapidly to market fluctuations, execute complex financial algorithms, and analyze vast datasets to make informed investment decisions. Effective process management in the financial sector is not only about optimizing computational resources but also about maintaining the integrity and security of financial transactions.

Healthcare is another domain where effective process management has a profound impact, influencing patient care, medical research, and administrative operations. In a hospital setting, for instance, electronic health record (EHR) systems manage numerous processes simultaneously, from updating patient records to facilitating communication among healthcare professionals. A well-designed process management system ensures that critical tasks, such as patient admissions, laboratory tests, and medication administration, occur seamlessly. It enhances the overall efficiency of healthcare delivery, reduces errors, and contributes to better patient outcomes. In medical research, process management is essential for handling complex simulations, analyzing genetic data, and running simulations of biological processes, accelerating the pace of scientific discovery and drug development.

The manufacturing industry is yet another arena where effective process management plays a transformative role. In a smart manufacturing environment, numerous processes, from production lines to supply chain management, must be orchestrated seamlessly to ensure optimal efficiency. Consider an assembly line where robots, conveyor belts, and automated systems collaborate in real-time to manufacture products. Effective process management ensures that each step in the production process is coordinated efficiently, minimizing downtime and optimizing resource utilization. Through real-time monitoring and adaptive process control, manufacturing systems can respond swiftly to changes in demand, reduce waste, and enhance overall productivity. The impact of effective process management is evident not only in traditional manufacturing but also in emerging fields such as Industry 4.0, where the integration of advanced technologies like the Internet of Things (IoT) and artificial intelligence further amplifies the importance of streamlined and adaptive processes.

In the field of telecommunications, where networks handle an ever-increasing volume of data and connections, effective process management is vital for ensuring reliable and responsive communication services. Telecommunication networks manage a multitude of processes, from routing data packets to handling voice calls and video streams. The ability to efficiently allocate network resources, manage concurrent connections, and adapt to changing traffic patterns is critical for providing high-quality communication services. Effective process management in telecommunications impacts not only individual users making calls but also enables the seamless functioning of applications like video conferencing, online gaming, and streaming services on a global scale.

In the transportation industry, effective process management is essential for optimizing logistics, tracking shipments, and ensuring the timely movement of goods. Consider a modern supply chain where multiple processes, including inventory management, order processing, and transportation coordination, must be synchronized seamlessly. Effective process management allows for real-time tracking of shipments, automated route optimization, and responsive communication between various stakeholders in the supply chain. This not only improves the efficiency of transportation systems but also enhances customer satisfaction through timely deliveries and accurate order fulfillment. In the context of smart cities and intelligent transportation systems, effective process management contributes to the optimization of traffic flow, public transportation services, and overall urban mobility.

The impact of effective process management is also evident in educational institutions, where administrative processes, classroom management, and online learning platforms rely on streamlined and efficient workflows. In a university, for instance, effective process management ensures smooth enrollment processes, timely grading of assignments, and seamless collaboration among students and faculty. Learning management systems (LMS) leverage process management to facilitate online courses, manage content delivery, and support collaborative learning environments. The ability to handle multiple processes concurrently enhances the educational experience for students and enables institutions to adapt to changing pedagogical approaches and technological advancements.

In the realm of customer service and support, effective process management is crucial for providing timely and personalized assistance to customers. Consider a customer support center where various processes, including ticketing systems, knowledge bases, and communication channels, need to be coordinated to address customer inquiries and issues. Effective process management ensures that customer requests are routed to the appropriate agents, relevant information is accessible in real-time, and service-level agreements are met consistently. Through automated workflows and adaptive process orchestration, customer service operations can handle diverse scenarios efficiently, enhancing customer satisfaction and loyalty.

The impact of effective process management extends to the entertainment industry, where content creation, distribution, and audience engagement rely on streamlined workflows. In a film production studio, for example, effective process management ensures that various tasks, from scriptwriting to post-production editing, occur in a coordinated and efficient manner. Content distribution platforms leverage process management to handle concurrent streaming requests, personalize content recommendations, and analyze user engagement patterns. The ability to manage complex processes in the entertainment industry not only influences the efficiency of content creation but also enhances the overall user experience for audiences worldwide.

In conclusion, the impact of effective process management is pervasive across diverse industries and domains, shaping the efficiency, reliability, and adaptability of systems and services. From operating systems orchestrating concurrent tasks to cloud platforms dynamically allocating resources, and from healthcare systems optimizing patient care workflows to manufacturing processes adapting to changing demands, effective process management is a linchpin for success. Its influence extends to fields as varied as finance, telecommunications, education, entertainment, and transportation, where optimized workflows and adaptive orchestration contribute to improved performance and outcomes. As technology continues to advance, the role of effective process management remains integral to addressing the challenges and opportunities presented by evolving computing environments and the complex interplay of interconnected systems.

Chapter 2: The Fundamentals of Operating Systems

Defining an operating system and its role in computer systems.

An operating system (OS) is a fundamental software component that serves as an intermediary between computer hardware and user-level applications. It is a critical system software that provides a cohesive and organized environment for the effective execution of diverse computing tasks. The primary role of an operating system is to manage and control the underlying hardware resources, ensuring that various software applications can run efficiently and concurrently on a computer system. It acts as a bridge between the complex hardware architecture and the user, providing an abstraction layer that simplifies interaction and resource utilization.

At its core, an operating system functions as a resource manager, overseeing the allocation and utilization of hardware resources such as the central processing unit (CPU), memory, storage, and input/output devices. It acts as a supervisor, ensuring that multiple processes and applications can coexist, share resources, and execute concurrently without interfering with one another. This resource management aspect is crucial for optimizing the overall performance and responsiveness of a computer system, allowing users to run diverse applications simultaneously without having to manually manage hardware resources.

One of the key functions of an operating system is process management. It facilitates the execution of multiple processes, which are independent units of program execution, on a single or multi-processor system. The operating system handles the creation, scheduling, and termination of processes, ensuring that they run efficiently and securely. Process management involves activities such as context switching, where the state of a process is saved and restored, allowing the CPU to seamlessly switch between different processes. Additionally, the operating system provides mechanisms for inter-process communication and synchronization, enabling processes to cooperate and share information.

Memory management is another critical aspect of an operating system's role. It is responsible for overseeing the allocation and deallocation of memory space, ensuring that each process has sufficient memory to execute without conflicting with other processes. The OS employs techniques such as virtual memory, paging, and segmentation to provide a virtualized and efficient memory environment. By abstracting the complexities of physical memory from applications, the operating system allows for the illusion of larger and more flexible memory spaces, contributing to the seamless execution of diverse software applications.

File system management is integral to an operating system's responsibilities. It involves the organization, storage, retrieval, and manipulation of data on storage devices. The OS abstracts the complexities of interacting with storage devices, presenting users and applications with a logical file system. File system management ensures data integrity, provides mechanisms for data protection, and facilitates efficient storage utilization. It allows users to create, modify, and organize files and directories, abstracting the intricacies of interacting with storage devices at the hardware level.

The role of an operating system extends to managing input and output (I/O) operations, facilitating communication between the computer and external devices such as keyboards, mice, printers, and network interfaces. I/O management involves handling diverse devices with varying speeds and communication protocols. The operating system abstracts the complexities of device interaction, providing a standardized interface for applications to perform I/O operations. This abstraction ensures that applications can access and utilize a wide range of devices without requiring detailed knowledge of their specific hardware characteristics.

Furthermore, an operating system plays a crucial role in providing a secure and protected computing environment. It implements security mechanisms to control access to resources, authenticate users, and protect data from unauthorized access. User authentication, file permissions, encryption, and secure communication protocols are integral components of an operating system's security features. The OS acts as a safeguard, preventing malicious software or unauthorized users from compromising the integrity and confidentiality of the system.

In the context of networked computing, an operating system facilitates network communication, allowing computers to connect and communicate with each other. Network protocols, such as TCP/IP, are implemented by the operating system to enable seamless communication over local area networks (LANs) and the broader internet. The OS provides networking services, such as the ability to establish connections, transmit data, and manage network configurations, enabling distributed computing and collaborative applications.

The concept of device drivers is vital in the operating system's role, especially concerning hardware compatibility. Device drivers are specialized programs that enable the operating system to communicate with and control hardware devices. Whether it's a printer, graphics card, or network adapter, the operating system relies on device drivers to abstract the hardware-specific details and provide a standardized interface for applications to interact with various devices. Device drivers ensure that the operating system can effectively manage and utilize a wide array of hardware components.

Moreover, an operating system contributes to system stability and fault tolerance. It includes error detection and recovery mechanisms to handle system failures, crashes, and unexpected errors. Features such as process isolation prevent a failure in one application or process from affecting the entire system. The operating system's ability to manage system resources efficiently and recover from errors enhances the overall reliability and robustness of the computer system.

The concept of multiprocessing and multi-user support is intrinsic to the role of an operating system. In a multiprocessing environment, the OS coordinates the execution of multiple processes concurrently on a single or multiple processors. This enables efficient resource utilization and enhances overall system performance. Additionally, an operating system supports multi-user environments, allowing multiple users to interact with the system simultaneously. User management, access control, and session isolation are essential components of multi-user support, enabling secure and collaborative computing.

In the contemporary computing landscape, the concept of graphical user interfaces (GUIs) has become integral to the user experience. An operating system often includes a graphical shell that provides users with a visual interface to interact with the system. GUIs offer a user-friendly environment, allowing users to navigate file systems, launch applications, and perform various tasks through graphical elements such as windows, icons, and menus. The operating system manages the graphical interface, ensuring a responsive and intuitive user experience.

The role of an operating system is not confined to traditional computing devices like personal computers or servers. With the proliferation of embedded systems, operating systems find application in a diverse range of devices, from smartphones and smart TVs to automotive control systems and IoT devices. Embedded operating systems provide the necessary abstractions and management capabilities tailored to the specific requirements of embedded environments, ensuring reliable and efficient operation in constrained and specialized computing platforms.

In conclusion, an operating system serves as the cornerstone of modern computer systems, providing a crucial layer of abstraction and management between hardware resources and user-level applications. Its multifaceted role encompasses resource management, process coordination, memory abstraction, file system organization, I/O operations, security enforcement, networking, device compatibility, fault tolerance, multiprocessing, multi-user support, and graphical user interfaces. The effectiveness of an operating system directly influences the efficiency, reliability, and user experience of a computer system. As technology continues to advance, the role of operating systems evolves to accommodate new computing paradigms, ensuring their continued relevance and significance in the ever-changing landscape of computing.

Exploring the kernel, shell, and file system components.

At the core of any operating system lies the kernel, a fundamental component responsible for managing hardware resources and providing essential services to user-level applications. The kernel acts as an intermediary, facilitating communication between the computer's hardware and the software running on it. Its primary functions include process scheduling, memory management, I/O operations, and system call handling. In essence, the kernel is the nucleus of the operating system, embodying its core functionalities. It serves as the bridge that allows user applications to interact with the underlying hardware seamlessly. The kernel is crucial for maintaining system stability, managing system resources efficiently, and ensuring a secure and reliable computing environment.

Complementing the kernel is the shell, a user interface that enables interaction between users and the operating system. The shell acts as a command-line interpreter or a graphical interface, allowing users to communicate with the operating system by entering commands or interacting with visual elements. It interprets user inputs, translates them into system calls, and communicates with the kernel to execute the desired actions. Shells can vary, with some providing more sophisticated scripting capabilities and others focusing on simplicity and ease of use. Examples include the Bash shell in Unix-like systems and the Command Prompt in Windows. The shell plays a pivotal role in making the power and capabilities of the operating system accessible to users, facilitating tasks ranging from file management to complex system administration tasks through a user-friendly interface.

The file system is a critical component that organizes and manages data on storage devices, providing a structured and hierarchical approach to storing and retrieving information. It serves as a repository for files, directories, and metadata, allowing users and applications to organize, access, and manipulate data efficiently. The file system abstracts the complexities of interacting with storage devices, presenting users with a logical and organized view of their data. Different operating systems may employ various file system types, such as NTFS in Windows, ext4 in Linux, or APFS in macOS, each with its own features and optimizations. The file system is integral to data integrity, ensuring that files are stored reliably, and data consistency is maintained even in the event of system failures or unexpected shutdowns.

Delving deeper into the kernel, its architecture is often modular, consisting of various components that collaborate to fulfill specific functions. Process management is a critical aspect, involving the creation, scheduling, and termination of processes. The kernel's scheduler allocates CPU time to different processes, ensuring a fair and efficient distribution of computing resources. Memory management is another core function, overseeing the allocation and deallocation of memory space, and utilizing techniques like virtual memory to provide an illusion of larger memory spaces. I/O management involves handling input and output operations, orchestrating communication between the CPU and external devices, ensuring efficient data transfer. The kernel's system call interface allows user-level applications to request services from the kernel, serving as a boundary between user space and kernel space.

Within the kernel, device drivers play a crucial role in facilitating communication between the operating system and hardware devices. Device drivers are specialized modules that enable the kernel to interact with various peripherals, such as printers, graphics cards, or network adapters. They abstract the intricate details of hardware communication, providing a standardized interface for the kernel to communicate with diverse hardware components. Device drivers are essential for ensuring hardware compatibility and enabling the operating system to effectively manage and utilize the full spectrum of available hardware resources.

The shell, as a user-facing interface, comes in different forms, each catering to distinct user preferences and requirements. Command-line shells, such as Bash in Unix-like systems or PowerShell in Windows, allow users to enter textual commands for system interaction. Users can execute a series of commands, automate tasks through scripting, and navigate the file system efficiently. Graphical shells, on the other hand, provide a visual environment, allowing users to interact with the system through graphical elements like icons, windows, and menus. Desktop environments, such as GNOME, KDE, or Windows Desktop, incorporate graphical shells, providing an intuitive and visually appealing user interface. The choice between command-line and graphical shells often depends on user preferences, the nature of tasks, and the level of technical expertise.

File systems, integral to data organization and retrieval, follow a hierarchical structure. Directories, also known as folders, provide a means to organize files into a structured tree-like hierarchy. Users can navigate through directories to locate and access files efficiently. File systems employ a naming convention for files, allowing users to differentiate between them based on names, extensions, or attributes. Metadata, associated with each file, includes information such as file size, creation date, and permissions. File systems also manage access control, determining which users or groups have permissions to read, write, or execute specific files. The hierarchical and organized nature of file systems simplifies data management, aiding users in locating and managing their files effectively.

The kernel, shell, and file system work cohesively to provide a comprehensive and efficient computing environment. Users interact with the shell, issuing commands or manipulating files, which the shell translates into system calls for the kernel. The kernel, in turn, manages processes, memory, and I/O operations, coordinating the execution of user-level tasks. It communicates with device drivers to control hardware devices and interacts with the file system to organize and retrieve data. The file system, with its hierarchical structure and metadata, ensures a systematic approach to data management. This symbiotic relationship between the kernel, shell, and file system is the foundation of the user experience in operating systems, providing the necessary abstractions and interfaces for users to harness the full potential of their computing devices.

In summary, the kernel, as the core of the operating system, manages hardware resources and provides essential services, acting as an intermediary between the hardware and user-level applications. The shell, serving as a user interface, allows users to interact with the operating system through commands or graphical elements. It interprets user inputs, translates them into system calls, and communicates with the kernel to execute desired actions. The file system organizes and manages data on storage devices, providing a structured and hierarchical approach to data storage and retrieval. Together, these components form the backbone of an operating system, orchestrating the interaction between users and the underlying hardware to create a cohesive and efficient computing environment.

Overview of different types such as batch, time-sharing, and distributed systems.

In the realm of operating systems, various types have evolved over time to cater to different computing needs and environments. One of the earliest types is the batch processing system, which emerged during the early days of computing when machines were primarily dedicated to executing a sequence of predefined tasks without user interaction. In a batch processing system, users submit jobs in batches, and the operating system processes them in a non-interactive manner, executing each job sequentially. This type of system is efficient for handling large-scale computations, such as scientific simulations and data processing, where a set of tasks can be executed without constant user intervention. However, batch processing lacks interactivity and responsiveness, making it less suitable for scenarios that require immediate user feedback or dynamic interaction.

As computing needs evolved and interactive computing became more prevalent, the time-sharing operating system emerged as a response to the demand for concurrent user access. Time-sharing systems aim to provide the illusion of multiple users simultaneously interacting with the computer, even though the underlying hardware can only execute one task at a time. These systems achieve concurrency by rapidly switching between different user tasks, giving each user a small time slice or time quantum for their interactions. Time-sharing allows users to work interactively, entering commands and receiving immediate responses. This model is particularly advantageous for scenarios like interactive programming, online transaction processing, and real-time applications, where users expect prompt system feedback.

Another significant development is the distributed operating system, which is designed to operate across multiple interconnected machines, often geographically dispersed. In a distributed system, resources such as computation, storage, and communication are distributed across the network, and the operating system orchestrates their usage seamlessly. This type of system offers several advantages, including improved reliability, increased availability, and enhanced scalability. Distributed operating systems facilitate efficient resource sharing and collaborative computing, allowing users and applications to harness the power of a networked environment. Examples of distributed systems include cloud computing platforms, where computing resources are provided as services over the internet, and cluster computing environments that leverage the combined power of multiple interconnected machines to solve complex problems.

Real-time operating systems (RTOS) represent another specialized type tailored for applications with stringent timing constraints. In real-time systems, tasks must be completed within predefined time limits to ensure correctness and reliability. RTOS prioritizes timely execution of tasks, providing mechanisms for predictable and deterministic response times. This type of operating system is crucial in domains like embedded systems, aerospace control, medical devices, and industrial automation, where precise timing and reliability are paramount. Real-time operating systems can be categorized into hard real-time systems, where missing deadlines is intolerable and could lead to catastrophic consequences, and soft real-time systems, where occasional delays are acceptable but impact system performance.

Microkernel operating systems take a different architectural approach by minimizing the kernel's functionality and delegating many tasks to user-space processes, often referred to as servers. The micro-kernel architecture aims to enhance system modularity, extensibility, and reliability by keeping the core kernel minimal and moving additional functionalities outside the kernel space. This allows for easier modification and addition of system components without affecting the core kernel, contributing to a more flexible and maintainable system. While microkernel architectures offer advantages in terms of customization and adaptability, they may introduce additional overhead due to increased inter-process communication.

Multimedia operating systems are designed to handle multimedia data, such as audio, video, and graphics, efficiently. These systems prioritize the real-time processing and delivery of multimedia content, ensuring smooth playback and responsiveness. Multimedia operating systems find applications in entertainment, gaming, video editing, and virtual reality, where the seamless handling of multimedia data is critical. These systems incorporate specialized components and algorithms to optimize multimedia processing, such as multimedia drivers, codecs, and scheduling mechanisms tailored for real-time multimedia applications.

Network operating systems are geared towards facilitating communication and resource sharing in networked environments. These systems enable computers to connect and collaborate over a network, sharing files, printers, and other resources. Network operating systems support features like file sharing, remote access, and network security. They are commonly used in business environments, where multiple computers need to communicate and share resources within an organization. Examples of network operating systems include Novell NetWare and Microsoft Windows Server, which provide functionalities for managing networked resources and user access.

Mobile operating systems power smartphones, tablets, and other mobile devices, catering to the unique requirements of portable computing. Mobile operating systems prioritize energy efficiency, responsiveness, and support for touch interfaces. They often include features such as app stores, security measures, and synchronization capabilities to enhance the mobile user experience. Prominent examples of mobile operating systems include Android, iOS, and HarmonyOS, each tailored for specific devices and ecosystems. These operating systems have played a transformative role in the way users interact with technology, providing a rich ecosystem of applications and services on portable devices.

Hybrid operating systems combine features of different types, incorporating elements from both monolithic and microkernel architectures. These systems aim to strike a balance between performance and flexibility, leveraging the advantages of diverse architectural models. A hybrid operating system may have a monolithic kernel while allowing certain functionalities to run in user space as separate modules. This approach provides the benefits of a monolithic kernel's performance while allowing for easier extension and modification of certain system components. Hybrid operating systems are designed to offer a compromise between the simplicity of monolithic kernels and the flexibility of microkernel architectures.

In conclusion, the diverse types of operating systems reflect the varied needs and contexts in which computing systems operate. From batch processing systems optimized for large-scale computations to time-sharing systems supporting interactive user environments, and from distributed systems facilitating collaboration across networks to real-time systems meeting stringent timing constraints, each type serves a specific purpose. As technology continues to advance, new types of operating systems are likely to emerge, addressing the evolving demands of computing in an ever-changing landscape. The rich tapestry of operating system types underscores the adaptability and versatility of these crucial software components, shaping the way users interact with and leverage the power of computing devices across diverse domains.

Breaking down the architecture into layers and modules.

The architecture of a computing system is intricately structured, typically organized into layers and modules, each serving a specific purpose and contributing to the overall functionality of the system. At the foundational layer is the hardware, comprising the physical components such as the central processing unit (CPU), memory, storage devices, input/output (I/O) devices, and the communication infrastructure that facilitates data transfer between these elements. This hardware layer forms the bedrock upon which the entire computing system is built, providing the raw computational power and storage capacity necessary for processing tasks.

Above the hardware layer lies the firmware, a layer that consists of low-level software embedded in hardware devices. Firmware serves as an intermediary between hardware and higher-level software, providing a bridge for communication and enabling the initialization and control of hardware components. Examples of firmware include the BIOS (Basic Input/Output System) or UEFI (Unified Extensible Firmware Interface) in personal computers, which initialize the system during boot and provide a basic interface for hardware configuration.

The operating system layer sits atop the firmware and serves as a crucial bridge between the hardware and user-level applications. It encompasses the kernel, responsible for managing hardware resources and providing essential services, and various system libraries and utilities that facilitate interaction between applications and the underlying hardware. The operating system establishes an abstraction layer, shielding applications from the complexities of hardware interactions. It manages processes, memory, file systems, and I/O operations, ensuring efficient resource utilization and providing a stable and secure environment for applications to run.

Within the operating system layer, the kernel is often modular, comprising various modules that handle specific functionalities.

Process management modules oversee the creation, scheduling, and termination of processes, managing their execution on the CPU. Memory management modules handle the allocation and deallocation of memory, implementing techniques like virtual memory for efficient memory usage. I/O management modules facilitate communication between the CPU and external devices, coordinating data transfer. The file system module organizes and manages data on storage devices, providing a logical structure for file storage and retrieval. The modular nature of the kernel allows for flexibility and ease of maintenance, as each module can be developed, updated, or replaced independently.

The shell, another component within the operating system layer, acts as a user interface, enabling interaction between users and the system. It interprets user commands, translates them into system calls, and communicates with the kernel to execute desired actions. The shell can be command-line based, where users input textual commands, or graphical, where users interact with visual elements like icons and menus. The shell plays a pivotal role in making the operating system accessible to users, providing a means for users to execute commands, manage files, and interact with the system in a user-friendly manner.

Above the operating system layer are the user-level applications, encompassing a diverse range of software that users interact with to perform specific tasks. Applications can include word processors, web browsers, multimedia players, development environments, and more. These applications leverage the services provided by the operating system, utilizing its abstractions and functionalities to execute tasks without having to interact directly with hardware components. The modular structure of the operating system allows applications to run independently, each having its own address space and resources, while the kernel manages their execution concurrently.

In a networked computing environment, an additional layer often exists to facilitate communication and resource sharing between multiple computers. The network layer encompasses protocols and services that enable data transmission across networks. This layer includes the TCP/IP protocol suite, routing algorithms, and network services. The network layer allows computers to communicate, share resources, and collaborate, forming the foundation for distributed and collaborative computing environments.

Security is a cross-cutting concern that permeates multiple layers of the architecture. Security mechanisms, such as authentication, authorization, and encryption, are integrated into the hardware, firmware, operating system, and application layers to safeguard against unauthorized access, data breaches, and malicious activities. Security modules within the operating system layer implement access control policies, secure communication protocols, and encryption algorithms to ensure the confidentiality and integrity of data.

The modular architecture extends beyond the operating system layer into the application layer, where applications are often designed with a modular structure to enhance maintainability and extensibility. Modular programming practices involve breaking down software into smaller, independent modules that encapsulate specific functionalities. Each module performs a well-defined task, and modules can be developed, tested, and updated independently, promoting code reusability and ease of maintenance.

In summary, the architecture of a computing system is structured into layers and modules, each serving a specific purpose and contributing to the overall functionality of the system. The hardware layer provides the foundational physical components, while the firmware layer acts as an intermediary between hardware and software. The operating system layer, comprising the kernel, system libraries, and utilities, manages hardware resources and provides essential services, shielding applications from hardware complexities.

User-level applications leverage the services of the operating system to perform specific tasks. The network layer facilitates communication between computers in a networked environment. Security mechanisms are integrated across multiple layers to protect against unauthorized access and malicious activities. The modular nature of the architecture, from the kernel's modular design to modular programming practices in applications, enhances flexibility, maintainability, and extensibility, contributing to the overall efficiency and robustness of the computing system.

Understanding the structure of file systems and directories.

The structure of file systems and directories is a fundamental aspect of modern computing, providing a systematic approach to organizing and managing data on storage devices. At the core of this structure is the concept of a file, a named collection of data that serves as a unit of storage. Files can contain a wide variety of information, ranging from text documents and images to executable programs and multimedia content. File systems, in turn, establish the rules and structures for storing, retrieving, and organizing these files on storage media such as hard drives, solid-state drives, or other storage devices.

The hierarchical organization of file systems is facilitated by directories, also known as folders. Directories serve as containers for files and other directories, creating a structured and easily navigable tree-like hierarchy. This hierarchical structure provides a logical way to organize data, allowing users to create a hierarchy of directories to suit their needs. For example, a user might have a directory named "Documents" that contains subdirectories like "Work," "Personal," and "Projects," each further organizing files related to those specific categories. This hierarchical arrangement simplifies file organization and retrieval, making it easier for users to locate and manage their data.

The root directory, positioned at the top of the hierarchy, serves as the starting point for the entire file system. It is the base directory from which all other directories and subdirectories stem. Each directory and subdirectory within the file system has a unique path, specifying its location within the hierarchy. Paths are expressed in a standardized format, such as "/home/user/Documents/Work," with each forward slash indicating a level in the hierarchy. This standardized approach ensures consistency and ease of reference, allowing users and applications to navigate the file system accurately.

Files within a directory are identified by their filenames, which are unique within the scope of the directory. Filenames can include a combination of letters, numbers, and special characters, providing flexibility for users to name files based on their content or purpose. Extensions, such as ".txt" for text files or ".jpg" for image files, are often used to denote the file type and assist in identifying the content at a glance.

Access control is a crucial aspect of file systems, governing which users or groups have permission to perform specific operations on files and directories. Permissions typically include the ability to read, write, and execute files, and users can be assigned different levels of access based on their roles or privileges. This access control mechanism ensures data security and privacy, allowing users to protect sensitive information from unauthorized access or modifications.

In addition to standard files and directories, file systems may include special files and directories that serve specific purposes. For instance, the root directory often contains system files and directories necessary for the functioning of the operating system. Hidden files, denoted by filenames starting with a dot (e.g., ".config"), are files that are not displayed by default in directory listings, providing a way to store configuration information or other system-related data.

File systems employ various data structures to efficiently manage and track the location of files and directories on storage devices.

A file allocation table (FAT), used in file systems like FAT16 and FAT32, maintains a table that maps file names to their physical locations on the storage medium. In contrast, more modern file systems like NTFS (New Technology File System) use a master file table (MFT) to store metadata and pointers to file data clusters. These data structures enable the file system to quickly locate and access files, contributing to efficient file retrieval and system performance.

File systems also implement techniques to optimize storage space and reduce fragmentation. Fragmentation occurs when a file is stored in non-contiguous blocks on a storage medium, impacting read and write speeds. File systems employ strategies such as clustering and file allocation algorithms to allocate contiguous blocks of storage whenever possible, minimizing fragmentation and enhancing overall system performance.

Journaling is a feature integrated into some file systems to improve reliability and data integrity. In a journaled file system, a journal records changes to the file system before they are applied. This journaling mechanism helps recover the file system to a consistent state in the event of a power failure or system crash, reducing the risk of data corruption.

Symbolic links and hard links are mechanisms within file systems that allow for the creation of pointers to files or directories. Symbolic links are references to the target file or directory, creating a separate entry that points to the original location. Hard links, on the other hand, create multiple directory entries that reference the same inode (index node) on the storage medium. Both types of links offer flexibility in organizing and referencing files and directories, enabling users to create alternative pathways to access data.

File systems are not limited to a single storage device; they can span multiple devices or partitions, creating a distributed file system. Distributed file systems enable seamless data sharing and access across multiple computers or nodes in a network. Examples of distributed file systems include NFS (Network File System) and CIFS (Common Internet File System), which allow users to access files stored on remote servers as if they were local.

The extensible nature of file systems allows for the incorporation of additional features and enhancements. For instance, some file systems support file compression, allowing users to reduce the storage space occupied by files. Encryption features enable the secure storage of sensitive data by encrypting files or entire directories, protecting them from unauthorized access. These extensible features cater to diverse user needs, making file systems adaptable to a wide range of applications and scenarios.

In conclusion, the structure of file systems and directories is a foundational aspect of computing, providing an organized and hierarchical framework for storing and retrieving data on storage devices. Directories create a hierarchical tree-like structure, offering a logical organization for files, while filenames, paths, and access control mechanisms contribute to effective data management and security. The use of data structures, such as file allocation tables and master file tables, enables efficient file retrieval and storage optimization. Advanced features like journaling, links, distributed file systems, and extensibility through compression and encryption further enhance the functionality of file systems, adapting them to diverse user requirements and technological advancements. The seamless integration of these elements ensures that file systems play a pivotal role in shaping the way users interact with and manage data in the digital landscape.

Exploring command-line interfaces (CLI) and graphical user interfaces (GUI).

Command-Line Interfaces (CLI) and Graphical User Interfaces (GUI) represent two distinct paradigms for interacting with computers and software, each offering unique advantages and catering to different user preferences. The Command-Line Interface, rooted in the early days of computing, relies on text-based commands entered by users to execute operations or interact with the system. CLI operates in a text-based environment, providing a command prompt where users can type specific commands to perform tasks. Commands are often precise and require a certain syntax, making them powerful tools for users with a technical background or those comfortable with coding. The CLI's strength lies in its efficiency for repetitive or scripted tasks, enabling users to automate processes through scripts or batch files. Operating systems like Unix, Linux, and the Windows Command Prompt exemplify the prevalence and versatility of command-line interfaces.

In contrast, Graphical User Interfaces revolutionized user interaction by introducing visual elements such as icons, windows, and menus to simplify the user experience. GUIs aim to provide a more intuitive and user-friendly interface, reducing the reliance on text-based commands. Users interact with the system by clicking on icons, dragging and dropping files, and navigating through menus using a mouse or touch input. GUIs offer a more visually appealing and accessible environment, making computing accessible to a broader audience. Operating systems like Microsoft Windows, macOS, and various Linux distributions leverage GUIs as the primary means of interaction. GUIs excel in scenarios where users prioritize ease of use, visual representation, and a more natural approach to navigation.

Command-Line Interfaces, although perceived by some as less user-friendly, have distinctive advantages. They offer precise control and scripting capabilities, making them favored by system administrators, developers, and power users. The ability to chain commands together and create complex scripts enables automation, streamlining repetitive tasks and enhancing productivity. CLI is often preferred in server environments or when working with remote systems, where a lightweight and text-based interface is more efficient than a graphical one. Moreover, CLI interfaces consume fewer system resources compared to GUIs, making them suitable for resource-constrained environments.

Graphical User Interfaces, on the other hand, prioritize accessibility and ease of use, making computing more approachable for a wider audience. GUIs leverage visual metaphors, such as icons representing applications or folders, and provide feedback through graphical elements like progress bars or dialog boxes. This visual representation helps users navigate and interact with the system intuitively, without the need to memorize complex commands. GUIs excel in applications like graphic design, video editing, and content creation, where visual feedback and manipulation are essential. They also provide a consistent and visually coherent environment for users across various applications and tasks.

The debate between CLI and GUI often revolves around user preferences, workflow requirements, and the nature of the task at hand. Some users find comfort and efficiency in the precision of command-line interfaces, where the direct input of commands offers a sense of control and immediacy. Others favor the visual clarity and ease of navigation provided by graphical interfaces, appreciating the ability to interact with the system through familiar visual metaphors.

Modern operating systems often strike a balance by incorporating both CLI and GUI elements, offering users the flexibility to choose based on their preferences and needs. This hybrid approach provides the best of both worlds, allowing users to leverage the efficiency of command-line tools when necessary while benefiting from the visual intuitiveness of graphical interfaces for everyday tasks. For example, PowerShell in Windows and the Terminal in macOS and Linux provide powerful command-line interfaces alongside rich graphical environments.

The command-line renaissance has witnessed the emergence of enhanced shells and tools that combine the efficiency of CLI with more intuitive features. Tools like Zsh and Fish introduce auto-completion, syntax highlighting, and other enhancements to make command-line interactions more user-friendly. Additionally, package managers like npm, pip, and apt have command-line interfaces that simplify the installation and management of software packages.

Accessibility and inclusivity are essential considerations in the design of user interfaces. While CLI interfaces may be daunting for users unfamiliar with coding or technical commands, GUIs often offer a more welcoming entry point to computing. The visual representation of tasks and the reduction of syntax-based interactions can empower users who may find a text-based interface challenging. The design principles of GUIs focus on creating interfaces that are intuitive, with visual cues guiding users through tasks and reducing the learning curve.

The evolution of technology has seen the rise of web-based interfaces, introducing a new dimension to the CLI vs. GUI discussion. Web interfaces often integrate command-line features accessible through a browser, offering a combination of both paradigms. This approach, exemplified by tools like Jupyter Notebooks, allows users to execute commands within a web browser while providing a visual representation of the results. Web-based interfaces extend the reach of command-line capabilities to a broader audience without the need for a local terminal.

Security considerations also play a role in the CLI vs. GUI debate. Command-line interfaces are often favored in server environments due to their reduced attack surface and lower resource consumption. GUIs, while offering convenience, may introduce additional complexities and potential vulnerabilities. System administrators and security professionals often prefer command-line tools for their efficiency and the ability to precisely control and audit system changes.

In conclusion, the choice between Command-Line Interfaces and Graphical User Interfaces is nuanced and depends on factors such as user preferences, the nature of the task, and the context in which computing occurs. Both paradigms have distinct strengths and weaknesses, and the ongoing evolution of technology has seen efforts to bridge the gap between them. The hybrid approach, blending the precision of command-line tools with the visual appeal of graphical interfaces, reflects a pragmatic understanding that different users and scenarios may benefit from different interaction models. Ultimately, the CLI vs. GUI debate is not about one being superior to the other but rather recognizing the diversity of user needs and providing interfaces that empower users to interact with computing systems in ways that suit their preferences and workflow requirements.

The role of device drivers in communication between hardware and the operating system.

Device drivers play a pivotal role in facilitating communication between hardware components and the operating system, serving as essential intermediaries that enable seamless interaction within a computing system. At its core, a device driver is a specialized software module designed to act as a bridge between the hardware devices connected to a computer and the operating system that manages and controls these devices. This communication is vital for ensuring that the diverse array of hardware components, ranging from peripheral devices to storage devices and network interfaces, can function cohesively within the broader computing environment.

One fundamental aspect of device drivers is their role in abstracting the complexities of hardware communication for the operating system. Hardware devices often have unique specifications, interfaces, and protocols, making direct communication between the operating system and each individual device impractical. Device drivers abstract these intricacies by providing a standardized interface that the operating system can interact with, shielding it from the specifics of each hardware component. This abstraction layer enhances compatibility, allowing the operating system to communicate with a wide variety of devices without requiring intricate knowledge of their internal workings.

In the context of the operating system's kernel, device drivers act as modules that extend its functionality to support diverse hardware. The kernel is responsible for core functions such as process management, memory allocation, and input/output operations. However, to communicate effectively with hardware peripherals, the kernel relies on device drivers to provide the necessary translation between its generic commands and the device-specific protocols. This modular architecture allows for flexibility and scalability, as new devices can be integrated into the system by adding or updating corresponding device drivers without necessitating changes to the entire operating system.

Device drivers also play a crucial role in the initialization and configuration of hardware components during the system's boot process. As the operating system boots, device drivers are loaded to initialize and configure the connected hardware devices, ensuring that they are in a suitable state for interaction with the operating system. This initialization process involves tasks such as setting up memory addresses, configuring interrupt requests, and establishing communication channels. By managing these low-level details, device drivers prepare the hardware for seamless integration into the operating system's environment, contributing to the overall stability and functionality of the system.

One of the primary functions of device drivers is to handle input and output operations between the operating system and hardware peripherals. This encompasses a wide range of activities, from reading data from storage devices and sending data to printers to managing communication with network interfaces. For example, a printer driver translates the generic print commands from the operating system into specific instructions for the connected printer, ensuring that the printed output accurately reflects the user's intent. Similarly, a storage device driver manages the reading and writing of data between the operating system and storage media, abstracting the intricacies of storage protocols and optimizing data transfer.

Device drivers are instrumental in enabling plug-and-play functionality, allowing users to connect and disconnect hardware devices without requiring manual intervention or system restarts. When a new device is connected, the corresponding device driver is automatically loaded, initializing and configuring the device for immediate use. Conversely, when a device is disconnected, the associated device driver can gracefully handle the removal of the device, ensuring that the operating system transitions seamlessly to the altered hardware environment. This plug-and-play capability enhances user convenience and promotes the interoperability of diverse hardware components.

Furthermore, device drivers contribute to the efficient utilization of hardware resources. By optimizing the communication between the operating system and hardware, device drivers help enhance performance, reduce latency, and improve the overall responsiveness of the system. For instance, graphics card drivers play a critical role in ensuring that the operating system can leverage the full capabilities of the graphics hardware, optimizing rendering and enabling features such as hardware-accelerated graphics processing. Similarly, network interface drivers facilitate efficient data transfer between the operating system and network devices, contributing to the system's overall responsiveness in networking tasks.

The life cycle of a device driver involves ongoing maintenance, updates, and compatibility enhancements. As hardware evolves and new devices are introduced, device drivers must be regularly updated to ensure compatibility and optimal performance. Operating system updates may also necessitate corresponding updates to device drivers to maintain seamless integration. Device driver developers work closely with hardware manufacturers to address issues, implement improvements, and ensure that the drivers evolve in tandem with both the hardware and the operating system.

Security considerations are paramount in the design and implementation of device drivers. Given their privileged position within the operating system, device drivers must undergo rigorous testing and validation to ensure they do not introduce vulnerabilities or compromise system security. The implementation of secure coding practices, robust validation mechanisms, and adherence to established security standards are essential aspects of device driver development. Security updates and patches are regularly released to address identified vulnerabilities and enhance the resilience of device drivers against potential threats.

In modern computing environments, device drivers extend beyond traditional desktops and laptops to include a wide range of devices in the Internet of Things (IoT) ecosystem. IoT devices, ranging from smart thermostats to industrial sensors, rely on specialized device drivers to enable communication with the underlying operating systems. The diversity of IoT hardware underscores the importance of flexible and extensible device driver architectures that can accommodate the unique requirements of emerging technologies.

In conclusion, device drivers serve as integral components that facilitate communication between hardware devices and the operating system, contributing to the seamless functionality, compatibility, and performance of computing systems. Their role in abstracting hardware complexities, managing initialization processes, handling input and output operations, enabling plug-and-play functionality, and ensuring ongoing compatibility underscores their significance in the broader landscape of system architecture. As technology continues to advance and new hardware innovations emerge, the role of device drivers remains critical in adapting and optimizing the interaction between operating systems and an ever-expanding array of hardware peripherals.

Overview of security features such as authentication and authorization.

Security features such as authentication and authorization form the bedrock of robust information security frameworks, playing a critical role in safeguarding digital assets and sensitive data across various computing environments. Authentication, the process of verifying the identity of users or entities attempting to access a system, is the initial line of defense against unauthorized access. This multifaceted process involves the presentation of credentials, typically in the form of usernames and passwords, biometric data, or cryptographic keys. Authentication mechanisms ensure that only authorized individuals or entities gain access to protected resources, mitigating the risk of unauthorized access and identity impersonation.

In the realm of authentication, multi-factor authentication (MFA) has emerged as a powerful strategy to enhance security. MFA requires users to present multiple forms of identification, combining factors such as something they know (password), something they have (security token or smart card), and something they are (biometric data like fingerprints or facial recognition). This layered approach significantly strengthens the authentication process, making it more resilient against various attack vectors, including password-based attacks and identity theft. MFA is widely adopted in contemporary security practices, providing an additional layer of defense in environments where sensitive data and critical systems are at stake.

Authorization, the subsequent phase in the security continuum, focuses on determining the level of access and permissions granted to authenticated users or entities. Once a user's identity is verified through the authentication process, authorization mechanisms come into play to define and enforce access control policies. Authorization is intricately linked to the concept of privilege management, which involves assigning specific privileges or roles to users based on their responsibilities within the organization. Role-based access control (RBAC) is a prevalent authorization model, where users are assigned roles, and each role is associated with specific permissions and access rights. This granular approach allows organizations to tailor access privileges to individual user roles, reducing the risk of unauthorized access and limiting the impact of security incidents.

The principle of least privilege (POLP) is a foundational concept in authorization, emphasizing the restriction of access rights for users to the minimum level necessary to perform their designated tasks. By adhering to the principle of least privilege, organizations minimize the potential impact of security breaches and limit the exposure of sensitive information. Fine-grained access controls enable administrators to define precisely what actions and resources each user or role can access, creating a more secure and manageable access environment.

Access control lists (ACLs) and capability systems are common mechanisms employed in authorization to define and manage access rights. ACLs specify which users or system processes are granted access to objects, files, or resources and what operations they can perform. Capability systems, on the other hand, involve the assignment of tokens or capabilities to users, granting access to specific resources based on the possession of these tokens. Both ACLs and capability systems contribute to the implementation of access controls tailored to organizational security policies.

Security policies, a critical component of authorization, provide a framework for defining and enforcing security rules within an organization. These policies articulate the acceptable use of resources, delineate access control requirements, and establish guidelines for data protection. Organizations often formulate and implement security policies to align with regulatory compliance requirements, industry standards, and best practices. Security policies are dynamic and should evolve in response to changing threat landscapes, emerging technologies, and organizational shifts.

Encryption is a fundamental security feature that protects data integrity and confidentiality during transmission and storage. Encryption algorithms transform plaintext data into ciphertext, rendering it unreadable without the appropriate decryption key. Transport Layer Security (TLS) and its predecessor, Secure Sockets Layer (SSL), are widely used cryptographic protocols that establish secure communication channels over the internet, ensuring that sensitive information, such as login credentials and financial transactions, remains confidential and secure from eavesdropping or tampering.

Digital signatures and certificates are cryptographic tools that enhance data integrity and authentication in digital communications. Digital signatures provide a means of verifying the authenticity and origin of a message or document, as they are uniquely tied to the signer's identity. Certificates, issued by trusted certificate authorities (CAs), validate the authenticity of digital signatures and facilitate secure communication by establishing a trust framework. Public key infrastructure (PKI) is a comprehensive system that incorporates digital signatures, certificates, and other cryptographic tools to manage and secure digital communication across networks.

Audit trails and logging mechanisms are essential security features that enable organizations to monitor and track user activities, system events, and security incidents. Audit trails capture a chronological record of actions performed within a system, facilitating forensic analysis and aiding in the detection of anomalous or malicious behavior. Logging mechanisms record events, errors, and system activities, providing administrators with valuable insights into the state of the system and potential security threats. Security Information and Event Management (SIEM) solutions integrate audit trails and logs, offering a centralized platform for real-time monitoring, analysis, and reporting of security-related events.

Vulnerability management and patch management are integral components of proactive security measures. Vulnerability management involves identifying, assessing, and prioritizing security vulnerabilities in software, systems, and networks. Organizations utilize vulnerability assessments and penetration testing to uncover weaknesses that could be exploited by attackers. Patch management focuses on the timely application of software updates, patches, and security fixes to address known vulnerabilities and enhance the resilience of systems against potential threats. Automated tools and processes streamline vulnerability and patch management efforts, reducing the window of exposure to security risks.

Incident response and security incident management are critical elements in handling security breaches and mitigating the impact of security incidents. Incident response involves the systematic approach to identifying, containing, eradicating, recovering from, and learning from security incidents. Organizations establish incident response plans that define roles, responsibilities, and procedures for responding to various types of incidents, ensuring a coordinated and effective response. Security incident management encompasses the broader strategy of managing security incidents throughout their lifecycle, from detection and analysis to resolution and post-incident assessment.

Network security features, including firewalls, intrusion detection and prevention systems (IDS/IPS), and Virtual Private Networks (VPNs), are fundamental components in safeguarding networked environments. Firewalls act as barriers between internal networks and external entities, controlling incoming and outgoing traffic based on predefined security rules. IDS/IPS systems monitor network and system activities, identifying and responding to potential security threats. VPNs establish secure, encrypted connections over public networks, allowing users to access private networks securely and ensuring the confidentiality of transmitted data.

Security awareness and training programs are crucial for building a security-conscious organizational culture. Educating users about security best practices, the risks associated with phishing, social engineering, and the importance of safeguarding sensitive information contributes to the human element of cybersecurity. Security awareness programs empower users to recognize and respond effectively to security threats, reducing the likelihood of human error as a vector for cyberattacks.

In conclusion, security features such as authentication, authorization, encryption, and others constitute the foundation of robust information security. These features collectively establish a multi-layered defense strategy, protecting against unauthorized access, data breaches, and various cyber threats. The integration of security policies, cryptographic tools, access controls, and proactive security measures reinforces the resilience of computing environments and ensures the confidentiality, integrity, and availability of critical assets. As the digital landscape continues to evolve, security features remain indispensable in safeguarding sensitive information and maintaining the trust and integrity of systems and networks.

Introduction to system calls and their importance in facilitating communication between applications and the operating system.

System calls are a fundamental aspect of the interaction between applications and the operating system, serving as crucial interfaces that enable programs to request services and resources from the underlying operating system kernel. At their core, system calls act as bridges between the user space, where applications run, and the kernel space, where the operating system's core functionalities are implemented. This essential communication facilitates a wide range of operations, from basic input/output and file manipulation to more complex tasks such as process management, memory allocation, and network communication. As a result, system calls play a central role in providing a standardized and controlled means for applications to access and utilize the underlying resources of the computer system.

The significance of system calls lies in their ability to abstract the complexities of hardware interaction, allowing applications to execute tasks without needing intricate knowledge of the underlying hardware architecture. Applications interact with the operating system through a set of predefined system call interfaces, presenting a consistent layer of abstraction regardless of the specific hardware configuration. This abstraction shields application developers from the intricacies of low-level hardware details, enabling them to focus on writing portable and platform-independent code. Consequently, software written to make system calls can run on different operating systems with minimal modifications, promoting code reusability and easing the development of cross-platform applications.

One of the fundamental categories of system calls involves file and input/output operations, which enable applications to read from and write to files, as well as perform various input and output activities. For instance, opening or closing files, reading or writing data to a file, and manipulating file attributes are common file-related system calls. These operations form the backbone of file management in computing systems, allowing applications to store, retrieve, and manipulate data persistently. This abstraction ensures that applications do not need to concern themselves with the intricacies of disk access, storage management, or specific file system implementations.

Process management is another critical domain facilitated by system calls, encompassing operations such as process creation, termination, and synchronization. System calls in this category allow applications to spawn new processes, manage their execution, and coordinate communication between them. Context switching, the mechanism by which the operating system transitions between executing processes, is also orchestrated through system calls. By providing these process management services, system calls ensure the effective utilization of system resources, the isolation of processes, and the overall stability of the computing environment.

Memory management system calls are integral to the dynamic allocation and deallocation of memory, enabling applications to request and release memory as needed. Allocating memory for variables, data structures, or dynamic arrays is a common operation performed through memory management system calls. These system calls contribute to efficient memory utilization, preventing memory leaks and ensuring that applications have the necessary resources for their execution. Additionally, memory protection mechanisms, enforced through system calls, safeguard against unauthorized access and manipulation of memory regions, enhancing system security and stability.

System calls are also pivotal in providing communication and synchronization mechanisms between processes, facilitating inter-process communication (IPC). This category includes system calls for creating and managing communication channels such as pipes, message queues, and shared memory segments. By leveraging these IPC mechanisms, applications can exchange data, synchronize their execution, and collaborate in complex computing scenarios. System calls related to IPC play a crucial role in building concurrent and distributed systems, where communication between processes is essential for achieving parallelism and responsiveness.

Network-related system calls form the backbone of networking capabilities in modern computing environments. These system calls allow applications to establish network connections, send and receive data over networks, and manage network configurations. Protocols like Transmission Control Protocol (TCP) and User Datagram Protocol (UDP) are implemented through network-related system calls, enabling applications to communicate seamlessly across local and global networks. As a result, system calls in this category are vital for the development of networked applications, internet services, and distributed computing systems.

The ability to interact with hardware devices is facilitated by device-related system calls, allowing applications to communicate with peripherals such as printers, storage devices, and input/output devices. For instance, printing a document, reading from a disk, or capturing input from a keyboard involve system calls that interface with the corresponding hardware devices. By abstracting the intricacies of device interaction, system calls in this category enable applications to utilize a diverse range of hardware components without needing to implement device-specific functionalities.

Error handling and signaling system calls are essential for managing exceptional conditions and events within the computing system. Applications can use these system calls to handle errors, exceptions, and signals gracefully. For example, signaling system calls enable applications to respond to specific events or interrupts, enhancing their responsiveness and adaptability. Error handling system calls provide mechanisms for applications to detect and respond to errors, ensuring robustness and preventing unintended consequences in the face of unexpected events.

The asynchronous and parallel execution of tasks is facilitated through system calls related to threads and synchronization. Threading system calls allow applications to create and manage multiple threads of execution, enabling parallelism and concurrency. Synchronization mechanisms, such as locks and semaphores implemented through system calls, ensure coordinated and orderly access to shared resources among threads. These system calls are instrumental in developing multi-threaded applications that harness the full computational power of modern processors and improve overall system responsiveness.

In the context of security, system calls contribute to enforcing access controls, user authentication, and process isolation. Security-related system calls enable the implementation of mandatory access controls, discretionary access controls, and other security policies defined by the operating system. User authentication system calls play a key role in verifying the identity of users, ensuring that only authorized individuals or processes access sensitive resources. Process isolation mechanisms, facilitated through system calls, contribute to the containment of security breaches and the protection of system integrity.

The efficiency and performance of system calls are crucial for the overall responsiveness of applications and the system as a whole. Operating systems optimize system call handling through techniques such as syscall optimization, reducing the overhead associated with transitioning between user space and kernel space. Efficient system call handling is particularly critical in high-performance computing environments, real-time systems, and scenarios where rapid response times are essential.

In conclusion, system calls form the linchpin of communication between applications and the operating system, providing a standardized interface for accessing the diverse functionalities offered by the underlying kernel. Their importance lies in abstracting the complexities of hardware interaction, enabling applications to execute tasks without intimate knowledge of the hardware architecture. System calls span a broad spectrum of operations, from file and process management to memory allocation, network communication, and security enforcement. By acting as the intermediary layer between user space and kernel space, system calls play an indispensable role in orchestrating the seamless interaction between applications and the operating system, contributing to the efficiency, portability, and reliability of computing systems.

Analyzing notable operating systems and their impact on the evolution of computing.

The evolution of computing has been significantly shaped by notable operating systems, each contributing distinct innovations and paradigms that have influenced the way we interact with and harness the power of computers. Microsoft Windows, a dominant player in the personal computer (PC) realm, has played a pivotal role in popularizing graphical user interfaces (GUIs) and bringing computing to a broad audience. The release of Windows 95 marked a watershed moment, introducing a visually appealing interface, the Start menu, and support for plug-and-play hardware. Windows 98 and subsequent versions further refined the user experience, solidifying Microsoft's position as a major player in the operating system landscape. The widespread adoption of Windows in homes, businesses, and educational institutions has made it a cornerstone of modern computing, contributing to the seamless integration of PCs into everyday life.

Similarly, the Unix operating system, conceived in the late 1960s at Bell Labs, has left an enduring impact on computing, especially in the realm of servers, mainframes, and academic environments. Unix's design philosophy, emphasizing modularity, simplicity, and the use of text-based interfaces, has influenced subsequent operating systems, including Linux and macOS. The open-source nature of Unix has led to the development of various Unix-like operating systems, fostering a rich ecosystem of tools and utilities. Linux, a Unix-like operating system kernel created by Linus Torvalds in the early 1990s, embodies the collaborative and community-driven ethos of open source. Linux distributions, such as Ubuntu, Debian, and Red Hat, power a significant portion of servers, embedded systems, and mobile devices, contributing to the prevalence of open-source software in the computing landscape.

Apple's macOS, built on a Unix-based foundation, has redefined the user experience by seamlessly integrating aesthetics, usability, and performance. The introduction of Mac OS X marked a significant departure from Apple's previous operating systems, combining the elegance of the Macintosh interface with the robustness of a Unix-based architecture. The macOS ecosystem has thrived on innovation, introducing features like Time Machine for effortless backups, Spotlight for powerful search capabilities, and the App Store for streamlined software distribution. The macOS approach to design, user experience, and seamless integration across devices has garnered a dedicated user base and influenced the design principles of other operating systems.

In the realm of mobile computing, Google's Android operating system has played a transformative role, powering a vast array of smartphones and tablets. Android's open-source nature, coupled with the extensive customization options it offers to device manufacturers and users, has contributed to its widespread adoption. The Android ecosystem, fueled by the Google Play Store, has facilitated the distribution of a vast range of applications, transforming smartphones into versatile computing devices. The prevalence of Android has reshaped the mobile landscape, fostering competition and innovation among device manufacturers while providing users with a diverse range of choices and functionalities.

The server-side dominance of Unix and its derivatives has been complemented by Microsoft's Windows Server operating systems. Windows Server has played a key role in enterprise computing, providing a platform for hosting applications, managing network services, and supporting critical business operations. The introduction of features like Active Directory has enhanced Windows Server's capabilities in user management and network administration. The ubiquity of Windows Server in corporate environments underscores its impact on the infrastructure that underpins modern business operations.

The emergence of cloud computing has brought forth a new breed of operating systems designed to harness the power of distributed and scalable computing environments. Linux distributions, such as CentOS and Ubuntu Server, have become staples in cloud infrastructure due to their stability, efficiency, and the availability of a wide range of software packages. Moreover, containerization technologies, exemplified by Docker and Kubernetes, have redefined how applications are deployed and managed across diverse computing environments. These technologies have transcended the traditional boundaries of operating systems, fostering a more portable and scalable approach to application development and deployment.

In the domain of real-time operating systems (RTOS), which are designed for applications requiring precise and predictable timing, QNX has stood out as a prominent player. QNX's microkernel architecture, characterized by a small and modular design, has found applications in embedded systems, automotive control systems, and medical devices. The reliability and deterministic behavior of QNX have made it a preferred choice in safety-critical applications where precise timing and fault tolerance are paramount.

The advent of mobile computing and the rise of tablets have propelled Apple's iOS into the spotlight, creating a new paradigm for mobile operating systems. iOS, known for its streamlined user interface, app-centric approach, and a tightly controlled ecosystem, has redefined the way users interact with mobile devices. The App Store, introduced with the launch of the iPhone in 2008, revolutionized software distribution for mobile applications, leading to the proliferation of a vast and diverse ecosystem of apps. The success of iOS has influenced the design principles of other mobile operating systems and set standards for user experience and application development in the mobile space.

A noteworthy mention goes to the FreeBSD operating system, a Unix-like system that has played a significant role in both server and desktop environments. Known for its advanced networking capabilities, scalability, and permissive open-source license, FreeBSD has been the foundation for various projects and operating systems, including the widely used macOS. FreeBSD's commitment to stability and performance has contributed to its longevity and its adoption in various niches, from web servers to embedded systems.

The impact of these operating systems extends beyond their technical attributes, influencing user expectations, developer practices, and the broader socio-economic landscape. The rise of open-source operating systems has fostered collaborative development models, enabling global communities to contribute to the enhancement and evolution of software. The democratization of computing, driven by diverse operating systems, has empowered users with choices, fostering competition and innovation.

Moreover, the security landscape has been significantly shaped by operating systems, with each facing its own set of challenges and adopting distinct security models. Windows, for instance, has been a target for malware and viruses due to its widespread use, leading to the development of robust antivirus and security solutions. In contrast, Unix-based systems have historically benefited from a security-oriented design, with principles such as least privilege and separation of duties contributing to their resilience against security threats.

The trajectory of operating systems reflects the dynamic interplay between technological advancements, user needs, and market forces. As computing continues to evolve, the role of operating systems in shaping the digital landscape remains central. The ongoing pursuit of efficiency, security, and user-centric design ensures that operating systems will continue to be at the forefront of technological innovation, influencing the way we work, communicate, and experience the digital realm.

Chapter 3: Synchronization Techniques for Seamless Operations

Defining synchronization and its significance in multi-process environments.

Synchronization in the context of computing refers to the coordination and control of multiple concurrent processes to ensure orderly and predictable execution. In multi-process environments, where multiple independent processes share resources and execute concurrently, synchronization becomes a critical aspect to prevent undesirable interactions, data inconsistencies, and conflicts. The significance of synchronization lies in its ability to establish a harmonious and organized execution flow among processes, ensuring that they cooperate effectively without leading to issues such as data corruption, race conditions, or deadlock scenarios.

One fundamental challenge in multi-process environments is the potential for concurrent access to shared resources, like memory, files, or data structures. Without proper synchronization mechanisms, simultaneous and uncoordinated access by multiple processes can result in unpredictable and erroneous behavior. For instance, consider a scenario where two processes attempt to update a shared variable simultaneously. Without synchronization, the final value of the variable may be inconsistent or depend on the timing of the updates. Synchronization mechanisms, such as locks, semaphores, and mutexes, provide a means to control access to shared resources, ensuring that only one process can access a resource at any given time, preventing data corruption and maintaining consistency.

Race conditions, a common challenge in multi-process environments, occur when the final outcome of a program depends on the relative timing of operations between concurrent processes. Synchronization mechanisms help mitigate race conditions by imposing order and control over the execution of processes. For instance, using locks ensures that only one process can enter a critical section of code at a time, preventing other processes from interfering with the execution of that section. By eliminating the non-deterministic nature of race conditions, synchronization mechanisms contribute to the reliability and predictability of multi-process systems.

Deadlocks represent another critical issue in multi-process environments, arising when two or more processes are unable to proceed because each is waiting for the other to release a resource. Synchronization mechanisms play a key role in deadlock prevention and resolution. Techniques such as deadlock detection algorithms and resource allocation policies help identify and break deadlocks, ensuring that the system remains responsive and does not grind to a halt due to conflicting resource dependencies. By addressing deadlocks, synchronization mechanisms contribute to the overall robustness and availability of multi-process systems.

In addition to preventing data inconsistencies and resolving conflicts, synchronization is crucial for achieving inter-process communication (IPC) and coordination. Processes often need to communicate, exchange data, or coordinate their activities to accomplish complex tasks. Synchronization primitives, such as semaphores and message passing mechanisms, facilitate reliable communication and coordination among processes. For instance, a producer-consumer scenario may involve synchronization mechanisms to ensure that the producer does not overwhelm the consumer with data or that the consumer does not access incomplete or inconsistent data.

Real-time systems, where tasks must meet stringent timing constraints, rely heavily on synchronization to ensure that processes execute within predefined time limits. Synchronization mechanisms in real-time systems help coordinate the execution of tasks to meet deadlines, prevent resource conflicts, and ensure that critical operations proceed in a timely and predictable manner. This is particularly crucial in applications such as embedded systems, automotive control systems, and industrial automation, where the consequences of missed deadlines or uncoordinated execution can be severe.

The significance of synchronization extends to parallel computing environments, where multiple processes or threads work concurrently to solve complex problems. In parallel computing, achieving efficient parallelism requires proper synchronization to coordinate the activities of individual processing units, avoid contention for shared resources, and ensure the correct sequencing of operations. Synchronization primitives like barriers and parallel loops aid in orchestrating the parallel execution of tasks, enhancing performance and scalability in parallel computing environments.

Moreover, synchronization is integral to ensuring the consistency and integrity of data in multi-process databases and distributed systems. In scenarios where multiple processes or nodes interact with a shared database, synchronization mechanisms prevent conflicts and race conditions that could lead to data corruption or inconsistency. Distributed systems, which span multiple machines or locations, rely on synchronization to maintain a globally consistent view of shared data, ensuring that updates from different nodes are applied in a coordinated and orderly fashion.

The implementation of synchronization mechanisms involves trade-offs between performance, scalability, and simplicity. Lock-based synchronization, where processes acquire and release locks to access shared resources, provides a straightforward and intuitive approach but may lead to contention and reduced parallelism. More advanced techniques, such as lock-free algorithms and transactional memory, aim to mitigate these issues by allowing processes to operate independently without explicit locks. However, these approaches may introduce additional complexity and overhead. The choice of synchronization strategy depends on the specific requirements and characteristics of the multi-process environment.

In conclusion, synchronization plays a pivotal role in multi-process environments, ensuring the orderly and predictable execution of concurrent processes. Its significance lies in mitigating data inconsistencies, resolving conflicts, preventing race conditions and deadlocks, facilitating inter-process communication, and coordinating the execution of tasks. Synchronization mechanisms provide the foundation for reliable and efficient operation in diverse computing scenarios, ranging from real-time systems and parallel computing environments to distributed systems and multi-process databases. As computing systems continue to evolve and leverage parallelism, the role of synchronization remains paramount in maintaining the integrity, predictability, and performance of concurrent operations.

Understanding race conditions and critical sections in concurrent processes.

Race conditions and critical sections represent fundamental challenges in concurrent processes, where multiple independent threads or processes execute concurrently, sharing resources and data. A race condition occurs when the behavior of a program depends on the relative timing of events, and the final outcome becomes unpredictable. This unpredictability arises from the interleaved execution of multiple threads or processes that access shared resources without proper coordination. Race conditions can lead to data inconsistencies, unexpected results, and even system failures. Addressing race conditions requires a deep understanding of the concept of critical sections, which are segments of code or operations that, when executed by one thread or process, must be protected to prevent interference from others.

Critical sections are integral to managing race conditions and ensuring the integrity of shared resources. A critical section is a portion of code that accesses shared data or resources, and only one thread or process is allowed to execute it at a time. The goal is to prevent concurrent access to critical data or operations, thereby avoiding race conditions and maintaining data consistency. To enforce mutual exclusion, the fundamental principle is that if one thread or process is executing in a critical section, others must be prevented from entering it until the current execution completes. Achieving this mutual exclusion is central to addressing race conditions and maintaining the correctness of concurrent programs.

Various synchronization mechanisms are employed to establish and manage critical sections effectively. One commonly used technique is the use of locks, such as mutexes (mutual exclusion locks) or semaphores, to control access to critical sections. When a thread or process wishes to enter a critical section, it must acquire the associated lock. If the lock is currently held by another thread, the requesting thread is blocked until the lock is released, ensuring that only one thread at a time can execute the critical section. Lock-based synchronization provides a straightforward and intuitive approach to enforcing mutual exclusion in critical sections, but it comes with challenges, such as the potential for deadlocks and performance overhead due to contention.

Another approach to managing critical sections involves atomic operations or atomicity, where certain operations are designed to execute as a single, indivisible unit. In this context, an operation is atomic if it appears to occur instantaneously to other threads or processes. Atomic operations are typically provided by hardware architectures or programming language constructs, and they offer a way to ensure that critical sections are executed without interruption. While atomic operations can be more efficient than lock-based approaches, they may have limitations in terms of the complexity of operations that can be made atomic and their applicability to certain scenarios.

Transaction-based mechanisms, such as those used in database systems, also provide a way to manage critical sections. Transactions encapsulate a series of operations, and the system ensures that either all operations in the transaction are executed, or none of them are. Transactions provide a higher-level abstraction for managing critical sections, as they ensure atomicity, consistency, isolation, and durability (ACID properties) across multiple operations. While transactions are powerful, they may introduce additional complexity and overhead, especially in scenarios where fine-grained synchronization is required.

The notion of critical sections extends beyond traditional single-processor systems to the realm of multiprocessor and multicore architectures. In these environments, the challenges of managing critical sections are exacerbated due to the increased potential for parallelism and contention. The traditional synchronization mechanisms, such as locks, must be adapted to handle the nuances of these architectures, considering factors like cache coherence, memory visibility, and the impact of multiple cores accessing shared data concurrently. Techniques like lock-free and wait-free algorithms aim to provide solutions that minimize contention and allow processes to progress even in the absence of locks, although they can introduce additional complexity in terms of design and implementation.

Understanding the principles of race conditions and critical sections is essential for designing concurrent programs that are correct, efficient, and scalable. Race conditions often manifest when multiple threads or processes access shared resources without proper synchronization, leading to scenarios where the outcome is unpredictable. Critical sections, by enforcing mutual exclusion, provide a means to address race conditions by ensuring that only one thread or process can execute a critical section at a time. The choice of synchronization mechanism, whether locks, atomic operations, transactions, or specialized algorithms, depends on the specific requirements of the concurrent program and the characteristics of the underlying hardware architecture.

One common scenario illustrating the importance of managing race conditions and critical sections is the classic example of the "producer-consumer problem." In this scenario, multiple producers generate data, and multiple consumers consume that data. The producers and consumers share a common buffer or queue. Without proper synchronization, race conditions can arise when producers and consumers attempt to access and modify the shared buffer concurrently. For instance, a producer might try to add data to the buffer while a consumer is simultaneously trying to remove data. Without coordination, this can lead to data corruption, inconsistent states, or even crashes.

To address this issue, a critical section can be introduced to ensure that only one thread (producer or consumer) can access the shared buffer at any given time. A lock or other synchronization mechanism is used to protect the critical section, preventing concurrent access and guaranteeing that operations within the critical section are executed atomically. This ensures the integrity of the shared data structure and eliminates race conditions.

The understanding of race conditions and critical sections is not confined to low-level programming or systems-level development. In high-level programming languages and frameworks, the principles of managing concurrent access to shared resources remain relevant. For example, in multithreaded applications developed in languages like Java or C#, synchronization constructs such as synchronized blocks or locks are employed to manage critical sections and avoid race conditions. Similarly, in web development, where multiple requests may be processed concurrently, mechanisms like mutexes or semaphores are used to coordinate access to shared resources.

In the context of parallel and distributed computing, managing race conditions and critical sections becomes even more challenging due to the potential for multiple processes running on different machines or nodes. Distributed systems must contend with issues such as network latency, message passing, and the lack of shared memory. Mechanisms like distributed locks and consensus algorithms become essential in these scenarios to ensure the orderly execution of critical sections across distributed entities.

In conclusion, the concepts of race conditions and critical sections are foundational to concurrent programming and parallel computing. Race conditions arise when multiple threads or processes concurrently access shared resources without proper synchronization, leading to unpredictable outcomes. Critical sections, managed through synchronization mechanisms such as locks, atomic operations, or transactions, provide a means to enforce mutual exclusion and prevent race conditions. Understanding these concepts is crucial for designing correct, efficient, and scalable concurrent programs across various domains, from low-level system programming to high-level application development and distributed computing. As technology continues to advance, the principles of managing race conditions and critical sections remain at the forefront of ensuring the reliability and correctness of concurrent systems.

In-depth exploration of semaphores and mutexes as synchronization mechanisms.

Semaphores and mutexes are essential synchronization mechanisms, playing a crucial role in managing access to shared resources and preventing race conditions in concurrent programming environments. A semaphore is a signaling mechanism that allows threads or processes to coordinate their activities by controlling access to shared resources. It maintains a counter, often initialized to a positive integer, which represents the number of available resources. Threads can request and release resources by manipulating this counter. When the counter is positive, indicating available resources, a thread can acquire a resource by decrementing the counter. Conversely, when the counter reaches zero, further attempts to acquire resources result in blocking until other threads release resources, incrementing the counter. Semaphores come in two types: binary semaphores, where the counter can only take values of 0 or 1, resembling mutexes, and counting semaphores, where the counter can have values greater than 1, allowing multiple threads to access a resource concurrently.

Mutexes, short for mutual exclusion, are synchronization primitives specifically designed to enforce mutual exclusion, ensuring that only one thread can access a critical section of code at a time. Unlike semaphores, mutexes are binary in nature, having only two states: locked or unlocked. When a thread acquires a mutex, it becomes locked, preventing other threads from entering the associated critical section until the mutex is released. Mutexes are often employed in scenarios where exclusive access to a shared resource or data is required to maintain consistency. The simplicity and effectiveness of mutexes make them a fundamental building block for managing critical sections and preventing race conditions in concurrent programs.

Understanding the differences between semaphores and mutexes is essential for choosing the appropriate synchronization mechanism based on the requirements of a given concurrent program. Semaphores, with their versatile counting mechanism, provide flexibility in scenarios where multiple threads might access a shared resource concurrently, up to a specified limit. This is particularly useful in resource management scenarios where a fixed number of instances of a resource, like database connections or buffers, are available for concurrent use. Counting semaphores allow for a more nuanced control over resource allocation, enabling dynamic adjustment of resource availability based on the program's needs.

On the other hand, mutexes are more specialized and are typically employed in situations where exclusive access to a critical section of code is paramount. Mutexes ensure that only one thread can execute the protected code segment at any given time, providing a straightforward and efficient means of preventing race conditions. Mutexes are well-suited for scenarios where the shared resource or data is sensitive to simultaneous access, and maintaining consistency is critical. The binary nature of mutexes simplifies their usage, making them easy to implement and reason about, especially in scenarios with a clear distinction between locked and unlocked states.

Both semaphores and mutexes operate based on the principles of mutual exclusion and can be used to coordinate access to shared resources or protect critical sections. The choice between them often depends on the specific requirements of the concurrent program and the nature of the shared resource being managed. It is worth noting that while semaphores can be used to implement mutex-like behavior (binary semaphores essentially become mutexes), using mutexes is generally more straightforward when the goal is to enforce mutual exclusion without the need for counting.

In practical terms, the usage of semaphores and mutexes extends to various programming environments and languages. In multi-threaded applications, where multiple threads share the same address space, synchronization mechanisms are crucial for coordinating their activities. For instance, in Java, the `synchronized` keyword is used to create mutex-like behavior, ensuring that only one thread can execute a synchronized block of code at a time. Java also provides the `Semaphore` class, which can be used for more general resource management scenarios.

In C and C++, the POSIX Threads (Pthreads) library is commonly used for multithreading. Pthreads provide functions for creating and manipulating both mutexes and semaphores. Mutexes can be created and initialized using functions like `pthread_mutex_init`, and operations such as locking and unlocking are performed using `pthread_mutex_lock` and `pthread_mutex_unlock`. Semaphores, introduced with the `**sem_init**` function, can be used for more complex coordination between threads.

The implementation of semaphores and mutexes involves careful consideration of potential issues, such as deadlock and priority inversion, to ensure the reliability and correctness of concurrent programs. Deadlock occurs when multiple threads are blocked, each waiting for a resource held by another, creating a cyclic dependency. Strategies like deadlock detection algorithms and careful resource allocation policies help mitigate the risk of deadlocks. Priority inversion, another concern, arises when a high-priority thread is blocked waiting for a resource held by a low-priority thread, leading to decreased overall system performance. Priority inheritance protocols and priority ceiling mechanisms address this issue by dynamically adjusting thread priorities to prevent inversion.

In real-time systems, where precise timing and responsiveness are critical, the choice between semaphores and mutexes can impact the system's performance. Semaphore-based synchronization may introduce more contention, especially in scenarios with high levels of concurrency, potentially leading to increased waiting times for threads. Mutexes, with their binary nature, may be more suitable for real-time systems where minimizing contention and ensuring quick access to critical sections are essential.

The concepts of semaphores and mutexes are not limited to traditional multithreaded programming but also extend to parallel and distributed computing environments. In parallel computing, where multiple processors work on a shared problem concurrently, synchronization mechanisms are crucial for coordinating the execution of tasks and managing access to shared data structures. Parallel algorithms often leverage mutexes and semaphores to ensure the correctness of computations and prevent data corruption. In distributed systems, which span multiple machines or nodes, synchronization mechanisms become even more challenging due to factors such as network latency and the lack of shared memory. Distributed lock services and consensus algorithms, inspired by the principles of semaphores and mutexes, provide solutions for managing shared resources across distributed entities.

In conclusion, semaphores and mutexes are foundational synchronization mechanisms that play a critical role in concurrent programming environments. Semaphores, with their counting mechanism, provide flexibility for managing resources in scenarios with varying levels of concurrency. Mutexes, binary in nature, excel at enforcing mutual exclusion in critical sections, preventing race conditions and maintaining data consistency. The careful consideration of the specific requirements of a concurrent program, potential issues like deadlock and priority inversion, and the characteristics of the underlying environment helps determine whether semaphores or mutexes are the more suitable synchronization mechanism. As technology continues to advance, the principles of semaphores and mutexes remain integral to designing correct, efficient, and scalable concurrent systems across diverse domains.

Analyzing the concept of deadlock and strategies for prevention.

Deadlock, a complex and potentially disruptive issue in concurrent systems, occurs when two or more processes are unable to proceed because each is waiting for the other to release a resource. This situation creates a cyclic dependency, where each process is withholding a resource that another process needs, leading to a standstill in the system. The concept of deadlock is particularly pertinent in environments where multiple processes or threads contend for shared resources, and managing access to these resources becomes crucial.

Understanding the conditions that give rise to deadlock is fundamental to devising effective prevention strategies. Deadlock typically involves four necessary conditions: mutual exclusion, where at least one resource must be held in a non-sharable mode; hold and wait, where a process holds one resource while waiting for another; no preemption, where resources cannot be forcibly taken from a process; and circular wait, where a cycle of processes exists, each waiting for a resource held by the next. The interplay of these conditions creates a scenario where processes are stuck in a perpetual state of waiting, unable to make progress.

One common strategy for preventing deadlocks is breaking one or more of the necessary conditions. Mutual exclusion can be addressed by allowing resources to be sharable or allowing multiple processes to access a resource simultaneously. However, this may not be applicable in scenarios where resources must be accessed exclusively to maintain consistency, such as modifying a critical section of code or writing to a file.

The hold and wait condition can be mitigated by requiring processes to request all the resources they need upfront, rather than acquiring them incrementally. If a process cannot obtain all the required resources, it releases any resources it has acquired, preventing it from holding resources while waiting for others. While this approach can reduce the risk of deadlock, it may lead to decreased system efficiency, as processes may be unable to utilize resources that they could have acquired incrementally.

Addressing the no preemption condition involves allowing the operating system to forcibly preempt resources from a process if necessary. While this approach can break a potential deadlock, it introduces complexities and challenges, particularly in scenarios where forcibly preempting resources may lead to inconsistent states or data corruption. Forcible preemption can also impact the fairness and predictability of the system.

Circular wait, the final necessary condition, can be mitigated by imposing a total ordering on resources and requiring processes to request resources in this predefined order. By ensuring that processes always request resources in the same order, the potential for cyclic dependencies is eliminated. However, enforcing a total ordering on resources may not always be feasible or practical, especially in systems with dynamic resource allocation patterns.

A more holistic approach to deadlock prevention involves combining multiple strategies to address each of the necessary conditions simultaneously. One such approach is the use of the Banker's algorithm, a resource allocation and deadlock avoidance algorithm. The Banker's algorithm employs a safety algorithm that checks whether granting a resource request will leave the system in a safe state, ensuring that deadlock conditions are not met. This algorithm considers the maximum and available resources, along with the current resource allocations, to make informed decisions about resource allocation.

Another preventive strategy involves utilizing resource allocation graphs, where processes and resources are represented as nodes and edges, respectively, in a directed graph. This graph visually depicts the relationships between processes and resources, making it easier to identify potential cyclic dependencies and take corrective actions. By periodically analyzing the resource allocation graph, the system can dynamically adjust resource allocations to prevent deadlock.

While these preventive strategies are effective in many scenarios, they come with trade-offs. Introducing additional checks and mechanisms to prevent deadlock can impose overhead on the system, potentially impacting performance. Moreover, preventive strategies may introduce complexities in resource management and may not be foolproof, especially in dynamic and unpredictable environments.

Another consideration in deadlock prevention is the role of timeouts and resource reclaiming. In scenarios where a process requests a resource but does not receive it within a specified time frame, the request may be automatically released, preventing the process from waiting indefinitely. Timeouts introduce a level of dynamism to the system, but setting appropriate timeout values and handling timeout scenarios gracefully are non-trivial challenges.

In distributed systems, where processes may span multiple machines or nodes, the challenges of deadlock prevention are exacerbated. Distributed systems must contend with issues such as network latency, message passing, and the lack of shared memory. Traditional deadlock prevention strategies need to be adapted to handle the nuances of distributed environments. Distributed lock services, which manage locks across multiple nodes, and consensus algorithms, which coordinate distributed processes, provide solutions for preventing deadlocks in such scenarios.

An alternative perspective on deadlock is to acknowledge its inevitability in certain cases and focus on detection and recovery strategies. Deadlock detection involves periodically examining the system's state to identify whether a deadlock has occurred. Once a deadlock is detected, recovery strategies can be employed to break the deadlock and allow the system to continue. One common approach is to forcibly preempt resources from one or more processes to release the necessary resources for others. However, this approach introduces complexities, such as the potential for inconsistent states and the need for careful resource rollback mechanisms.

In real-time systems, where precise timing constraints are crucial, the prevention and detection of deadlocks become even more critical. Traditional deadlock prevention mechanisms may not be suitable for real-time systems, as they may introduce unpredictable delays and compromise the system's ability to meet deadlines. Real-time systems often rely on static analysis and scheduling techniques to ensure that resources are allocated in a manner that avoids deadlock scenarios.

The impact of deadlock goes beyond mere system inefficiency; it can have severe consequences in safety-critical systems, such as those used in healthcare, transportation, and industrial automation. In such contexts, the prevention, detection, and recovery from deadlocks become paramount to ensure the reliability and safety of the system. The choice of deadlock prevention or detection strategy depends on the specific requirements of the application, the nature of the resources involved, and the criticality of the system.

In conclusion, deadlock is a challenging issue in concurrent systems that arises from cyclic dependencies between processes contending for resources. Strategies for preventing deadlock involve addressing the necessary conditions, such as mutual exclusion, hold and wait, no preemption, and circular wait. While breaking one or more of these conditions can mitigate the risk of deadlock, preventive strategies come with trade-offs in terms of system complexity and efficiency. Holistic approaches, such as the Banker's algorithm and resource allocation graphs, aim to simultaneously address multiple conditions. In distributed systems, deadlock prevention must consider the challenges of network communication and lack of shared memory. Timeouts, distributed lock services, and consensus algorithms provide additional tools for preventing deadlocks in such environments. Alternatively, acknowledging the inevitability of deadlock in certain scenarios leads to the exploration of detection and recovery strategies. Real-time systems, with their stringent timing constraints, require specialized approaches to deadlock prevention. The choice between prevention and detection strategies depends on the specific requirements and criticality of the system. As technology advances and concurrent systems become more prevalent, the effective management of deadlock remains a critical aspect of designing robust and reliable computing systems.

Exploring methods for controlling concurrent access to shared resources.

Controlling concurrent access to shared resources is a fundamental challenge in concurrent programming, where multiple threads or processes contend for access to common data structures, files, or critical sections of code. The goal is to ensure that access to shared resources is coordinated in a way that prevents race conditions, maintains data consistency, and avoids conflicts between concurrent operations. Various methods and synchronization mechanisms are employed to address this challenge, each with its advantages, limitations, and suitability for different scenarios.

One of the primary methods for controlling concurrent access is the use of locks, specifically mutexes (mutual exclusion locks). Mutexes act as gatekeepers, allowing only one thread or process at a time to enter a critical section of code or access a shared resource. When a thread acquires a mutex, it gains exclusive access to the protected region, preventing other threads from entering until the mutex is released. This mechanism ensures mutual exclusion and simplifies the coordination of concurrent operations. While mutexes provide a straightforward and effective means of controlling access, they can introduce issues such as contention, where multiple threads compete for the same lock, potentially leading to performance bottlenecks.

To address the limitations of simple locks, more advanced synchronization mechanisms, such as semaphores, are employed. Semaphores extend the concept of locks by introducing a counter that represents the number of available resources or slots. Threads can acquire and release resources by manipulating this counter. Binary semaphores, a special case where the counter can only take values of 0 or 1, resemble mutexes and provide a way to control access to critical sections. Counting semaphores, with counters greater than 1, allow for more flexible resource management, enabling multiple threads to access a resource concurrently, up to a specified limit. Semaphores provide a higher level of control over resource allocation, especially in scenarios where the number of available resources varies dynamically.

Another approach to controlling concurrent access involves atomic operations, which are designed to execute as a single, indivisible unit. Atomic operations guarantee that the operation is completed without interruption, making them well-suited for scenarios where fine-grained synchronization is required. For example, compare-and-swap (CAS) is an atomic operation that updates a value if it matches an expected value. CAS is often used in lock-free and wait-free algorithms, where multiple threads can make progress without explicit locks. While atomic operations can enhance concurrency by minimizing contention, they may have limitations in terms of the complexity of operations that can be made atomic.

Transactional memory represents a more abstract and high-level method for controlling concurrent access. In transactional memory systems, a series of operations are treated as a transaction, and the system ensures that either all operations in the transaction are executed, or none of them are. This atomicity property simplifies the programming model, allowing developers to reason about concurrent operations without explicitly managing locks. Transactional memory systems aim to provide the benefits of atomicity, consistency, isolation, and durability (ACID properties), similar to database transactions, in the context of shared memory. However, implementing efficient and scalable transactional memory systems poses challenges, and their adoption in practical programming scenarios is still an area of ongoing research.

Concurrency control also extends to scenarios where processes or threads communicate and exchange data through inter-process communication (IPC) mechanisms. Message passing is a common method where processes communicate by sending and receiving messages. Synchronization in message-passing systems involves ensuring that messages are exchanged in a coordinated manner to avoid data corruption or inconsistencies. Techniques such as message queues, channels, and rendezvous points provide mechanisms for orderly communication between concurrent processes.

In addition to these methods, the concept of lock-free and wait-free algorithms aims to maximize concurrency by allowing multiple threads to make progress without waiting for locks. Lock-free algorithms guarantee that at least one thread will make progress within a finite number of steps, while wait-free algorithms ensure that every thread will make progress within a bounded number of steps. These algorithms often rely on low-level atomic operations and advanced data structures to achieve their goals. While lock-free and wait-free algorithms can enhance scalability and responsiveness, designing and implementing them correctly requires a deep understanding of concurrency and memory consistency models.

Concurrency control becomes even more challenging in distributed systems, where processes or threads span multiple machines or nodes. Distributed systems must contend with issues such as network latency, communication failures, and lack of shared memory. Consensus algorithms, such as the Paxos algorithm and the Raft consensus algorithm, provide methods for coordinating distributed processes and achieving agreement on shared values. Distributed lock services, like Apache ZooKeeper, offer solutions for managing distributed locks, enabling processes to coordinate access to shared resources across multiple nodes.

The choice of method for controlling concurrent access depends on the specific requirements and characteristics of the application, the nature of the shared resources, and the desired level of concurrency. Lock-based approaches, while simple and effective, may introduce contention and reduce parallelism. More advanced mechanisms, such as semaphores and atomic operations, provide greater flexibility and scalability but may require careful design and consideration of potential issues such as deadlock. Transactional memory and lock-free/wait-free algorithms offer high-level abstractions and increased concurrency but may come with additional complexity and performance considerations.

Concurrency control methods also need to address challenges such as deadlock prevention, priority inversion, and fairness. Deadlock prevention involves strategies to avoid situations where processes are unable to make progress due to cyclic dependencies. Priority inversion occurs when a high-priority process is blocked waiting for a resource held by a lower-priority process, leading to decreased system performance. Techniques like priority inheritance and priority ceiling protocols help mitigate priority inversion issues. Fairness concerns ensuring that all processes have an opportunity to access shared resources without being unfairly delayed.

In conclusion, controlling concurrent access to shared resources is a critical aspect of concurrent programming, influencing the correctness, efficiency, and scalability of systems. Various methods, ranging from simple locks and semaphores to atomic operations, transactional memory, and sophisticated lock-free/wait-free algorithms, provide a spectrum of tools for managing concurrency. The choice of method depends on the specific requirements of the application, the nature of shared resources, and the desired level of concurrency. Additionally, the challenges of distributed systems introduce additional considerations for controlling concurrent access across multiple nodes. As technology continues to advance and systems become more concurrent and distributed, effective concurrency control methods remain essential for designing robust and scalable computing systems.

Overview of synchronization models, including producer-consumer and reader-writer.

Synchronization models play a crucial role in concurrent programming, providing frameworks and patterns to manage the coordination of multiple threads or processes accessing shared resources. Two fundamental synchronization models are the producer-consumer model and the reader-writer model, each addressing specific scenarios and challenges in concurrent systems.

The producer-consumer model revolves around the coordination between threads or processes involved in producing data (producers) and those consuming it (consumers). This model is commonly employed in scenarios where a shared buffer or queue is utilized to transfer data from producers to consumers. The primary challenge in the producer-consumer model is to ensure that producers do not overflow the buffer and consumers do not access empty slots. Semaphores, mutexes, or other synchronization primitives are often used to coordinate access to the shared buffer. Producers, before depositing data, must check whether there is space available in the buffer, and consumers, before retrieving data, must ensure that the buffer is not empty. The coordination ensures a seamless flow of data between producers and consumers, preventing race conditions and maintaining the integrity of the shared buffer.

In the reader-writer model, the synchronization challenge arises when multiple threads or processes aim to access shared data, differentiating between those only reading (readers) and those modifying the data (writers). The primary goal is to allow concurrent read access while ensuring exclusive write access to maintain data consistency. A straightforward approach is to use locks or mutexes to achieve mutual exclusion, allowing either one reader or one writer at a time. However, this approach can lead to inefficiency, particularly in scenarios where there are frequent reads and infrequent writes. To enhance concurrency, more advanced synchronization mechanisms, such as read-write locks, are employed. Read-write locks permit multiple readers to access the shared data concurrently but restrict exclusive write access. This enables a balance between concurrent read access and exclusive write access, improving the overall throughput of the system. However, it introduces challenges related to fairness and potential writer starvation, as readers may continuously access the shared data, delaying writers.

The producer-consumer and reader-writer models represent fundamental synchronization patterns, but their variations and combinations are employed to address diverse scenarios in concurrent systems. For instance, a system may require a combination of producer-consumer and reader-writer synchronization within different components or modules to handle distinct functionalities. Advanced synchronization constructs, such as condition variables and barriers, are often integrated into these models to cater to specific coordination requirements.

Condition variables provide a mechanism for threads to wait until a particular condition is met before proceeding. In the context of the producer-consumer model, condition variables can be employed to signal when the buffer is not empty (for consumers) or not full (for producers), allowing threads to wait efficiently without continuous polling. In the reader-writer model, condition variables might be used to signal when data is available for reading or when a write operation has completed, optimizing resource utilization and responsiveness.

Barriers are synchronization constructs that enable a group of threads to synchronize at a predefined point in their execution. This is particularly useful in scenarios where threads need to coordinate and synchronize their progress before proceeding with further tasks. In the context of the producer-consumer model, barriers may be employed to ensure that all consumers have processed their data before allowing the producers to deposit new data into the shared buffer, preventing potential race conditions. In the reader-writer model, barriers could be used to coordinate a group of readers to collectively synchronize with a writer, ensuring a consistent snapshot of the shared data.

The choice of synchronization model depends on the specific requirements of the application, the characteristics of shared resources, and the desired level of concurrency. While the producer-consumer and reader-writer models provide fundamental coordination patterns, real-world concurrent systems often require more sophisticated synchronization strategies that leverage a combination of these models and additional constructs. Factors such as fairness, throughput, and responsiveness influence the design choices, and careful consideration is necessary to strike a balance between efficient resource utilization and avoiding synchronization bottlenecks.

In practical applications, these synchronization models find diverse use cases. For example, in a multi-threaded web server, the producer-consumer model can be applied to handle incoming requests. Incoming requests (producers) are added to a shared queue, and worker threads (consumers) process the requests from the queue. This ensures that requests are efficiently handled without the need for each thread to contend for incoming connections.

In database systems, the reader-writer model is often employed to manage concurrent access to data. Multiple queries (readers) can be executed concurrently, ensuring that data consistency is maintained. However, when a write operation is requested, exclusive access is enforced to prevent potential conflicts and ensure the integrity of the database. Read-write locks are commonly used to strike a balance between concurrent read access and exclusive write access in database management systems.

These synchronization models also play a significant role in real-time systems, where precise timing and responsiveness are critical. For instance, in a real-time data acquisition system, producers may represent sensor data sources, and consumers may be responsible for processing and transmitting the acquired data. Synchronization mechanisms, aligned with the producer-consumer model, ensure that data is processed and transmitted within specified time constraints.

In conclusion, synchronization models, exemplified by the producer-consumer and reader-writer models, are foundational concepts in concurrent programming, providing essential frameworks for coordinating access to shared resources. These models address specific challenges arising from concurrent access patterns and serve as building blocks for more complex synchronization strategies. Through the use of synchronization primitives such as locks, condition variables, and barriers, these models help ensure the orderly execution of concurrent operations, preventing race conditions and maintaining the integrity of shared resources. As concurrent systems become increasingly prevalent and complex, a nuanced understanding of synchronization models and their application is vital for designing robust, efficient, and responsive concurrent software.

Understanding synchronization challenges in multithreading environments.

Synchronization challenges in multithreading environments arise from the concurrent execution of multiple threads that share access to shared resources, such as data structures, variables, or critical sections of code. These challenges are fundamental to the field of concurrent programming and require careful consideration to ensure correct and efficient execution. One of the primary synchronization challenges is the risk of race conditions, where the outcome of a computation depends on the interleaving of instructions from different threads. Race conditions can lead to unpredictable and erroneous behavior, as threads may read and write shared data simultaneously, resulting in inconsistent states. The management of access to shared resources becomes crucial to prevent race conditions and maintain data consistency.

Mutexes, or mutual exclusion locks, are a common synchronization primitive used to address race conditions by ensuring that only one thread at a time can access a critical section of code or a shared resource. While mutexes effectively prevent race conditions, they introduce challenges of their own, such as the potential for deadlock. Deadlock occurs when two or more threads are blocked, each waiting for a resource held by another, creating a cyclic dependency. Strategies for deadlock prevention, detection, and recovery are essential to address these challenges and ensure the reliability of multithreading environments.

Another synchronization challenge is priority inversion, where a high-priority thread is blocked waiting for a resource held by a lower-priority thread. This phenomenon can lead to decreased system performance and violates the expected execution priorities. Priority inheritance protocols and priority ceiling mechanisms are strategies employed to mitigate priority inversion, dynamically adjusting thread priorities to ensure fair and efficient execution. These mechanisms help maintain the intended order of thread execution and prevent scenarios where high-priority threads are indefinitely delayed.

Fairness in resource allocation is another aspect of synchronization challenges, where threads must be given equal opportunities to access shared resources. Unfairness may lead to certain threads experiencing prolonged delays, impacting the overall system performance and responsiveness. Synchronization constructs such as semaphores and condition variables, along with careful design considerations, are used to achieve fairness in resource allocation, ensuring that threads are not unfairly delayed in accessing critical resources.

The A-B-A problem is a subtle synchronization challenge that arises in scenarios involving shared data updates. It occurs when a thread reads a value (A), another thread modifies the value (B), and the original thread re-reads the value (A) assuming it is unchanged. This can lead to unexpected behavior as the thread may not be aware of the intermediate modification (B). Atomic operations and memory barriers are employed to address the A-B-A problem by ensuring that the sequence of read-modify-write operations is executed atomically or with well-defined ordering constraints, preventing inconsistencies in shared data.

Cache coherence introduces synchronization challenges in multithreading environments, particularly in systems with multiple processors or cores. Caches at different levels of the memory hierarchy may hold copies of shared data, leading to inconsistencies if not managed properly. Cache coherence protocols, such as MESI (Modified, Exclusive, Shared, Invalid) and MOESI (Modified, Owned, Exclusive, Shared, Invalid), are implemented to maintain consistency across caches. These protocols ensure that when one thread modifies a shared variable, the changes are reflected in all caches to prevent stale or inconsistent data.

Thread starvation and contention are additional synchronization challenges that impact the overall performance of multithreading environments. Thread starvation occurs when a thread is unable to acquire a required resource or access a critical section due to continuous contention. This can lead to reduced throughput and response times. Strategies like fair scheduling, adaptive locking mechanisms, and load balancing are employed to mitigate thread starvation and contention, ensuring a more equitable distribution of resources among threads.

Lock-free and wait-free algorithms present an advanced set of synchronization challenges that focus on achieving progress in the absence of locks. Lock-free algorithms ensure that at least one thread makes progress within a finite number of steps, while wait-free algorithms guarantee that every thread makes progress within a bounded number of steps. These algorithms leverage atomic operations and advanced data structures to avoid traditional locks, enhancing concurrency and responsiveness. However, their design and implementation are intricate, demanding a deep understanding of memory consistency models and low-level hardware interactions.

Real-time systems introduce synchronization challenges that emphasize meeting precise timing constraints. These systems must guarantee not only correctness but also timely execution of tasks. Synchronization mechanisms in real-time systems include techniques such as priority scheduling, rate monotonic scheduling, and deadline monotonic scheduling. Meeting deadlines and ensuring predictable behavior become paramount concerns, requiring specialized synchronization strategies tailored to the unique requirements of real-time environments.

In distributed systems, where threads or processes span multiple machines or nodes, synchronization challenges expand to incorporate issues such as network latency, communication failures, and lack of shared memory. Distributed lock services, consensus algorithms, and distributed synchronization primitives address challenges related to coordinating access to shared resources across distributed entities. Ensuring consistency and coordination in the face of network uncertainties adds complexity to synchronization strategies in distributed multithreading environments.

The dynamic nature of synchronization challenges calls for continuous advancements and innovations in concurrent programming. The emergence of transactional memory, which treats a sequence of operations as a transaction with ACID properties (Atomicity, Consistency, Isolation, Durability), presents a promising avenue for simplifying the development of concurrent systems. Transactional memory aims to provide a higher-level abstraction for managing shared data, reducing the intricacies associated with manual synchronization.

In conclusion, synchronization challenges in multithreading environments are diverse and multifaceted, encompassing race conditions, deadlock, priority inversion, fairness, the A-B-A problem, cache coherence, thread starvation, contention, lock-free/wait-free algorithms, real-time constraints, and distributed systems complexities. Addressing these challenges requires a comprehensive understanding of concurrency, synchronization primitives, and the intricacies of shared resource management. The choice of synchronization strategies depends on the specific requirements of the application, the characteristics of shared resources, and the desired level of concurrency. As technology advances and multithreading becomes increasingly pervasive, the effective management of synchronization challenges remains integral to designing robust, efficient, and responsive concurrent systems.

Challenges and strategies in synchronizing processes across distributed systems.

Synchronizing processes across distributed systems presents a myriad of challenges rooted in the complexities of communication, coordination, and the lack of a shared memory space. One of the primary challenges is network latency, as distributed systems involve processes running on different machines or nodes connected by a network. The time required for communication between nodes introduces delays, and variations in latency can lead to unpredictable synchronization behavior. Mitigating network latency challenges involves optimizing communication protocols, employing efficient data serialization techniques, and selecting appropriate network architectures. Additionally, addressing communication failures and ensuring fault tolerance become crucial aspects of synchronization strategies in distributed systems.

Consistency in shared data across distributed processes poses another significant challenge. In a distributed environment, processes may update shared data concurrently, leading to inconsistencies if not managed appropriately. Maintaining consistency requires the implementation of distributed consistency models, such as eventual consistency or strong consistency, depending on the application requirements. Techniques like distributed transactions, distributed locks, and consensus algorithms, such as Paxos and Raft, are em ployed to ensure that updates to shared data are coordinated and consistent across distributed processes. However, achieving strong consistency often comes at the cost of increased latency and reduced availability, necessitating careful trade-offs in design.

The lack of a shared memory space complicates the implementation of traditional synchronization primitives, such as locks and semaphores, across distributed processes. Coordinating access to shared resources becomes challenging when processes do not have direct access to each other's memory. Distributed lock services, like Apache ZooKeeper, provide a solution by offering a centralized service for managing distributed locks. These services enable processes to synchronize their actions by acquiring and releasing distributed locks, ensuring mutual exclusion and preventing race conditions. However, reliance on a centralized service introduces a single point of failure and potential bottlenecks, demanding careful consideration in system design.

Ensuring fairness in resource allocation becomes a pertinent challenge in distributed systems, where processes contend for shared resources across different nodes. Unfairness may arise due to variations in network latencies or differences in the computational capacities of nodes. Load balancing mechanisms, dynamic resource allocation strategies, and distributed scheduling algorithms are employed to distribute the workload evenly and ensure that all processes have equitable access to shared resources. Achieving fairness contributes to enhanced system performance, responsiveness, and overall efficiency.

Concurrency control in distributed systems is intricately tied to the challenges of ensuring atomicity, consistency, isolation, and durability (ACID properties) across distributed transactions. Coordinating transactions that involve multiple processes across different nodes requires sophisticated distributed transaction management protocols. Two-phase commit (2PC) and three-phase commit

(3PC) are classic examples of distributed transaction protocols that ensure that either all nodes commit or all nodes abort a transaction, preserving consistency. However, these protocols may introduce challenges related to blocking, scalability, and increased latency, prompting the exploration of alternative approaches such as optimistic concurrency control and distributed snapshot isolation.

The CAP theorem (Consistency, Availability, Partition Tolerance) introduces a fundamental trade-off in distributed systems, stating that it is impossible to simultaneously achieve strong consistency, high availability, and partition tolerance in a distributed system. Processes must make trade-offs between these three properties based on the system's requirements and the specific challenges it faces. For example, systems may opt for eventual consistency and prioritize availability in the face of network partitions, accepting the possibility of temporary inconsistencies. Understanding and navigating the implications of the CAP theorem is essential in designing distributed systems that align with the desired trade-offs.

Scalability challenges in distributed synchronization arise when the system needs to handle an increasing number of processes or nodes. Ensuring that synchronization mechanisms can scale horizontally with the addition of new nodes becomes crucial for accommodating growing workloads. Techniques such as sharding, partitioning, and decentralized architectures help distribute the synchronization load efficiently, enabling the system to scale gracefully. However, achieving scalability often involves complex engineering considerations, and the design must strike a balance between consistency and performance.

The complexities of distributed systems further extend to challenges in clock synchronization. Processes running on different nodes may have independent clocks with variations in time, leading to difficulties in ordering events consistently across the system. Distributed systems rely on algorithms such as the Network Time Protocol (NTP) or vector clocks to establish a coordinated sense of time among processes. However, addressing clock synchronization challenges involves considerations of clock drift, network delays, and the need for robust algorithms to order events accurately.

Asynchronous communication models introduce challenges related to ensuring the delivery and ordering of messages between distributed processes. In scenarios where processes communicate through asynchronous messaging, guaranteeing the reliable delivery of messages becomes a challenge, and ensuring a consistent order of message arrival may require additional coordination. Techniques like message queues, publish-subscribe patterns, and reliable messaging protocols contribute to addressing these challenges by providing reliable and ordered communication between distributed processes.

Distributed consensus algorithms, like Paxos and Raft, play a pivotal role in achieving agreement among distributed processes, especially in scenarios where nodes may fail or experience network partitions. Consensus algorithms help ensure that a majority of nodes agree on a particular value or decision, providing fault tolerance and consistency guarantees. However, these algorithms introduce challenges related to their complexity, the need for a majority of nodes to be available, and the impact on system performance.

In conclusion, synchronizing processes across distributed systems is a multifaceted challenge, encompassing issues of network latency, consistency, lack of shared memory, fairness, concurrency control, the CAP theorem trade-offs, scalability, clock synchronization, asynchronous communication, and distributed consensus. Addressing these challenges requires a nuanced understanding of distributed systems principles, the careful selection of synchronization mechanisms, and the consideration of trade-offs based on the specific requirements of the application. As distributed systems become increasingly prevalent in modern computing environments, the effective management of synchronization challenges remains a critical aspect of designing robust, reliable, and scalable distributed systems.

Examining the performance implications of synchronization techniques.

Examining the performance implications of synchronization techniques in concurrent programming reveals a nuanced landscape where choices made in managing shared resources significantly impact the efficiency, scalability, and responsiveness of systems. One of the fundamental synchronization techniques is the use of locks, such as mutexes, to achieve mutual exclusion and prevent race conditions. While locks effectively ensure data consistency by allowing only one thread at a time to access a critical section, they introduce performance implications. Lock contention, where multiple threads compete for the same lock, can lead to bottlenecks and reduced parallelism. Fine-grained locks may alleviate contention but introduce overhead due to increased lock acquisition and release operations. Balancing between granularity and contention becomes crucial for optimizing performance.

In contrast to locks, lock-free and wait-free synchronization techniques aim to enhance performance by allowing threads to make progress without waiting for locks. Lock-free algorithms ensure that at least one thread makes progress within a finite number of steps, while wait-free algorithms guarantee that every thread makes progress within a bounded number of steps. These techniques often leverage low-level atomic operations and advanced data structures. While lock-free and wait-free algorithms can enhance scalability and responsiveness, their design and implementation are complex, requiring a deep understanding of memory consistency models and careful consideration of potential contention and resource utilization.

Transactional memory represents an alternative approach with performance implications, offering a high-level abstraction for managing shared data. In transactional memory systems, a sequence of operations is treated as a transaction, and the system ensures that either all operations in the transaction are executed, or none of them are. This atomicity property simplifies the programming model and may lead to improved performance by reducing the need for explicit locks. However, the overhead of transaction management, contention in high-contention scenarios, and challenges in ensuring efficient rollbacks introduce trade-offs that impact the overall performance.

The granularity of synchronization is a critical factor influencing performance. Coarse-grained synchronization involves protecting large sections of code or data structures with locks, simplifying coordination but potentially introducing contention. Fine-grained synchronization, on the other hand, focuses on protecting smaller sections, minimizing contention but increasing the overhead of lock management. Striking the right balance between coarse-grained and fine-grained synchronization requires careful consideration of the application's characteristics, the nature of shared resources, and the anticipated concurrency levels.

Concurrency control mechanisms, such as read-write locks, introduce performance considerations in scenarios where multiple threads access shared data. Read-write locks permit multiple readers to access the shared data concurrently, enhancing parallelism. However, the need for exclusive write access introduces complexity and potential bottlenecks. Optimistic concurrency control strategies, like optimistic locking, allow multiple threads to proceed with their operations without acquiring locks, only validating consistency at the end. While this approach can improve performance by reducing contention, it may result in increased rollbacks and complexity in handling conflicting updates.

Cache coherence, particularly in systems with multiple processors or cores, plays a crucial role in synchronization performance. Inconsistent caches holding copies of shared data across different levels of the memory hierarchy can lead to performance degradation. Cache coherence protocols, such as MESI (Modified, Exclusive, Shared, Invalid) or MOESI (Modified, Owned, Exclusive, Shared, Invalid), ensure that changes to shared data are propagated across caches. Efficiently managing cache coherence enhances performance by minimizing cache misses and reducing the time spent on data retrieval and updates.

Asynchronous communication models, common in distributed systems, introduce performance implications related to message delivery and ordering. Ensuring reliable and ordered communication between distributed processes often involves trade-offs between performance and guarantees. Message queues and publish-subscribe patterns may enhance performance by decoupling sender and receiver processes, but they may introduce latency. Selecting the appropriate communication model depends on the application's requirements, the expected message volume, and the desired level of reliability.

Distributed synchronization techniques face additional performance challenges due to network latency and the lack of a shared memory space. Coordinating processes across different nodes introduces delays, and the choice between strong consistency and eventual consistency affects performance. Distributed consensus algorithms, like Paxos and Raft, ensure agreement among distributed processes but may incur overhead, impacting latency and throughput. The CAP theorem introduces trade-offs, emphasizing the need to balance consistency, availability, and partition tolerance based on the specific requirements of the distributed system.

In real-time systems, where precise timing is crucial, synchronization techniques impact not only correctness but also performance. Priority scheduling, rate monotonic scheduling, and deadline monotonic scheduling are used to allocate resources based on task priorities and timing constraints. Efficient synchronization mechanisms and algorithms are essential for meeting deadlines and ensuring the predictable execution of real-time tasks. The performance implications of synchronization decisions become particularly critical in domains where delays can have severe consequences, such as aerospace, healthcare, or industrial control systems.

Understanding the impact of synchronization techniques on performance extends to the exploration of hardware-level support for concurrency. Transactional memory, lock elision, and hardware-based atomic operations are examples of hardware-level features designed to optimize synchronization. These features aim to reduce the overhead associated with software-based synchronization techniques and enhance the performance of concurrent applications. However, leveraging hardware support requires compatibility with specific architectures and careful consideration of the application's characteristics.

In conclusion, examining the performance implications of synchronization techniques in concurrent programming involves navigating a complex landscape of trade-offs, considerations, and challenges. Choices made in synchronization impact contention, parallelism, scalability, and responsiveness. The context-specific nature of performance considerations requires a deep understanding of the application's requirements, the characteristics of shared resources, and the expected concurrency levels. As technology evolves, and concurrency remains a crucial aspect of modern computing, the optimization of synchronization techniques continues to be a dynamic area of research and engineering, aiming to strike the right balance between correctness and performance in diverse application domains.

Real-world examples illustrating the impact of effective synchronization.

Effective synchronization in real-world scenarios plays a pivotal role in ensuring the reliability, efficiency, and responsiveness of systems across various domains. One compelling example can be found in the realm of database management systems, where multiple transactions concurrently access and modify shared data. Synchronization mechanisms, such as locks and transaction isolation levels, are employed to prevent data inconsistencies and ensure the integrity of the database. For instance, in an e-commerce platform, simultaneous updates to product inventory and customer orders must be synchronized to avoid scenarios where conflicting transactions lead to inaccurate stock levels or order fulfillment. The effective coordination of these concurrent processes through synchronization mechanisms ensures a consistent and reliable representation of the system's state.

In the context of real-time systems, synchronization is crucial for meeting precise timing constraints and ensuring the predictable execution of critical tasks. Consider an automotive control system where multiple components, such as engine control units and anti-lock braking systems, must work in tandem to guarantee the safety and performance of the vehicle. Synchronization mechanisms, including priority scheduling and real-time synchronization protocols, enable these components to coordinate their actions, ensuring that time-critical operations, such as braking or acceleration, are executed within the required time frames. The impact of effective synchronization in such systems is profound, directly influencing the safety and reliability of real-time applications where split-second decisions are paramount.

Concurrency is a fundamental aspect of modern web servers handling a multitude of simultaneous requests. In a scenario where a web server receives concurrent requests for accessing and updating user data, synchronization is vital to prevent data corruption and inconsistencies. For instance, consider a social media platform where users simultaneously update their profiles or post content. Synchronization mechanisms ensure that updates to user profiles, comments, and other shared resources occur in a controlled and consistent manner. Without effective synchronization, race conditions could lead to scenarios where conflicting updates result in lost data or inaccurate user representations. The impact of synchronization in web servers is evident in maintaining data integrity, user experience, and the overall reliability of the platform.

Distributed systems, exemplified by cloud computing environments, showcase the impact of synchronization across geographically distributed nodes. In a cloud-based file storage service, multiple users may concurrently access and modify shared files stored across different servers. Synchronization mechanisms, such as distributed locks or consensus algorithms, are employed to coordinate access to these shared resources. Effective synchronization ensures that updates to files are consistent and propagated across distributed nodes, maintaining a coherent view of the file system. Without robust synchronization strategies, conflicts, and inconsistencies could arise, impacting the reliability and availability of cloud-based file storage services.

The gaming industry provides a compelling example where synchronization is essential for creating immersive and responsive multiplayer experiences. In online multiplayer games, players from different locations interact in real-time, necessitating synchronization to ensure a consistent game state for all participants. Synchronization mechanisms manage the concurrent execution of game events, such as player movements, interactions, and changes to the game environment. The impact of effective synchronization is evident in the seamless and coherent gameplay experience, where all players perceive a consistent representation of the game world. Ineffective synchronization could lead to scenarios where players observe divergent game states, compromising the fairness and quality of the gaming experience.

Financial trading platforms represent another domain where effective synchronization is critical. In high-frequency trading systems, multiple trading algorithms concurrently analyze market data and execute trades at high speeds. Synchronization mechanisms are employed to coordinate these algorithms and ensure that trades are executed in a well-ordered manner. The impact of synchronization in financial trading is evident in preventing race conditions and order execution conflicts that could lead to financial losses. The reliability and efficiency of high-frequency trading systems rely on effective synchronization to maintain the integrity of market transactions and respond swiftly to market changes.

Healthcare systems, particularly in the context of electronic health records (EHR) and medical data management, highlight the impact of synchronization on patient care. In a hospital setting, multiple healthcare professionals may simultaneously access and update patient records. Synchronization mechanisms, including record locking and transaction management, are crucial to prevent conflicting updates and ensure the accuracy of medical information. The impact of effective synchronization is evident in providing healthcare practitioners with reliable and up-to-date patient records, contributing to informed decision-making, patient safety, and overall healthcare quality.

Autonomous vehicles exemplify the intersection of synchronization and emerging technologies. In a scenario where multiple autonomous vehicles navigate through an urban environment, effective synchronization is essential to prevent collisions and ensure smooth traffic flow. Coordination mechanisms, facilitated by vehicle-to-vehicle communication and advanced sensor technologies, enable autonomous vehicles to synchronize their movements and respond collaboratively to dynamic traffic conditions. The impact of synchronization in autonomous vehicles is profound, influencing the safety, efficiency, and feasibility of widespread adoption of autonomous driving technologies.

Smart grid systems, designed to optimize energy distribution in electrical networks, rely on effective synchronization for efficient operation. In a smart grid, various devices, such as sensors, meters, and control systems, must synchronize their activities to balance energy supply and demand dynamically. Synchronization mechanisms ensure that devices coordinate their actions, responding to changes in energy consumption or generation. The impact of effective synchronization in smart grids is evident in optimizing energy utilization, reducing wastage, and enhancing the overall resilience and sustainability of electrical grids.

Overall, these real-world examples illustrate the diverse impact of effective synchronization across different domains. Whether it is ensuring data consistency in databases, enabling responsive real-time systems, coordinating concurrent access in distributed environments, or enhancing immersive experiences in gaming, synchronization is a foundational element. The success of applications and systems hinges on the careful implementation of synchronization mechanisms tailored to the specific requirements of each domain, showcasing the pervasive influence of synchronization on the reliability, efficiency, and performance of modern computing ecosystems.

Chapter 4: Task Scheduling Strategies for Optimal Performance

Defining task scheduling and its role in optimizing system performance.

Task scheduling is a fundamental aspect of operating systems and computing environments, playing a pivotal role in optimizing system performance by efficiently managing the execution of tasks or processes. At its core, task scheduling involves the allocation of system resources, such as CPU time and memory, to various tasks, ensuring that they are executed in a manner that maximizes overall system throughput, responsiveness, and fairness. The scheduler, a key component of the operating system, orchestrates the order in which tasks are executed, determining when each task gets access to the CPU and for how long. This dynamic allocation of resources is critical in both single-processor and multi-processor systems, where multiple tasks compete for limited resources.

In the context of a single-processor system, task scheduling aims to optimize the utilization of the CPU by interleaving the execution of tasks in a way that minimizes idle time. A preemptive scheduler, for instance, can interrupt the currently running task to give another task a chance to execute. This preemptive approach enhances responsiveness and ensures that no task monopolizes the CPU for an extended period. In contrast, a non-preemptive scheduler allows a task to run until completion or until it voluntarily yields control. The choice between preemptive and non-preemptive scheduling depends on system requirements, application characteristics, and the desired trade-off between responsiveness and simplicity.

In multi-processor or multi-core systems, task scheduling becomes even more intricate as multiple tasks can be executed concurrently. Here, the scheduler faces the challenge of distributing tasks across available processors to achieve load balancing and exploit parallelism. The goal is to minimize CPU idle time and enhance overall system throughput. Multi-processor task scheduling involves decisions such as which tasks to run on which processors, how to allocate shared resources, and how to synchronize tasks to prevent data inconsistencies or conflicts. The scheduler must adapt dynamically to changes in system load, the arrival of new tasks, or the completion of existing tasks, making real-time decisions to maintain optimal performance.

One key aspect of task scheduling is the consideration of task priorities. Different tasks may have varying levels of importance or urgency, and the scheduler must allocate resources accordingly. Priority scheduling allows tasks with higher priorities to be executed before those with lower priorities, ensuring that critical or time-sensitive operations are promptly addressed. However, priority scheduling introduces challenges related to fairness, as lower-priority tasks may be starved of resources if higher-priority tasks are continuously introduced. Balancing priority-based scheduling with fairness mechanisms is essential to prevent resource monopolization and ensure a responsive and equitable system.

Real-time task scheduling is a specialized domain where tasks must meet specific timing constraints or deadlines. In industries such as avionics, healthcare, or industrial control systems, the timely execution of tasks is critical. Real-time schedulers prioritize tasks based on their deadlines and ensure that they meet their timing requirements consistently. The scheduler must guarantee that critical tasks receive the necessary resources to execute within their deadlines, preventing catastrophic consequences in safety-critical applications. Meeting real-time constraints requires a deterministic and predictable scheduling approach, where the scheduler considers task deadlines as a primary factor in resource allocation.

Task scheduling also intersects with energy efficiency considerations, particularly in the context of mobile devices and battery-powered systems. Dynamic Voltage and Frequency Scaling (DVFS) is a technique employed by schedulers to adjust the operating frequency and voltage of the CPU based on the workload. By dynamically scaling these parameters, the scheduler can optimize energy consumption without sacrificing performance. For example, during periods of low activity, the scheduler may reduce the CPU frequency to conserve energy, and as demand increases, it can scale up to deliver higher performance. This dynamic adaptation to workload variations contributes to prolonged battery life and more sustainable operation in energy-constrained environments.

The role of task scheduling extends beyond CPU management to include I/O operations, disk access, and network communication. Input/Output-bound tasks, which spend a significant amount of time waiting for external resources, require efficient scheduling to prevent unnecessary idle time. Schedulers use techniques such as asynchronous I/O, I/O buffering, and overlapping I/O operations with CPU-bound tasks to optimize overall system performance. Disk scheduling, a critical component of storage management, determines the order in which disk requests are serviced, aiming to minimize seek times and maximize throughput. Network schedulers prioritize communication tasks, considering factors like Quality of Service (QoS) requirements to optimize data transfer rates and minimize latency.

In distributed systems, where tasks may be distributed across multiple nodes or servers, task scheduling involves coordinating the execution of tasks to achieve load balancing, fault tolerance, and overall system efficiency. Distributed task scheduling must account for the variability in network latencies, potential failures of nodes, and the dynamic nature of distributed environments. Techniques such as work stealing, where idle processors request tasks from busy ones, contribute to load balancing in distributed systems. Additionally, distributed schedulers must address the challenges of data consistency and synchronization, ensuring that tasks accessing shared data coordinate their actions effectively.

Task scheduling is integral to optimizing system performance in cloud computing environments as well. Cloud schedulers manage the allocation of virtual machines or containers across a pool of physical servers, orchestrating the execution of tasks in a way that maximizes resource utilization, scalability, and cost efficiency. Load balancing algorithms dynamically distribute tasks among available resources, adapting to changing demand and minimizing response times. Cloud schedulers also play a role in task migration, allowing tasks to be moved between servers to address load imbalances or hardware failures. The optimization of task scheduling in cloud environments is essential for delivering responsive services, efficient resource utilization, and cost-effective cloud computing solutions.

In conclusion, task scheduling is a multifaceted and essential aspect of operating systems that profoundly influences system performance across a range of computing environments. Whether in single-processor systems, multi-processor configurations, real-time applications, energy-constrained devices, or distributed and cloud computing environments, the scheduler's decisions impact responsiveness, throughput, fairness, and resource utilization. Task scheduling algorithms and strategies continue to evolve, adapting to the changing landscape of computing technologies and application requirements. As computing systems become increasingly diverse and complex, the role of task scheduling remains central to the optimization of system performance and the delivery of efficient, reliable, and responsive computing experiences.

Exploring different scheduling algorithms such as FCFS, Round Robin, and Priority Scheduling.

Exploring different scheduling algorithms provides insights into the diverse approaches employed by operating systems to manage the execution of tasks and optimize system performance. First-Come, First-Served (FCFS) is a simple and intuitive scheduling algorithm where tasks are executed in the order they arrive in the ready queue. While straightforward, FCFS may lead to the "convoy effect," where short tasks get stuck waiting behind long tasks, causing potential delays and poor utilization of CPU time. This algorithm is non-preemptive, meaning once a task starts executing, it continues until completion or it voluntarily relinquishes control.

Round Robin (RR) scheduling introduces a preemptive and time-sliced approach to task execution. Each task is assigned a fixed time quantum, and the scheduler cycles through the ready queue, allowing each task to execute for its allotted time. If a task doesn't complete within its time quantum, it is placed back in the ready queue, and the scheduler moves on to the next task. Round Robin ensures fairness by providing each task an equal opportunity to run, preventing any single task from monopolizing the CPU for an extended period. However, it may lead to inefficiencies with short tasks waiting for their turn and longer tasks incurring high context-switching overhead.

Priority Scheduling assigns priority levels to tasks, and the scheduler selects the highest-priority task for execution. In this algorithm, tasks with higher priority values are given precedence, and ties may be resolved based on other factors such as arrival time. Priority scheduling can be both preemptive and non-preemptive, depending on the system's requirements. While priority scheduling is effective in addressing the convoy effect and ensuring responsive execution for high-priority tasks, it may suffer from issues like priority inversion, where a low-priority task holds a resource required by a high-priority task, leading to potential delays.

In addition to these fundamental scheduling algorithms, several variations and enhancements have been developed to address specific challenges. Shortest Job Next (SJN) or Shortest Job First (SJF) scheduling selects the task with the shortest estimated runtime for execution next. This approach minimizes waiting times and optimizes turnaround, making it suitable for scenarios where task execution times are known or can be estimated accurately. However, predicting the exact runtime of tasks may be challenging in practice.

Multilevel Queue Scheduling organizes tasks into multiple queues based on priority levels, and each queue may have its own scheduling algorithm. High-priority tasks are assigned to the highest-priority queue and are scheduled first. This approach provides a balance between priority-based execution and fairness, allowing different classes of tasks to be managed effectively.

Multilevel Feedback Queue Scheduling extends the concept of multilevel queues by allowing tasks to move between queues dynamically based on their behavior. Tasks that use less CPU time may move to higher-priority queues, while CPU-bound tasks may move to lower-priority queues. This adaptive approach aims to optimize both CPU utilization and responsiveness, adapting to the characteristics of individual tasks over time.

Fair Share Scheduling is designed to ensure that each user or group receives a fair share of the system resources over time. This approach is particularly relevant in shared computing environments where multiple users or applications coexist. Fair share schedulers consider resource usage patterns and dynamically adjust priorities to distribute resources equitably among users or groups.

Real-Time Scheduling addresses the requirements of time-sensitive tasks in critical applications. Hard real-time scheduling guarantees that tasks meet their deadlines consistently, crucial in systems where missing deadlines can have severe consequences. Soft real-time scheduling provides a degree of flexibility, allowing tasks to miss occasional deadlines without catastrophic outcomes. Rate Monotonic Scheduling (RMS) assigns priorities based on task periods, ensuring that tasks with shorter periods receive higher priority. Earliest Deadline First (EDF) scheduling selects the task with the earliest deadline for execution, offering flexibility but requiring dynamic priority adjustments.

Weighted Round Robin Scheduling extends the basic Round Robin algorithm by assigning weights to tasks, influencing their share of CPU time. This approach is commonly used in network traffic scheduling, where different flows or users may have varying priorities or bandwidth requirements. Weighted Round Robin allows for the proportional allocation of resources based on task weights, ensuring that higher-priority tasks receive a larger share of CPU time.

Dynamic Priority Scheduling dynamically adjusts task priorities based on their behavior or resource usage. This approach aims to adapt to changing workload conditions and optimize system performance. The Linux Completely Fair Scheduler (CFS) is an example of a dynamic priority scheduler that uses the concept of virtual runtime to determine task priorities and maintain fairness.

In conclusion, exploring different scheduling algorithms reveals the diversity of approaches employed by operating systems to manage the execution of tasks and optimize system performance. FCFS, Round Robin, and Priority Scheduling represent fundamental scheduling strategies, each with its strengths and weaknesses. Variations such as SJF, Multilevel Queue, Multilevel Feedback Queue, Fair Share, Real-Time, Weighted Round Robin, and Dynamic Priority Scheduling address specific challenges and requirements in different computing environments. The choice of a scheduling algorithm depends on the characteristics of the tasks, the system's objectives, and the trade-offs between factors such as fairness, responsiveness, and resource utilization. As computing systems evolve, new scheduling algorithms and refinements continue to emerge, contributing to the ongoing quest for efficient and adaptive task scheduling strategies in diverse computing scenarios.

Understanding the concept of multilevel queue scheduling.

Multilevel queue scheduling is a dynamic and hierarchical approach used by operating systems to manage and prioritize tasks efficiently. This concept organizes tasks into multiple queues based on predefined priority levels, each representing a distinct class of tasks with similar characteristics or requirements. The primary objective of multilevel queue scheduling is to provide a balance between responsiveness and fairness, ensuring that tasks with different priorities are handled appropriately to optimize overall system performance.

At its core, a multilevel queue consists of several priority queues, each assigned a specific priority level. The number of priority levels and the scheduling algorithm associated with each queue may vary based on the design and requirements of the operating system. Generally, the highest-priority queue is given precedence, and tasks within this queue are scheduled for execution first. If the highest-priority queue is empty, the scheduler moves to the next lower-priority queue and continues this process until it finds a task to execute or reaches the lowest-priority queue.

Each queue may employ a different scheduling algorithm, tailoring the task management approach to the characteristics of the tasks within that priority level. For instance, the highest-priority queue might use a preemptive algorithm to ensure rapid response times for critical tasks, while lower-priority queues may utilize non-preemptive algorithms to avoid unnecessary context switching and overhead. This adaptability allows the scheduler to address the diverse needs of tasks within the system.

Multilevel queue scheduling is particularly suitable for environments where tasks can be categorized into distinct classes based on their importance, urgency, or resource requirements. This classification allows for a more granular control over the execution order and resource allocation. Real-time systems often benefit from multilevel queue scheduling, as it enables the prioritization of time-sensitive tasks over less critical ones.

One of the key advantages of multilevel queue scheduling is its ability to prevent resource starvation and the "convoy effect" that may occur in simpler scheduling algorithms. The "convoy effect" refers to a scenario where a long-running task monopolizes the CPU, causing shorter tasks to wait for an extended period. By segregating tasks into priority levels, multilevel queue scheduling ensures that lower-priority tasks are not indefinitely delayed by higher-priority ones. This results in improved fairness and responsiveness across different classes of tasks.

However, the effectiveness of multilevel queue scheduling depends on the proper assignment of tasks to priority levels and the choice of scheduling algorithms for each queue. Misjudgments in priority assignment or inappropriate scheduling algorithms can lead to suboptimal performance. Striking the right balance between responsiveness and fairness requires a thorough understanding of the workload characteristics and the system's objectives.

One common variation of multilevel queue scheduling is the Multilevel Feedback Queue Scheduling. In this approach, tasks are initially assigned to a specific queue based on their priority. However, as tasks execute, they may be moved between queues dynamically based on their behavior. For example, a task that uses a minimal amount of CPU time may be moved to a higher-priority queue, allowing it to receive quicker attention. On the other hand, CPU-bound tasks may be demoted to lower-priority queues to prevent them from monopolizing resources. This adaptive nature allows the scheduler to respond dynamically to the evolving resource needs and behaviors of tasks.

Multilevel queue scheduling finds applications in various computing environments. In time-sharing systems, where multiple users interact with a shared system concurrently, multilevel queue scheduling helps allocate CPU time fairly among users. Each user's tasks are placed in a separate queue, and the scheduler ensures that all users receive a reasonable share of system resources, preventing any single user from dominating the system.

In systems with varied task characteristics, such as batch processing environments, multilevel queue scheduling enables efficient resource allocation. Long-running batch tasks can be assigned to lower-priority queues, while more interactive or critical tasks occupy higher-priority queues. This arrangement ensures that both types of tasks coexist without one adversely affecting the other.

Multilevel queue scheduling is also beneficial in environments where tasks have distinct resource requirements, such as scientific computing or simulations. Different priority levels can be associated with specific computational or memory resources, allowing the scheduler to allocate resources according to the needs of the tasks.

Despite its advantages, multilevel queue scheduling has its challenges. The design of an effective multilevel queue system requires careful consideration of factors such as priority assignment, queue management policies, and the impact of dynamic task movement between queues. Additionally, determining the optimal number of priority levels and the right balance between preemptive and non-preemptive scheduling within each queue involves trade-offs that must align with the system's goals and workload characteristics.

In conclusion, multilevel queue scheduling stands as a versatile and adaptive approach in managing tasks within operating systems. By categorizing tasks into distinct priority levels and applying different scheduling algorithms to each queue, multilevel queue scheduling achieves a balance between responsiveness and fairness. This approach is particularly relevant in environments with diverse task characteristics, such as time-sharing systems, batch processing, and scientific computing. The dynamic nature of multilevel queue scheduling, along with variations like Multilevel Feedback Queue Scheduling, allows for effective resource allocation, preventing resource starvation and enhancing overall system performance. However, its successful implementation requires a nuanced understanding of workload characteristics and careful consideration of design choices to ensure optimal results in diverse computing scenarios.

Exploring real-time scheduling requirements and challenges. Real-time scheduling involves the management of tasks in computing systems where timely and predictable execution is critical. The unique requirements of real-time systems span various domains, including industrial automation, avionics, healthcare, telecommunications, and more. The primary objective of real-time scheduling is to ensure that tasks meet their deadlines consistently, as missing deadlines can have severe consequences in safety-critical applications. Real-time scheduling faces a set of distinctive challenges, ranging from stringent timing constraints to the need for deterministic and predictable task execution.

One of the fundamental requirements in real-time scheduling is meeting strict deadlines. Tasks in real-time systems are often associated with specific time constraints, and their completion times directly impact the system's functionality or safety. Hard real-time systems necessitate that tasks consistently meet their deadlines, as any deviation could lead to system failure or compromise safety. For example, in automotive control systems, real-time scheduling ensures that tasks responsible for functions like brake control or airbag deployment respond within the required time frames to guarantee passenger safety.

Predictability is a crucial aspect of real-time scheduling. Deterministic behavior ensures that the time taken to start and complete a task is known in advance. This predictability is essential for coordinating tasks with external events or for synchronization purposes. In applications like digital signal processing, where real-time constraints are prevalent, predictable execution times are critical to maintaining the integrity of signal processing algorithms and meeting timing requirements.

Real-time systems often operate in dynamic environments where the workload can change rapidly. Adapting to varying workloads while maintaining real-time guarantees is a significant challenge. Dynamic real-time scheduling involves adjusting task priorities or allocating resources based on the changing system conditions. This adaptability is vital in scenarios like server farms, where the workload can fluctuate due to varying user demands, and real-time tasks must still meet their deadlines despite these changes.

In preemptive real-time scheduling, tasks can be interrupted by higher-priority tasks, ensuring that the most critical tasks are promptly executed. Preemption is essential for guaranteeing timely response to urgent events. However, preemptive scheduling introduces challenges related to minimizing context-switching overhead. Excessive context switches can lead to increased latency and reduced overall system performance. Striking the right balance between preemption and minimizing context-switching overhead is crucial in preemptive real-time scheduling.

Resource contention is a common challenge in real-time systems, particularly in scenarios where multiple tasks compete for shared resources. Access to resources, such as communication channels, memory, or I/O devices, must be carefully managed to prevent conflicts and ensure that real-time tasks can access necessary resources within their deadlines. Resource-aware scheduling algorithms are employed to optimize resource allocation and mitigate contention issues in real-time systems.

Guaranteeing fairness among tasks is another challenge in real-time scheduling. While meeting deadlines for high-priority tasks is paramount, ensuring that lower-priority tasks receive their fair share of resources is essential for system balance. Fair real-time scheduling mechanisms prevent resource starvation, where lower-priority tasks are consistently delayed or even indefinitely postponed due to the continuous execution of high-priority tasks.

Real-time scheduling must address the issue of clock accuracy and precision. The accuracy of the system clock directly impacts the precision with which time-sensitive tasks can be scheduled. In applications like telecommunications, where precise timing is crucial, clock synchronization mechanisms are employed to maintain accurate time references across distributed systems. Ensuring a reliable and synchronized clock is fundamental for achieving the timing requirements of real-time tasks.

Another challenge in real-time scheduling is dealing with aperiodic tasks—tasks that do not follow a regular or periodic execution pattern. Aperiodic tasks may be triggered by external events or user interactions and must be accommodated within the real-time scheduling framework. The challenge lies in integrating aperiodic tasks with periodic ones while still ensuring timely execution for both. Techniques like Earliest Deadline First (EDF) scheduling aim to handle aperiodic tasks effectively by prioritizing tasks with the earliest deadlines.

Soft real-time systems introduce additional complexity by allowing occasional deadline misses without catastrophic consequences. While soft real-time scheduling provides some flexibility, managing and controlling the frequency of deadline misses present challenges. Balancing the reliability of task completion within specified timeframes and accommodating occasional delays is a delicate trade-off in soft real-time systems.

The integration of multicore processors in real-time systems introduces both opportunities and challenges. While multicore architectures can potentially improve overall system performance, efficiently managing task allocation and synchronization across multiple cores becomes essential. Load balancing, minimizing inter-core communication delays, and ensuring cache coherence are critical aspects of real-time scheduling in multicore environments.

Ensuring fault tolerance in real-time systems is crucial for applications where system failures can have severe consequences. Redundancy and fault recovery mechanisms are integrated into real-time scheduling strategies to detect and mitigate errors. In avionics, for instance, where reliability is paramount, real-time systems incorporate mechanisms like triple modular redundancy to ensure continued operation even in the presence of hardware faults.

Security considerations pose challenges in real-time systems, particularly in applications where tasks must execute in secure and isolated environments. Techniques for ensuring task isolation, preventing unauthorized access to critical resources, and maintaining data integrity are integral to secure real-time scheduling. Security measures must be seamlessly integrated without compromising the timing guarantees of real-time tasks.

The certification of real-time systems, especially in safety-critical domains like aviation or medical devices, adds an additional layer of complexity. Meeting certification standards such as DO-178C for avionics software involves rigorous testing, verification, and documentation to ensure that the real-time system adheres to safety and reliability requirements. Certification processes aim to instill confidence in the reliability and predictability of real-time systems used in critical applications.

In conclusion, real-time scheduling in computing systems is a complex and challenging endeavor that must balance the demands of meeting strict deadlines, providing predictable execution, adapting to dynamic workloads, and addressing issues of resource contention and fairness. The challenges evolve as real-time systems become more integrated, incorporating multicore architectures, handling a mix of periodic and aperiodic tasks, and ensuring fault tolerance and security. Real-time scheduling plays a crucial role in enabling the functionality and safety of applications in diverse domains, and addressing these challenges requires careful consideration of system requirements, design choices, and ongoing advancements in scheduling algorithms and techniques. As technology continues to advance, the evolution of real-time scheduling mechanisms will play a pivotal role in shaping the capabilities and reliability of future computing systems.

Scheduling challenges in multithreading environments.

Scheduling challenges in multithreading environments present a multifaceted landscape where the complexities of managing concurrent threads introduce a host of issues that impact system performance, responsiveness, and resource utilization. Multithreading, a programming and execution model that enables the concurrent execution of multiple threads within a single process, brings both opportunities and challenges to the realm of task scheduling. One of the primary challenges lies in the efficient allocation of CPU time among competing threads. With multiple threads vying for processor resources, contention arises, and the scheduler must make decisions to balance the execution of threads to avoid resource starvation or unfairness. This challenge is further compounded by the need for synchronization mechanisms to coordinate access to shared resources, preventing data inconsistencies or conflicts that may arise when multiple threads attempt to access and modify shared data simultaneously.

Context switching, a fundamental operation in multithreading environments, introduces scheduling challenges related to overhead and efficiency. Context switching occurs when the scheduler interrupts the execution of one thread and switches to another. While context switching is necessary for managing multiple threads, it comes with a cost. The overhead associated with saving and restoring thread contexts, updating data structures, and performing associated operations can impact overall system performance. Minimizing context-switching overhead is a crucial consideration in multithreading scheduling algorithms to ensure that the benefits of concurrency are not outweighed by the costs of frequent context switches.

The dynamic nature of multithreading introduces challenges related to load balancing. Load balancing aims to distribute the computational workload evenly among available processors or cores to maximize resource utilization. In multithreading environments, uneven distribution of threads across processors can lead to suboptimal performance, where some processors are underutilized while others are overloaded. Load balancing algorithms must adapt to changing workloads and thread behaviors to achieve an equitable distribution of computational tasks, ensuring that all processors contribute effectively to overall system throughput.

Priority inversion is a scheduling challenge that arises when a higher-priority thread is blocked by a lower-priority thread holding a shared resource. This situation can lead to unexpected delays for high-priority tasks, compromising the responsiveness of the system. Priority inversion can be mitigated through techniques such as priority inheritance, where the priority of a lower-priority thread is temporarily elevated to that of a higher-priority thread waiting for a shared resource. Managing priority inversion is essential in real-time systems or applications with stringent timing requirements, where predictable execution is paramount.

Deadlocks, a classic concurrency issue, also pose challenges in multithreading environments. Deadlocks occur when two or more threads are blocked, each waiting for a resource held by another, resulting in a circular waiting scenario. The scheduler must employ deadlock detection and prevention mechanisms to identify and resolve potential deadlocks, ensuring that threads can make progress and preventing the system from reaching a state where no thread can proceed.

Multithreading environments introduce challenges related to thread synchronization, as threads often need to coordinate their activities to achieve correct and predictable behavior. Synchronization mechanisms such as locks, semaphores, and barriers are employed to control access to shared resources and establish order among threads. However, improper use of synchronization primitives can lead to issues like race conditions, where the outcome of a program depends on the timing of thread execution, potentially resulting in unpredictable behavior. Designing effective and efficient synchronization strategies is crucial for maintaining the integrity of shared data and preventing data races.

Cache coherence poses a specific challenge in multithreading environments, particularly in systems with multiple processors or cores sharing a common memory hierarchy. Incoherent caches across different threads can lead to inconsistencies in the data observed by each thread, impacting program correctness. Cache coherence protocols, such as MESI (Modified, Exclusive, Shared, Invalid), are implemented to manage the state of cache lines and ensure that changes made by one thread are visible to others. Coordinating cache coherence in multithreading environments involves careful consideration of cache management policies and communication protocols to maintain data consistency.

The presence of non-uniform memory access (NUMA) architectures introduces scheduling challenges in multithreading environments. NUMA architectures feature multiple memory nodes, and threads may experience varying access latencies depending on their proximity to memory. Efficiently scheduling threads in NUMA environments requires an awareness of memory locality to minimize access latencies and optimize overall system performance. Thread migration between different NUMA nodes introduces additional complexities, as the scheduler must balance the benefits of proximity to memory with the potential costs of migration.

Power and energy considerations are increasingly relevant challenges in modern multithreading environments, particularly in mobile devices and energy-constrained systems. Dynamic Voltage and Frequency Scaling (DVFS) techniques are employed to adjust the operating frequency and voltage of processors based on workload demands. Schedulers must consider power-efficient thread placement and migration strategies to optimize energy consumption while maintaining performance. Balancing the trade-off between performance and power efficiency becomes a critical aspect of multithreading scheduling in battery-powered devices.

Real-time multithreading introduces challenges related to meeting stringent timing constraints for concurrent tasks. Thread priorities, deadlines, and execution times must be carefully managed to ensure that real-time tasks complete within their required timeframes. Schedulers in real-time multithreading environments often employ priority-based algorithms, deadline scheduling, and techniques like Earliest Deadline First (EDF) to guarantee timely execution and prevent deadline misses.

Asynchronous programming models, which leverage multithreading for responsiveness, introduce challenges related to coordination and control flow. Managing callbacks, event handlers, and asynchronous tasks requires effective scheduling strategies to balance concurrency with the need for orderly and predictable execution. Coordinating asynchronous threads and ensuring proper synchronization in response to events become critical aspects of multithreading scheduling in environments where responsiveness is paramount.

In conclusion, scheduling challenges in multithreading environments are diverse and multifaceted, ranging from efficient resource allocation and load balancing to addressing issues like priority inversion, deadlocks, and cache coherence. The complexities introduced by the dynamic nature of multithreading require sophisticated scheduling algorithms that adapt to changing workloads, prioritize responsiveness, and mitigate concurrency issues. The design of effective multithreading schedulers involves careful consideration of system architecture, synchronization mechanisms, power constraints, and real-time requirements. As computing systems continue to embrace parallelism and concurrency, addressing these scheduling challenges becomes instrumental in achieving optimal performance, responsiveness, and resource utilization in multithreading environments across diverse application domains.

Importance of load balancing in distributed systems.

Load balancing is a critical aspect of distributed systems, playing a pivotal role in ensuring optimal performance, resource utilization, and reliability. As these systems are designed to handle large-scale applications and services, the distribution of tasks and resources among multiple nodes becomes a complex challenge. Load balancing addresses this challenge by dynamically allocating incoming requests and computational workloads across the nodes of the system, preventing any single node from being overwhelmed and ensuring that the overall system operates efficiently.

One primary importance of load balancing lies in its ability to enhance system scalability. In a distributed environment, scalability refers to the system's capability to handle an increasing number of requests or workloads without sacrificing performance. Load balancing achieves scalability by intelligently distributing tasks among nodes, preventing any individual node from becoming a bottleneck.

This dynamic distribution ensures that the system can seamlessly scale up to accommodate higher demands, maintaining responsiveness and meeting user expectations.

Moreover, load balancing contributes significantly to resource utilization and optimization. In a distributed system, resources such as processing power, memory, and network bandwidth are finite. Efficient utilization of these resources is crucial for maximizing the system's overall throughput and minimizing resource wastage. Load balancing algorithms analyze the current state of each node, considering factors like CPU usage, memory availability, and network traffic, to allocate tasks in a way that optimizes resource utilization. By balancing the workload across nodes, the system can make the most effective use of available resources, thereby improving efficiency and reducing the risk of resource exhaustion.

Load balancing also plays a vital role in enhancing fault tolerance and system reliability. In a distributed system, hardware failures, software glitches, or network issues can occur unexpectedly. Load balancing helps mitigate these challenges by distributing tasks across multiple nodes, reducing the impact of a potential failure on the overall system. If one node becomes unavailable or experiences a malfunction, the load balancing mechanism redirects incoming requests to other healthy nodes, ensuring uninterrupted service delivery. This inherent fault tolerance contributes to the system's resilience, minimizing downtime and enhancing overall reliability.

Furthermore, load balancing contributes to improved response times and user experience. By evenly distributing tasks among nodes, the system can handle each request more efficiently, reducing the time it takes to process and respond. This results in faster response times for end-users, enhancing the overall user experience. Whether it's a web application, a cloud service, or any other distributed system, the ability to deliver prompt and consistent responses is crucial for user satisfaction. Load balancing, by preventing any single node from becoming overloaded, ensures that the system can maintain low-latency interactions with users, even during peak usage periods.

In the context of cost efficiency, load balancing proves to be a valuable strategy for optimizing resource usage and, consequently, reducing operational costs. Efficient resource allocation means that organizations can achieve more with their existing infrastructure, avoiding the need for excessive hardware investments to handle peak loads. By dynamically distributing workloads based on real-time conditions, load balancing enables organizations to scale their services without incurring unnecessary expenses, aligning resource provisioning with actual demand and promoting cost-effective operations.

Load balancing also facilitates easier system maintenance and upgrades. In a dynamic and distributed environment, routine maintenance tasks or system upgrades can be challenging without disrupting ongoing operations. Load balancing allows organizations to redirect traffic away from specific nodes that require maintenance, enabling seamless updates without affecting the overall user experience. This capability enhances the agility of distributed systems, making it easier for organizations to implement changes, apply patches, or upgrade software components without causing downtime or service interruptions.

Another significant aspect of load balancing is its contribution to security and mitigating the impact of potential security threats. In a distributed system, security is a paramount concern, and load balancing can be leveraged as a defense mechanism. By dispersing the workload across multiple nodes, load balancing makes it more challenging for malicious actors to target a specific point of vulnerability. In the event of a security incident or a distributed denial-of-service (DDoS) attack, load balancing can help distribute and absorb the malicious traffic, preventing it from overwhelming any single node and ensuring the overall system remains operational and secure.

In conclusion, load balancing stands as a cornerstone in the architecture of distributed systems, providing a multitude of benefits that collectively contribute to the system's efficiency, scalability, reliability, and security. By dynamically distributing tasks and workloads across nodes, load balancing optimizes resource utilization, enhances fault tolerance, improves response times, and supports cost-effective operations. In an era where distributed systems are integral to the functioning of applications and services, the importance of load balancing cannot be overstated, as it continues to be a key enabler for the seamless and robust operation of these complex and interconnected systems.

The role of interrupts in task scheduling.

Interrupts play a pivotal role in the intricate process of task scheduling within a computer system. Task scheduling, a fundamental aspect of operating systems, involves the efficient management of processes and their execution on the central processing unit (CPU). Interrupts serve as mechanisms that disrupt the normal flow of a CPU's execution to address specific events, and they are closely intertwined with task scheduling to ensure the effective utilization of system resources and responsiveness to various events.

One of the primary roles of interrupts in task scheduling is to handle external events and asynchronous processes. External events, such as hardware interrupts triggered by input/output devices or timer interrupts that mark the passage of time, necessitate immediate attention from the operating system. When an interrupt occurs, the CPU temporarily suspends its current execution to respond promptly to the event. In the context of task scheduling, interrupts enable the operating system to preempt the currently running process and switch to a different task that requires immediate attention. This preemptive capability ensures that time-critical processes, such as handling user input or managing hardware events, are promptly addressed without compromising system responsiveness.

Moreover, interrupts are integral to supporting multitasking and time-sharing in operating systems. In a multitasking environment, where multiple processes compete for CPU time, interrupts allow the operating system to switch between tasks seamlessly. Time-sharing, a technique that allocates CPU time to different processes in a fair and efficient manner, relies on interrupts to enforce time limits and context switches. Timer interrupts, for example, enable the operating system to interrupt a running process after a predefined time slice, redistributing CPU time among competing tasks. This preemptive task scheduling ensures that no single task monopolizes the CPU, promoting fairness and responsiveness in a multitasking environment.

Interrupt-driven task scheduling also enhances the overall system efficiency by facilitating asynchronous input/output operations. When a process initiates an input/output operation, it can continue its execution without waiting for the operation to complete. However, once the operation finishes, an interrupt is generated to signal the completion. Task scheduling takes advantage of this interrupt-driven approach to efficiently manage processes, allowing the CPU to switch to other tasks while waiting for input/output operations to conclude. This overlap of computation and I/O operations optimizes CPU utilization and contributes to the overall throughput of the system.

Furthermore, interrupts are crucial for handling exceptional conditions and error scenarios in a timely manner. When an error or an exceptional event occurs, such as a divide-by-zero error or a page fault, interrupts enable the operating system to swiftly intervene and manage the situation. By generating an interrupt, the system can suspend the faulty process, execute an error-handling routine, and take corrective actions. This preemptive handling of exceptions through interrupts prevents the propagation of errors, enhances system stability, and ensures a more robust computing environment.

In the realm of real-time systems, interrupts play a vital role in meeting stringent timing requirements. Real-time operating systems often need to respond to external events within specific deadlines to guarantee the correct and timely execution of critical tasks. Interrupts enable the operating system to prioritize and preempt non-critical processes in favor of real-time tasks. This capability ensures that time-sensitive operations, such as controlling industrial processes or managing critical communications, are executed with precision and meet the specified timing constraints.

In the context of interrupt prioritization, task scheduling relies on interrupt controllers to manage the hierarchy of interrupts and their corresponding priorities. Different types of interrupts may have varying levels of urgency and importance. For example, a hardware interrupt signaling a critical hardware failure may take precedence over a timer interrupt indicating a regular time slice expiration. Interrupt controllers prioritize and manage these interrupts, allowing the operating system to make informed decisions about task scheduling based on the urgency and significance of the events.

Despite the numerous advantages of interrupts in task scheduling, their improper handling can lead to potential challenges such as interrupt storms and priority inversion. An interrupt storm occurs when a system is bombarded with a high rate of interrupts, overwhelming the CPU and hindering normal processing. Priority inversion, on the other hand, is a situation where a lower-priority task holds a resource needed by a higher-priority task, leading to inefficient resource utilization. To address these challenges, sophisticated interrupt handling mechanisms and scheduling algorithms are employed, ensuring that interrupts are managed effectively without compromising system stability or performance.

In conclusion, interrupts play a multifaceted and indispensable role in the intricate landscape of task scheduling within operating systems. From responding to external events and managing asynchronous processes to supporting multitasking, time-sharing, and handling exceptional conditions, interrupts are the linchpin that enables the operating system to orchestrate the efficient execution of tasks on the CPU. Their preemptive nature ensures timely responsiveness, facilitates efficient resource utilization, and contributes to the overall stability and reliability of computer systems. As technology continues to advance, the role of interrupts in task scheduling remains a crucial element in the design and optimization of modern operating systems.

Exploring dynamic scheduling techniques based on system workload.

Dynamic scheduling techniques based on system workload are instrumental in optimizing the performance and resource utilization of computer systems by adapting to varying workloads in real-time. In the dynamic scheduling paradigm, the allocation of resources and assignment of tasks are not predetermined but are adjusted dynamically based on the current system state and workload characteristics. This approach contrasts with static scheduling, where task assignments and resource allocations are fixed before execution. Dynamic scheduling techniques prove particularly beneficial in environments with fluctuating workloads, where the demand for resources varies dynamically, requiring a responsive and adaptive scheduling mechanism to ensure efficient system operation.

One of the key aspects of dynamic scheduling techniques is their ability to consider the current workload and adapt the allocation of resources accordingly. Workload characterization involves analyzing the nature of tasks, their computational requirements, and their dependencies. Dynamic schedulers continuously monitor the system's workload, collecting real-time data on the demands placed on the CPU, memory, and other resources. By leveraging this information, dynamic scheduling algorithms make informed decisions about task prioritization, resource allocation, and load balancing. This adaptability ensures that the system can respond to changing workload patterns, allocating resources more effectively and minimizing resource contention.

Load balancing is a critical component of dynamic scheduling, aiming to distribute tasks evenly across the available resources to prevent overloading or underutilization of specific components. Dynamic load balancing techniques take into account the current state of the system, including the CPU and memory usage, to intelligently distribute tasks among nodes. For example, in a distributed system, a dynamic load balancer may analyze the computational load on each node and migrate tasks from overloaded nodes to underutilized ones. This proactive redistribution of tasks optimizes resource utilization, enhances system throughput, and ensures that no single component is overwhelmed, contributing to improved overall system efficiency.

Another aspect of dynamic scheduling involves task prioritization based on the urgency and criticality of different tasks in the workload. Dynamic priority scheduling assigns priorities dynamically, taking into account factors such as deadlines, task dependencies, and the overall system state. Real-time systems, in particular, benefit from dynamic priority scheduling as it allows for the timely execution of time-sensitive tasks. For instance, in an embedded system controlling a robotic arm, tasks related to sensor data processing and motor control may be dynamically prioritized to meet stringent timing requirements, ensuring that the system responds promptly to external stimuli.

Adaptive scheduling algorithms, a subset of dynamic scheduling techniques, dynamically adjust their behavior based on feedback from the system. These algorithms continuously assess the performance of tasks and the system as a whole, refining their strategies over time. Adaptive techniques can be particularly effective in environments where workload characteristics change gradually or unpredictably. For example, machine learning-based scheduling algorithms may learn from historical data to predict future workload patterns and adjust their scheduling decisions accordingly. This self-tuning capability enhances the resilience and adaptability of the scheduling mechanism, allowing it to optimize system performance in the face of evolving workload dynamics.

In cloud computing environments, dynamic scheduling is crucial for efficiently managing resources and meeting service-level agreements (SLAs). Cloud platforms handle diverse workloads from various users, and the demand for resources can fluctuate dramatically. Dynamic scheduling in the cloud involves elastic resource provisioning, automatic scaling, and workload migration to ensure that resources are allocated according to current demands. Auto-scaling mechanisms, for instance, dynamically adjust the number of virtual machines based on the current workload, scaling up during peak demand and scaling down during periods of low activity. This elasticity allows cloud providers to optimize resource usage, improve cost-efficiency, and deliver reliable services to users with varying computational needs.

Furthermore, energy-aware dynamic scheduling techniques have gained prominence in recent years, particularly in the context of green computing and sustainability. These techniques aim to optimize energy consumption by dynamically adjusting the operation of computing resources based on workload characteristics. For instance, dynamic voltage and frequency scaling (DVFS) algorithms dynamically adjust the voltage and clock frequency of processors to match the current workload. By scaling down during periods of low activity and scaling up during high-demand phases, energy-aware scheduling contributes to reducing overall power consumption, lowering operational costs, and minimizing the environmental impact of computing infrastructure.

In the context of parallel and distributed computing, dynamic scheduling is crucial for maximizing parallelism and minimizing idle times. Dynamic parallelism refers to the ability to adaptively allocate computational resources to parallel tasks based on their availability and readiness to execute. Task-stealing algorithms, a common dynamic scheduling technique in parallel computing, allow idle processors to "steal" tasks from busy processors, ensuring a more balanced distribution of computational work. This approach enhances parallel application performance by minimizing the impact of load imbalance and improving overall system efficiency.

Despite the numerous advantages of dynamic scheduling, challenges and trade-offs exist. Overhead introduced by dynamic decision-making processes and runtime adjustments can impact system performance. Additionally, the complexity of dynamic scheduling algorithms may lead to increased computational requirements. Striking the right balance between adaptability and efficiency is a key consideration in the design and implementation of dynamic scheduling techniques. Moreover, issues such as task migration costs, contention for shared resources, and maintaining fairness in task execution need to be carefully addressed to ensure the successful deployment of dynamic scheduling in diverse computing environments.

In conclusion, dynamic scheduling techniques based on system workload represent a versatile and adaptive approach to optimizing the performance of computer systems across various domains. These techniques leverage real-time information about the workload to dynamically adjust task assignments, resource allocations, and scheduling decisions. From load balancing and adaptive scheduling to energy-aware strategies and dynamic parallelism, the realm of dynamic scheduling encompasses a diverse set of methodologies tailored to address the specific challenges posed by varying workloads. As computing environments continue to evolve, the role of dynamic scheduling remains pivotal in ensuring efficient resource utilization, responsiveness, and adaptability to the dynamic nature of modern computing workloads.

Challenges and strategies in scheduling tasks in cloud computing environments.

Scheduling tasks in cloud computing environments poses a myriad of challenges that stem from the dynamic and distributed nature of these platforms. Cloud computing, characterized by on-demand resource provisioning and scalable services, necessitates effective task scheduling strategies to ensure optimal resource utilization, meet service-level agreements (SLAs), and address the unique challenges inherent in these environments.

One prominent challenge in cloud task scheduling revolves around the dynamic nature of workloads. Workload variability, influenced by factors such as user demand, application characteristics, and external events, requires adaptive scheduling mechanisms. The fluctuating nature of workloads in the cloud makes it challenging to predict resource requirements accurately. Dynamic scheduling strategies are essential to handle these variations, ensuring that resources are allocated efficiently to accommodate varying levels of demand. Reactive approaches, such as auto-scaling and load balancing, play a crucial role in dynamically adjusting resource allocations based on real-time workload changes.

Another significant challenge pertains to the heterogeneity of cloud resources. Cloud environments encompass a diverse set of hardware configurations, including virtual machines with different processing capabilities, memory sizes, and storage capacities. Efficiently scheduling tasks across such heterogeneous infrastructure poses challenges related to resource compatibility and optimization. Scheduling strategies must consider the characteristics of available resources and intelligently match them with the requirements of tasks to maximize resource utilization. Additionally, strategies like bin-packing algorithms are employed to allocate tasks to the most suitable resources, minimizing resource fragmentation and enhancing overall efficiency.

Resource contention constitutes a critical challenge in cloud task scheduling, particularly in multi-tenant environments where multiple users and applications share the same infrastructure. Competition for shared resources, such as CPU, memory, and network bandwidth, can lead to performance degradation and violation of SLAs. Scheduling algorithms need to effectively mitigate resource contention by considering factors like priority, fairness, and isolation. Techniques such as quota-based scheduling and resource reservation mechanisms help allocate resources in a manner that ensures fairness among competing tasks while preventing any single tenant from monopolizing shared resources.

The inherent scalability of cloud environments introduces challenges related to massive-scale task scheduling. With a vast number of resources available, scheduling algorithms must efficiently handle large-scale deployments to meet the demands of cloud-scale applications. Distributed scheduling mechanisms, leveraging techniques like parallel scheduling and decentralized decision-making, are crucial for orchestrating the execution of tasks across a multitude of resources. These strategies help distribute the scheduling workload, avoid bottlenecks, and scale horizontally to accommodate the ever-expanding cloud infrastructure.

Deadline constraints and real-time task requirements add another layer of complexity to cloud task scheduling. Certain applications, such as those in the domains of finance, telecommunications, and online gaming, have stringent timing requirements. Meeting these deadlines is crucial for ensuring the desired quality of service. Real-time task scheduling strategies must consider factors like task priorities, deadlines, and temporal constraints to guarantee timely execution. Techniques such as earliest deadline first (EDF) scheduling and deadline-driven approaches play a vital role in managing real-time tasks in the cloud.

Energy efficiency and sustainability are increasingly important considerations in cloud task scheduling due to the environmental impact and operational costs associated with data centers. Green computing initiatives aim to minimize energy consumption and reduce the carbon footprint of cloud infrastructures. Task scheduling strategies must incorporate energy-aware algorithms, such as dynamic voltage and frequency scaling (DVFS) and consolidation of tasks on fewer active servers, to optimize energy usage without compromising performance. These strategies contribute to achieving a balance between performance objectives and ecological responsibility in cloud computing environments.

Security and privacy concerns present additional challenges in cloud task scheduling. As tasks are distributed across multiple servers and may involve sensitive data, ensuring the confidentiality, integrity, and availability of information is paramount. Scheduling mechanisms must incorporate security measures, such as encryption, access controls, and secure communication protocols, to safeguard data during task execution. Privacy-aware scheduling strategies also address concerns related to data residency and compliance with regulatory requirements, ensuring that sensitive tasks are processed in accordance with legal and contractual obligations.

The complexity of managing inter-task dependencies and communication further complicates cloud task scheduling. Many applications are composed of multiple interdependent tasks that require coordination and communication during execution. Scheduling strategies must consider these dependencies to prevent bottlenecks, minimize communication overhead, and optimize overall task completion times. Techniques like gang scheduling and data locality optimizations aim to co-locate dependent tasks on the same resources, reducing communication latency and improving the efficiency of task execution.

Furthermore, the economic aspects of cloud computing introduce challenges related to cost optimization and resource allocation. Cloud users typically pay for the resources they consume, making cost-effective task scheduling a critical consideration. Scheduling strategies must balance performance objectives with cost considerations, dynamically adjusting resource allocations based on pricing models and user preferences. Techniques like spot instance utilization, which leverages temporary, cost-efficient resources, and predictive pricing models contribute to optimizing resource costs in cloud environments.

In response to these challenges, various strategies and approaches have been developed to enhance the effectiveness of task scheduling in cloud computing environments. Machine learning and predictive analytics are increasingly integrated into scheduling algorithms to forecast workload patterns, optimize resource allocations, and improve overall system efficiency. Reinforcement learning techniques enable scheduling systems to learn and adapt to changing conditions over time, enhancing their ability to make informed decisions in dynamic environments.

Moreover, containerization technologies, such as Docker and Kubernetes, have emerged as powerful tools for task scheduling and resource management in cloud environments. Containers provide lightweight, portable units that encapsulate applications and their dependencies, facilitating efficient deployment and scaling. Container orchestration platforms enable automated scheduling, scaling, and management of containerized applications, offering flexibility and agility in adapting to changing workload demands.

In conclusion, the challenges in scheduling tasks in cloud computing environments are diverse and multifaceted, stemming from the dynamic, distributed, and heterogeneous nature of these platforms. Efficient task scheduling is essential for maximizing resource utilization, meeting performance objectives, and ensuring cost-effective operation in the cloud. Strategies addressing workload variability, resource contention, real-time requirements, security, energy efficiency, and economic considerations are crucial for the success of cloud computing deployments. As cloud technologies continue to evolve, ongoing research and innovation in task scheduling will be essential to address emerging challenges and optimize the performance of cloud-based applications and services.

Analyzing instances where effective task scheduling contributed to system efficiency.

Effective task scheduling has played a pivotal role in enhancing system efficiency across various domains, contributing to improved resource utilization, reduced response times, and overall optimization of computational processes. One notable instance of the impact of task scheduling on system efficiency is observed in the context of parallel and distributed computing. In scientific simulations and data-intensive applications, where tasks can be parallelized, efficient allocation of computational resources is crucial. Task scheduling algorithms, such as dynamic load balancing and parallel task decomposition, ensure that parallel tasks are distributed evenly across available processors. This not only minimizes idle times but also maximizes the utilization of processing power, accelerating the overall execution of parallelized applications. Efficient task scheduling in parallel and distributed computing environments has been instrumental in unlocking the full potential of high-performance computing systems, allowing researchers and engineers to tackle complex problems with unprecedented speed and scalability.

In cloud computing, effective task scheduling has become a linchpin for optimizing resource usage and meeting user demands. Cloud environments are characterized by their on-demand nature and the ability to scale resources dynamically. Task scheduling strategies in the cloud aim to allocate virtual machines and distribute tasks across the available infrastructure efficiently. This adaptability is particularly evident in auto-scaling mechanisms, where the number of virtual machines is automatically adjusted based on current workload and demand. The dynamic allocation of resources ensures that users receive the necessary computational power precisely when needed, minimizing costs during periods of low demand and providing responsiveness during peak usage. Effective task scheduling in the cloud not only optimizes resource utilization but also contributes to the economic sustainability of cloud services by aligning resource allocation with actual demand patterns.

Real-time systems provide another compelling example of the impact of effective task scheduling on system efficiency. In industries such as aviation, healthcare, and industrial automation, where timely response to events is critical, real-time operating systems employ sophisticated scheduling algorithms to meet stringent deadlines. The earliest deadline first (EDF) scheduling algorithm, for instance, assigns priorities to tasks based on their deadlines, ensuring that the most time-critical tasks are executed first. This prioritization guarantees that critical operations, such as sensor data processing, control signals, and feedback loops, are handled promptly. Effective real-time task scheduling is paramount in preventing system failures, reducing latency, and ensuring the reliability of systems where timely and predictable responses are non-negotiable.

In the realm of multimedia applications and streaming services, efficient task scheduling is imperative for delivering a seamless and high-quality user experience. Video encoding, decoding, and streaming involve computationally intensive tasks that require timely execution to prevent buffering and latency issues. Task scheduling algorithms in multimedia systems prioritize video processing tasks, ensuring that frames are processed in the correct order and delivered to users without interruptions. Additionally, adaptive streaming services dynamically adjust video quality based on network conditions and device capabilities. Task scheduling strategies play a crucial role in orchestrating these adaptive mechanisms, optimizing the delivery of multimedia content to users and enhancing the overall efficiency of streaming services.

Database management systems represent another domain where task scheduling significantly impacts system efficiency. In large-scale data warehouses and transactional databases, numerous concurrent queries and transactions contend for access to database resources. Effective query scheduling algorithms, such as multi-level feedback queues and shortest job first (SJF) scheduling, prioritize and allocate resources to queries based on their characteristics and urgency. This ensures that critical queries receive prompt attention and that resources are distributed fairly among competing tasks. Efficient task scheduling in database systems contributes to reduced query response times, improved throughput, and enhanced overall performance, allowing organizations to extract valuable insights from their data with minimal latency.

The field of high-performance computing (HPC) offers further instances where effective task scheduling is a cornerstone of system efficiency. Supercomputers and computing clusters, utilized in scientific research, weather modeling, and simulations, handle intricate tasks that demand massive computational power. Task scheduling algorithms in HPC systems aim to optimize the allocation of computing resources and minimize the time-to-solution for complex problems. Techniques such as gang scheduling, which coordinates the simultaneous execution of related tasks, and checkpointing, which periodically saves the state of a computation, contribute to efficient resource utilization and fault tolerance. By orchestrating the execution of parallel tasks across multiple processors, effective task scheduling in HPC environments accelerates scientific discovery, simulations, and computations that would be infeasible without the efficient distribution of computational workloads.

In the context of embedded systems, task scheduling is vital for ensuring the dependable operation of devices with real-time requirements. Embedded systems, found in automotive electronics, medical devices, and consumer electronics, often involve a mix of real-time and non-real-time tasks. Task scheduling algorithms in these systems must prioritize time-critical tasks while efficiently handling less time-sensitive operations. For instance, in an anti-lock braking system (ABS) in a car, the scheduling algorithm ensures that tasks related to monitoring wheel speed and applying brakes are prioritized to guarantee immediate responses. Effective task scheduling in embedded systems not only enhances the reliability of critical functionalities but also contributes to the energy efficiency of devices, extending battery life and minimizing resource consumption.

Moreover, in the context of grid and cluster computing, where resources are distributed across multiple nodes, task scheduling strategies are crucial for balancing workloads and optimizing resource utilization. Grid computing often involves collaboration among geographically dispersed resources, and efficient task scheduling ensures that computational tasks are assigned to appropriate nodes based on their capabilities and availability. By minimizing communication overhead and load imbalances, effective task scheduling in grid and cluster environments contributes to improved scalability and overall system efficiency. This is particularly evident in scientific collaborations that leverage grid computing for large-scale simulations and data analyses, where tasks are distributed across a network of interconnected resources.

In the emerging field of edge computing, where computational tasks are performed closer to the data source, effective task scheduling is essential for maximizing the benefits of low-latency processing and reducing the burden on central data centers. Edge computing applications, such as smart cities, Internet of Things (IoT) devices, and autonomous vehicles, require responsive and efficient task scheduling mechanisms. Decentralized scheduling algorithms and edge-aware strategies contribute to minimizing latency, conserving bandwidth, and enhancing the overall efficiency of edge computing systems. These advancements allow edge devices to process data locally, reducing the need for round-trip communication to centralized servers and improving the real-time responsiveness of applications.

In conclusion, effective task scheduling has proven to be a linchpin for enhancing system efficiency across diverse computing environments. From parallel and distributed computing to real-time systems, multimedia applications, database management, high-performance computing, embedded systems, and emerging paradigms like edge computing, task scheduling strategies play a pivotal role in optimizing resource utilization, meeting performance objectives, and ensuring cost-effective operation. The ability to orchestrate the execution of tasks, balance workloads, and prioritize critical operations contributes to the overall efficiency, responsiveness, and reliability of computing systems across various domains, ultimately shaping the landscape of modern computing.

Chapter 5: Memory Management in Operating Systems

Defining memory management and its critical role in system performance.

Memory management is a crucial aspect of computer systems that plays a pivotal role in determining overall system performance. It encompasses a set of processes and techniques employed by operating systems to organize, allocate, and deallocate memory resources efficiently. The primary goal of memory management is to ensure optimal utilization of the available memory, allowing programs to run smoothly while avoiding conflicts and errors. In essence, it is the backbone of a computer's functionality, influencing the execution of applications, responsiveness, and overall user experience.

At its core, memory management involves the allocation of memory space to different programs and processes, dynamically adapting to the changing needs of the system. This dynamic allocation is essential for multitasking, where multiple programs run concurrently, sharing the limited resources of the computer. Effective memory management ensures that each program receives the necessary space for execution without encroaching on the territories of other processes, thus preventing unintended interference and potential crashes.

One of the key components of memory management is the concept of virtual memory. Virtual memory allows the system to use a combination of RAM (Random Access Memory) and secondary storage (usually a hard disk) to create an illusion of a larger and contiguous memory space than physically available. This enables the execution of larger programs that may not fit entirely into the RAM, thereby enhancing the system's capability to handle complex tasks and applications. However, the effective utilization of virtual memory requires efficient algorithms and mechanisms for swapping data between the RAM and the secondary storage, avoiding performance bottlenecks and delays.

Memory management is closely tied to the concept of memory hierarchy, which encompasses various levels of memory with different speeds and sizes. Caches, registers, RAM, and secondary storage form a hierarchical structure, with each level serving a specific purpose in storing and retrieving data. Efficient memory management involves optimizing the use of these different levels, considering factors such as access times, cost, and capacity. Strategies such as caching algorithms and memory hierarchy design contribute significantly to reducing latency and improving the overall responsiveness of the system.

Furthermore, memory management plays a critical role in maintaining data integrity and preventing unauthorized access. Security mechanisms, such as memory protection, segmentation, and access controls, are integral components of memory management systems. These mechanisms ensure that programs cannot access the memory space allocated to other processes, preventing potential security breaches and unauthorized data modifications. Additionally, memory management is instrumental in detecting and handling memory-related errors, such as segmentation faults, to maintain system stability and reliability.

The impact of memory management on system performance is evident in various scenarios, ranging from basic everyday tasks to resource-intensive applications. In a multitasking environment, efficient memory management allows seamless switching between applications, ensuring a responsive user experience. Conversely, poor memory management can lead to system slowdowns, freezes, and crashes, hindering productivity and frustrating users. In resource-intensive applications like video editing or 3D rendering, effective memory management becomes even more critical, as these tasks demand substantial memory resources for optimal performance.

Optimizing memory usage involves implementing advanced algorithms for memory allocation and deallocation, garbage collection, and memory compaction. These algorithms aim to minimize fragmentation, both internal and external, which can lead to inefficient use of memory space. Fragmentation occurs when memory is allocated and deallocated in a way that leaves small, non-contiguous gaps, making it challenging to allocate larger blocks of memory when needed. Efficient memory management algorithms, such as those used in modern operating systems, mitigate fragmentation issues and contribute to the overall stability and performance of the system.

The impact of memory management extends beyond the realm of traditional desktop or laptop computing to encompass server environments and cloud computing. In server environments, where multiple users or applications may simultaneously access the same resources, effective memory management is paramount for maintaining consistent and reliable service. Cloud computing, with its distributed and virtualized nature, relies heavily on robust memory management to ensure efficient resource allocation among virtual machines and containers.

In conclusion, memory management is a foundational element in computer systems, shaping their performance, reliability, and security. Its role in orchestrating the allocation and deallocation of memory resources, managing virtual memory, and optimizing memory hierarchy is indispensable for the seamless operation of modern computing devices. As technology evolves and the demand for computational power increases, the importance of efficient memory management becomes even more pronounced. A well-designed and implemented memory management system is not just a technical detail but a fundamental determinant of the user experience and the overall success of computing systems in diverse and demanding environments.

Understanding the concept of address spaces and memory segmentation.

Address spaces and memory segmentation are fundamental concepts in computer architecture and memory management, playing a crucial role in organizing and utilizing memory efficiently. An address space refers to the range of memory addresses that a computer system or a process can use to store and retrieve data. In essence, it defines the boundaries within which a program operates in terms of memory access. The concept of address spaces is instrumental in ensuring the isolation of processes and preventing interference between them. Each process is allocated its own distinct address space, shielding it from the memory activities of other processes. This isolation is essential for maintaining data integrity, security, and preventing unintended conflicts that could arise if processes shared the same memory addresses.

Memory segmentation is a technique employed in memory management to divide a process's address space into distinct segments, each serving a specific purpose. These segments typically include code, data, stack, and heap segments, each catering to different aspects of program execution. The code segment contains the program instructions, the data segment stores initialized and static data, the stack segment manages function call information and local variables, and the heap segment is responsible for dynamic memory allocation during runtime. Segmentation enhances the organization and efficiency of memory usage by providing a structured approach to managing different types of data within a process.

The segmentation process involves assigning a base address and a limit to each segment, defining the starting point and size of the memory area allocated for that segment. This segmentation approach allows for flexibility in memory allocation, as each segment can grow or shrink dynamically based on the program's requirements. However, it also introduces challenges, such as potential fragmentation and the need for effective management strategies. Segmentation can lead to both internal fragmentation, where memory within a segment is not fully utilized, and external fragmentation, where free memory is scattered throughout the address space, making it challenging to allocate contiguous blocks of memory.

To overcome the limitations of segmentation, a concept known as paging is often employed. Paging involves dividing the physical memory and the process's virtual address space into fixed-size blocks called pages. These pages serve as the basic unit of memory allocation and are managed independently. Unlike segmentation, paging eliminates external fragmentation by dividing the memory into uniform-sized pages, simplifying the allocation and deallocation processes. However, it introduces the possibility of internal fragmentation within pages, as a page may be only partially filled with data.

A combination of segmentation and paging, known as segmented paging or hierarchical paging, seeks to harness the advantages of both approaches while mitigating their respective drawbacks. In this hybrid model, the address space is divided into segments, and each segment is further divided into pages. This hierarchical structure allows for efficient memory management, reducing both internal and external fragmentation. Moreover, it provides a flexible and organized framework for handling diverse memory requirements within a process.

The concept of address spaces and memory segmentation becomes particularly relevant in the context of modern operating systems, where multitasking is a common practice. Operating systems must manage the memory spaces of multiple processes concurrently, ensuring their isolation and preventing conflicts. The use of address spaces and segmentation allows the operating system to create a virtual environment for each process, providing the illusion of a dedicated and isolated memory space. This virtualization of memory enables the concurrent execution of multiple processes without the risk of memory interference, contributing to system stability and user experience.

In addition to managing the memory of individual processes, address spaces play a critical role in facilitating inter-process communication (IPC). Address spaces provide a means for processes to share data and communicate with each other, either through shared memory regions or by passing messages. IPC mechanisms rely on well-defined address spaces to enable secure and controlled data exchange between processes, fostering collaboration and coordination in complex computing environments.

The concept of address spaces and memory segmentation is not limited to traditional desktop or server computing but extends to embedded systems, real-time systems, and distributed systems. In embedded systems, where resources are often limited, efficient memory management is essential for optimizing performance and ensuring reliable operation. Real-time systems, with stringent timing requirements, benefit from well-organized address spaces to minimize delays in memory access. In distributed systems, where processes may run on different machines, the concept of address spaces helps in coordinating memory access and communication across the network.

In conclusion, the understanding of address spaces and memory segmentation is fundamental to the design and operation of computer systems. These concepts provide a structured framework for organizing and managing memory, ensuring the isolation of processes, supporting multitasking, and enabling efficient memory utilization. While segmentation allows for the logical division of a process's address space into meaningful segments, paging and hybrid approaches address the challenges associated with fragmentation. The role of address spaces extends beyond individual processes to encompass inter-process communication and is pivotal in diverse computing environments, from embedded systems to distributed computing. As technology continues to evolve, the principles of address spaces and memory segmentation remain integral to the development of efficient and scalable computer systems.

Exploring memory allocation techniques such as contiguous and non-contiguous allocation.

Memory allocation techniques are fundamental aspects of memory management in computer systems, determining how programs access and utilize memory during their execution. Two prominent approaches to memory allocation are contiguous and non-contiguous allocation. Contiguous memory allocation involves assigning a single, continuous block of memory to a process. This method simplifies the memory management process, as the entire address space required by a program is allocated as a contiguous block. The starting address of the block and its size are crucial parameters, defining the entire range of memory addresses accessible to the program. While this approach is straightforward and efficient in terms of memory access, it poses challenges in accommodating multiple processes concurrently. As processes are allocated contiguous blocks, fragmentation can occur, leading to both internal fragmentation within the allocated block and external fragmentation in the unallocated spaces between blocks. Contiguous allocation is commonly employed in simple memory management systems and real-mode operating systems, where processes can be loaded into contiguous physical memory without virtualization.

Non-contiguous memory allocation, on the other hand, allows a process's memory to be scattered throughout the physical memory space. This method overcomes the limitations of contiguous allocation, providing more flexibility in memory utilization. Non-contiguous allocation techniques include paging and segmentation. In paging, the physical memory is divided into fixed-size blocks called pages, and the virtual memory of a process is divided into corresponding pages. Each page of the process can be allocated to any available physical page, enabling efficient use of memory resources. This approach minimizes external fragmentation by allowing for dynamic allocation of pages, but it may introduce internal fragmentation if a page is only partially filled. Paging is widely used in modern operating systems and provides a balance between simplicity and flexibility in memory management.

Segmentation, another non-contiguous memory allocation technique, divides a process's address space into distinct segments based on the type of data stored, such as code, data, stack, and heap segments. Each segment is allocated independently, and the sizes of segments can vary dynamically during program execution. Segmentation enhances memory management by organizing data logically, but it may lead to external fragmentation. To address this issue, a combination of segmentation and paging, known as segmented paging or hierarchical paging, is often employed. This hybrid approach combines the benefits of both segmentation and paging, providing a structured and flexible memory management system.

The choice between contiguous and non-contiguous memory allocation depends on the specific requirements of the system and the nature of the processes it needs to handle. Contiguous allocation is suitable for simpler systems with limited memory and straightforward memory access requirements. In contrast, non-contiguous allocation techniques are more suitable for complex systems with multitasking capabilities and dynamic memory needs. The evolution of computer systems has seen a shift towards non-contiguous memory allocation due to the advantages it offers in terms of flexibility, efficient use of memory, and support for multitasking.

One significant challenge in memory allocation is fragmentation, which refers to the scattering of unused memory space across the system. Contiguous allocation can lead to external fragmentation as processes are loaded and unloaded, leaving gaps of unused memory. To address this issue, compaction techniques may be employed, involving the relocation of processes to eliminate or reduce fragmentation. However, compaction introduces additional overhead and may not be practical in real-time or resource-constrained systems.

In non-contiguous allocation, fragmentation is also a concern, but it manifests differently. Paging minimizes external fragmentation by allocating memory in fixed-size blocks, but it may introduce internal fragmentation if a page is not fully utilized. Segmentation, while providing logical organization, can lead to external fragmentation if segments of varying sizes are allocated independently. The challenge is to find a balance between logical organization and efficient use of memory, considering factors such as process size, memory requirements, and the need for dynamic memory allocation.

Moreover, memory allocation techniques are closely tied to the concept of virtual memory, which extends the available memory beyond physical RAM by using secondary storage, typically a hard disk. Virtual memory allows processes to execute even if the total memory requirements exceed the physical RAM capacity. Paging plays a crucial role in implementing virtual memory, as it allows the operating system to swap pages between physical RAM and the secondary storage, ensuring that the active pages are in RAM while less frequently accessed pages reside on the disk. This mechanism is transparent to the executing processes, providing the illusion of a vast and contiguous address space while efficiently managing physical memory resources.

Non-contiguous memory allocation techniques, particularly paging and segmentation, contribute to the efficiency and stability of modern operating systems. They enable the dynamic allocation and deallocation of memory, support multitasking, and facilitate the execution of diverse applications with varying memory requirements. The development of sophisticated algorithms for page replacement, such as the Least Recently Used (LRU) algorithm, enhances the performance of non-contiguous memory allocation by optimizing the placement of pages in physical memory. These algorithms consider factors like access frequency and recency to decide which pages to keep in RAM, minimizing page faults and improving overall system responsiveness.

In conclusion, memory allocation techniques, whether contiguous or non-contiguous, are essential components of memory management in computer systems. Contiguous allocation simplifies memory access but may lead to fragmentation issues, making it suitable for simpler systems. Non-contiguous allocation techniques, such as paging and segmentation, offer flexibility, efficient use of memory, and support for multitasking in complex systems. The choice between these techniques depends on the specific requirements of the system and the nature of the processes it handles. As computer systems continue to evolve, memory management remains a critical aspect, and advancements in allocation techniques contribute to the optimization of system performance and resource utilization.

Introduction to virtual memory and its importance in modern operating systems.

Virtual memory is a pivotal concept in modern operating systems, revolutionizing the way computers manage memory resources and execute programs. At its core, virtual memory is a memory management technique that provides an abstraction layer between the physical memory (RAM) and the storage devices, allowing the computer to utilize secondary storage, typically a hard disk, as an extension of the available RAM. This abstraction creates an illusion of a vast and contiguous address space for each process, even if the physical RAM is limited. Virtual memory serves as a bridge between the demands of applications and the constraints of physical hardware, offering a solution to the challenge of efficiently managing memory in complex computing environments.

The importance of virtual memory in modern operating systems stems from its ability to address several key issues inherent in traditional memory management. One primary challenge is the limited physical RAM available in a computer system. As applications and processes become more sophisticated, their memory requirements increase, often surpassing the available physical memory. Virtual memory mitigates this limitation by allowing processes to use more memory than is physically present, effectively extending the system's capacity and enabling the execution of larger and more complex programs.

In addition to overcoming physical memory limitations, virtual memory facilitates multitasking, a fundamental capability in modern operating systems. In a multitasking environment, where multiple processes run concurrently, each process expects its own dedicated memory space. Virtual memory provides a means to isolate processes, ensuring that they have the illusion of a dedicated and contiguous memory space, even if they are sharing the same physical memory. This isolation prevents unintended interference between processes, enhancing system stability and security.

The concept of virtual memory is closely tied to the idea of demand paging. Demand paging is a mechanism where the operating system loads only the necessary portions of a program into physical memory when they are actively being used. Instead of loading the entire program into RAM at the start, the operating system loads specific pages as they are requested during program execution. This dynamic loading and unloading of pages allow for efficient use of physical memory resources, optimizing the overall performance of the system.

Another crucial aspect of virtual memory is the handling of page faults. When a program attempts to access a memory page that is not currently in physical RAM, a page fault occurs. The operating system then responds by bringing the required page into RAM from the secondary storage. This seamless page fault handling is transparent to the running processes, providing the illusion of a continuous and abundant memory space. Effective algorithms, such as those based on page replacement policies like Least Recently Used (LRU), contribute to the efficient management of page faults, minimizing their impact on system performance.

Furthermore, virtual memory plays a vital role in enhancing the overall responsiveness of the system. As processes share the limited physical memory, the operating system must make intelligent decisions about which pages to keep in RAM and which to move to the secondary storage. The ability to swap pages in and out of physical memory ensures that the active and frequently accessed pages remain in RAM, reducing the likelihood of page faults and maintaining optimal system responsiveness. Virtual memory, with its demand paging and page replacement mechanisms, contributes significantly to creating a smooth and efficient user experience, even in resource-constrained environments.

The implementation of virtual memory introduces the concept of the page table, a data structure that maps the virtual addresses used by a process to the corresponding physical addresses in RAM. The page table is crucial for the operating system to track the location of pages in both virtual and physical memory. It enables the translation of virtual addresses into physical addresses during program execution, ensuring that processes interact with the correct physical memory locations. The efficiency of the page table management is essential for the overall performance of virtual memory systems, and modern operating systems employ sophisticated algorithms to optimize page table access.

The impact of virtual memory extends beyond traditional desktop or server computing environments to various computing platforms, including embedded systems, real-time systems, and cloud computing. In embedded systems, where resources are often constrained, virtual memory allows for the efficient use of limited physical memory while supporting the execution of complex applications. Real-time systems, with stringent timing requirements, benefit from virtual memory's ability to manage memory dynamically without causing significant delays. In cloud computing, where virtualization is a key component, virtual memory enables the efficient allocation and management of resources among virtual machines and containers.

Moreover, the use of virtual memory contributes to system reliability and fault tolerance. In scenarios where a process or application encounters a critical error, the operating system can isolate the affected process without disrupting the entire system. Virtual memory allows for the segmentation and isolation of processes, limiting the impact of failures to the specific processes involved. This isolation enhances the robustness of the system, ensuring that a failure in one application does not lead to a system-wide crash.

In conclusion, virtual memory stands as a cornerstone in modern operating systems, providing an effective solution to the challenges posed by limited physical memory and the demands of complex applications. Through techniques like demand paging, page fault handling, and efficient page table management, virtual memory enables the illusion of a vast and contiguous address space for each process. This abstraction not only supports multitasking and efficient memory utilization but also contributes to system responsiveness and fault tolerance. As technology continues to advance, the principles of virtual memory remain integral to the design and optimization of operating systems across a diverse range of computing environments.

In-depth analysis of page replacement algorithms like LRU and FIFO.

Page replacement algorithms play a pivotal role in the efficient management of virtual memory in computer systems, determining which pages to retain in physical memory and which to swap out to secondary storage. Two widely used page replacement algorithms are Least Recently Used (LRU) and First-In-First-Out (FIFO). LRU is based on the principle of discarding the page that has not been accessed for the longest period, assuming that pages accessed more recently are likely to be used again in the near future. This algorithm aims to minimize the number of page faults by retaining the most recently used pages in physical memory. LRU operates on the principle of temporal locality, reflecting the tendency of programs to access the same memory locations repeatedly within a short time frame. While LRU is conceptually straightforward, its practical implementation involves challenges in maintaining an accurate and up-to-date record of page access history.

One common approach to implementing LRU is the use of counters or stacks. In the counter-based implementation, each page has an associated counter that is incremented every time the page is accessed. The page with the lowest counter value represents the least recently used page and is a candidate for replacement. While this approach provides a direct measure of recency, it requires additional hardware support and introduces overhead due to frequent counter updates. Another method involves maintaining a stack of page numbers in the order of their access, where the most recently used page is at the top. However, updating and maintaining the stack for each memory access can be computationally expensive, impacting system performance. Despite these challenges, LRU remains a widely used and well-regarded page replacement algorithm due to its theoretical optimality in minimizing page faults.

FIFO, on the other hand, is a simpler page replacement algorithm that follows a first-in-first-out approach. In FIFO, the page that has been in physical memory the longest is selected for replacement. This algorithm operates on the assumption that pages that have been in memory for an extended period are less likely to be accessed in the near future. FIFO maintains a queue of pages in the order they were brought into physical memory, and when a page needs to be replaced, the one at the front of the queue is selected. While FIFO is easy to implement and requires minimal computational overhead, it suffers from the lack of consideration for actual page access patterns. It may perform poorly in scenarios where pages are accessed in a non-uniform distribution or when there is a significant variance in the access frequencies of different pages.

Comparing LRU and FIFO reveals their distinct advantages and limitations. LRU, with its focus on recency, tends to perform well in scenarios where there is a high degree of temporal locality, and pages that were accessed recently are likely to be accessed again soon. However, its implementation complexity and potential for high overhead can be drawbacks in certain environments. FIFO, being a simpler algorithm, is computationally less expensive and easy to implement. It is suitable for scenarios where the temporal order of page access is less critical, and the page access patterns do not exhibit strong temporal locality. However, FIFO may lead to poor performance in situations with varying access frequencies and uneven distributions.

Efforts to enhance the practicality of LRU and address its implementation challenges have led to the development of approximations and variations. One such approach is the Clock algorithm, which uses a circular list of pages and a hand that moves around the circle. When a page fault occurs, the hand is moved, and the page it points to is considered for replacement. If the page has been accessed, it is given a second chance and the hand moves to the next page. This process continues until a page without a second chance is found. The Clock algorithm offers a compromise between the simplicity of FIFO and the theoretical optimality of LRU.

In contrast, variations of LRU attempt to strike a balance between accuracy and computational efficiency. The Not Recently Used (NRU) algorithm, for example, categorizes pages into different classes based on their access history. Pages are periodically reset to the least recently used class, allowing for a dynamic adjustment of the recency measure. While NRU simplifies the implementation compared to true LRU, it introduces the challenge of selecting appropriate parameters for classifying pages, influencing its effectiveness.

The practical choice between LRU and FIFO, or their variations, depends on the characteristics of the workload and the system requirements. In scenarios where recency of access is critical and temporal locality is high, LRU or its approximations may be preferred. However, the associated overhead and complexity should be carefully considered. FIFO, with its simplicity, may be suitable for environments where the order of page access is less relevant, and computational efficiency is a primary concern. The choice also depends on the specific use case, as certain applications and workloads may exhibit distinct access patterns that align better with one algorithm over the other.

It is essential to acknowledge that the effectiveness of page replacement algorithms is influenced by various factors, including the size of physical memory, the nature of the workload, and the characteristics of the accessed data. The optimal choice of a page replacement algorithm may involve a trade-off between theoretical optimality and practical implementation considerations. As computer systems continue to evolve and the demands on memory management become more diverse, ongoing research aims to develop adaptive and intelligent page replacement algorithms that can dynamically adjust their strategies based on the evolving characteristics of workloads and access patterns.

In conclusion, page replacement algorithms like LRU and FIFO play a critical role in the effective management of virtual memory, impacting the performance and responsiveness of computer systems. LRU, with its focus on recency, strives for optimal performance by retaining the most recently used pages in physical memory. However, its practical implementation complexity and potential for high overhead have led to the development of approximations and variations. FIFO, while simpler and computationally less expensive, may lack adaptability to varying access patterns. The choice between LRU and FIFO depends on the specific requirements of the system, the characteristics of the workload, and the balance between theoretical optimality and practical implementation considerations. Ongoing research continues to explore adaptive page replacement strategies that can dynamically adjust to the evolving demands of modern computing environments.

The role of memory mapping in linking files to memory locations.

Memory mapping serves as a fundamental and powerful mechanism in computer systems, playing a crucial role in linking files to memory locations and facilitating efficient data access and manipulation. At its essence, memory mapping establishes a direct correspondence between the content of a file and a range of memory addresses, enabling seamless integration of file operations with standard memory access mechanisms. This concept is particularly significant in modern operating systems and applications, providing a versatile and efficient means of handling data that is stored persistently on secondary storage devices, such as hard drives or SSDs.

One of the key advantages of memory mapping is the elimination of the need for explicit read and write operations between files and programs. Instead of relying on traditional file input/output (I/

O) operations, memory mapping allows the contents of a file to be treated as if it were an array in memory. This approach simplifies the programming model and enhances performance by reducing the overhead associated with explicit I/O operations. The memory mapping mechanism essentially extends the uniformity of memory access to include file data, promoting a seamless and unified approach to handling both volatile and persistent data within a program's address space.

In practical terms, the process of memory mapping involves associating a region of virtual memory with the content of a file. This virtual memory region, known as a memory-mapped file, mirrors the structure and organization of the file, enabling the program to manipulate the file's data using standard memory access operations. The operating system takes on the responsibility of managing the synchronization between the in-memory representation and the actual file on disk. As a result, any modifications made to the memory-mapped file are automatically reflected in the underlying file, and vice versa, eliminating the need for explicit file I/O calls.

Memory mapping offers two primary modes of access: read-only and read-write. In a read-only mapping, the program can access the file's contents in a manner analogous to reading from standard memory, providing a convenient mechanism for efficiently sharing data between multiple processes or instances of an application. On the other hand, read-write mapping enables both reading and writing, allowing programs to update the file directly in memory, with the changes persisting back to the file on disk. This flexibility is particularly valuable in scenarios where frequent modifications to the file's content are required.

An essential aspect of memory mapping is the role of the memory-mapped file as a shared memory region that can be accessed by multiple processes simultaneously. This feature facilitates inter-process communication, enabling efficient data exchange between independent processes running on the same system. Shared memory through memory mapping is more efficient than traditional inter-process communication mechanisms, such as message passing, as it avoids the need for data serialization and deserialization. Additionally, since memory-mapped files are managed by the operating system, changes made by one process are immediately visible to others, providing a real-time and synchronized view of shared data.

The performance benefits of memory mapping are further exemplified in scenarios involving large datasets or frequently accessed files. By mapping a file into memory, the operating system can employ its virtual memory management mechanisms, such as demand paging, to load only the portions of the file that are actively accessed into physical memory. This on-demand loading minimizes the initial loading time and optimizes memory usage by bringing into memory only the portions needed for the ongoing computation. Consequently, memory mapping is particularly advantageous for applications dealing with extensive datasets, databases, or multimedia files, where efficient access to specific portions of the file is crucial for performance.

The use of memory mapping is not limited to regular files; it extends to other system objects as well. For instance, memory-mapped I/O allows mapping memory regions directly to hardware devices, treating them as if they were regular memory addresses. This technique is especially relevant in scenarios involving devices like graphics cards, where direct access to memory-mapped regions enhances performance by eliminating the need for intermediate buffers and reducing data transfer overhead.

Despite its numerous advantages, memory mapping does present certain considerations and challenges. One notable concern is the potential for unintentional modification of memory-mapped files. Since changes in memory are automatically reflected in the corresponding file, there is a risk of inadvertently altering the file's content.

To address this, operating systems and programming frameworks often provide mechanisms to mark memory-mapped regions as read-only or employ other safeguards to prevent unintended modifications.

Another consideration is the potential for increased memory consumption when working with large files. While memory mapping offers the advantage of on-demand loading, mapping a sizable file may lead to higher memory usage, especially in scenarios where only a small portion of the file is actively accessed. Careful consideration of the file size and access patterns is necessary to optimize memory utilization and prevent unnecessary resource consumption.

In conclusion, memory mapping stands as a versatile and powerful mechanism in computer systems, bridging the gap between persistent storage and volatile memory. By establishing a direct linkage between files and memory locations, memory mapping facilitates seamless and efficient data access, manipulation, and sharing. Its ability to eliminate the need for explicit file I/O operations, support shared memory among processes, and optimize the handling of large datasets positions it as a crucial component in modern operating systems and applications. As technology continues to advance, the principles of memory mapping remain integral to the development of efficient and high-performance computing systems.

Importance of memory protection in preventing unauthorized access.

Memory protection is a fundamental aspect of computer systems, playing a pivotal role in safeguarding the integrity, security, and stability of both the operating system and the user applications that run on it. At its core, memory protection involves mechanisms and techniques implemented by the operating system to prevent unauthorized access, modification, or execution of memory regions. The importance of memory protection cannot be overstated, as it serves as a critical line of defense against various security threats and ensures that processes operate within their designated boundaries.

One of the primary functions of memory protection is to isolate processes and prevent them from interfering with each other's memory space. In a multitasking environment where multiple processes run concurrently, each process expects to have exclusive access to its allocated memory without being able to inadvertently or maliciously access the memory of other processes. Without proper memory protection, processes could potentially overwrite each other's data, leading to data corruption, crashes, and security vulnerabilities. Memory protection mechanisms, enforced by the hardware and the operating system, establish boundaries between processes, ensuring that each process operates within its own protected memory space.

The concept of memory protection extends beyond processes to include the protection of the operating system's kernel memory. The kernel, as the core component of the operating system, manages system resources and provides essential services. Unauthorized access or modification of kernel memory can have severe consequences, potentially compromising the entire system's stability and security. Memory protection mechanisms restrict user-level processes from directly accessing or modifying kernel memory, enforcing a clear boundary between user space and kernel space. This separation prevents user processes from tampering with critical system data structures and code, safeguarding the integrity of the operating system.

Moreover, memory protection plays a crucial role in preventing buffer overflow attacks, a common type of security vulnerability where an attacker exploits a programming error to overwrite adjacent memory regions. By manipulating the contents of a buffer beyond its intended boundaries, attackers can inject malicious code or data into the process's memory space, potentially gaining unauthorized access or executing arbitrary commands. Memory protection mechanisms, such as address space layout randomization (ASLR) and the use of non-executable memory regions, help mitigate the impact of buffer overflow attacks by introducing unpredictability into the memory layout and preventing the execution of injected code.

In the context of virtual memory systems, memory protection is closely tied to the concept of access control. Access control mechanisms define the permissions associated with different memory regions, specifying whether a process can read, write, or execute specific portions of its address space. This fine-grained control enables the operating system to enforce security policies at the memory level, ensuring that processes adhere to their designated access permissions. Unauthorized attempts to access or modify memory trigger exceptions or segmentation faults, alerting the operating system to potential security breaches and preventing the exploitation of vulnerabilities.

Furthermore, memory protection is essential for securing sensitive information, such as user credentials, cryptographic keys, and confidential data. Many applications handle sensitive information that should be kept private and protected from unauthorized access. Memory protection mechanisms help ensure that this sensitive data remains inaccessible to unauthorized processes or users. Encryption and secure key management, integrated with memory protection, contribute to the overall security posture by safeguarding the confidentiality of critical information stored in memory.

In shared environments, where multiple users may have concurrent access to a system, memory protection becomes a crucial component of user isolation and security. Each user's processes must operate within their designated memory space, preventing accidental or intentional interference with the data or code belonging to other users. Memory protection mechanisms, combined with user-level access controls, contribute to a secure multi-user environment, ensuring that one user's activities do not compromise the security or privacy of another user's data.

In the realm of modern computing, the increasing prevalence of cloud computing and virtualization further underscores the importance of memory protection. In virtualized environments, multiple virtual machines or containers share the same physical hardware. Memory protection mechanisms become instrumental in maintaining the isolation between virtualized instances, preventing one virtual machine from accessing or affecting the memory of another. This becomes especially critical in cloud computing scenarios, where multiple users or organizations share the same underlying infrastructure. Memory protection ensures that the coexistence of diverse workloads on shared hardware does not introduce security vulnerabilities or compromise the confidentiality and integrity of user data.

The evolving landscape of cybersecurity threats highlights the ongoing importance of robust memory protection. Sophisticated attacks, including privilege escalation exploits, malware injection, and memory-based attacks, underscore the need for proactive measures to secure memory resources. Memory protection mechanisms continually evolve to address emerging threats, incorporating advanced features such as hardware-based memory encryption, runtime integrity checks, and secure enclave technologies. These advancements aim to raise the bar for attackers, making it more challenging to compromise the security of computer systems through memory-related vulnerabilities.

In conclusion, memory protection stands as a cornerstone of computer system security, providing essential safeguards against unauthorized access, data corruption, and malicious activities. By establishing boundaries between processes, protecting kernel memory, preventing buffer overflow attacks, and enforcing access controls, memory protection mechanisms contribute to the overall stability, integrity, and security of operating systems and applications. As computing environments become increasingly complex and interconnected, the ongoing evolution of memory protection techniques remains critical to addressing emerging security challenges and ensuring the resilience of modern computer systems against a diverse range of threats.

Challenges posed by fragmented memory and strategies for compaction.

Fragmented memory poses significant challenges to the efficient utilization and management of computer system resources. Memory fragmentation occurs when the free memory space in a computer system is scattered in non-contiguous segments, leading to suboptimal use of available memory. There are two main types of fragmentation: internal fragmentation, where memory is allocated but not fully utilized within a block, and external fragmentation, where free memory is scattered throughout the system, making it challenging to allocate contiguous blocks of memory for larger processes. These challenges impact system performance, responsiveness, and the ability to accommodate processes with varying memory requirements.

Internal fragmentation arises from the allocation of memory in fixed-size blocks, leading to situations where a process may not fully occupy the entire allocated block. This inefficiency is particularly evident in scenarios where memory is allocated in fixed-size pages or blocks, and a process's memory requirements do not align precisely with these fixed sizes. As a result, portions of allocated memory remain unused, leading to a wastage of resources. Internal fragmentation can be exacerbated in scenarios involving dynamic memory allocation, where the size of allocated memory may exceed the actual needs of the process, resulting in suboptimal usage.

External fragmentation, on the other hand, occurs when free memory is scattered across the system, making it difficult to find contiguous blocks of memory for larger processes. This fragmentation can be attributed to the dynamic allocation and deallocation of memory during the execution of processes. As processes are loaded and unloaded, gaps or holes are created in the memory space, and these gaps may not align in a way that allows for the allocation of larger contiguous blocks. Over time, the accumulation of external fragmentation can severely limit the system's ability to allocate memory for new processes, leading to memory shortages and degraded performance.

To address the challenges posed by fragmented memory, memory compaction strategies are employed to reclaim scattered memory and create contiguous blocks. Compaction involves rearranging the allocated and free memory spaces to reduce fragmentation and create larger contiguous blocks of free memory. However, memory compaction introduces its own set of challenges and considerations.

One common compaction strategy is compaction at allocation time, where the allocator actively seeks and compacts memory before allocating a new block. This strategy aims to reduce external fragmentation by compacting memory in real-time as new processes are loaded. While this approach helps maintain a more contiguous memory space, it introduces additional overhead, as memory compaction activities are performed synchronously with memory allocation. This overhead can impact system responsiveness and may not be suitable for real-time systems or scenarios with stringent performance requirements.

Another compaction strategy involves periodic compaction, where memory compaction activities are performed at scheduled intervals or during periods of low system activity. Periodic compaction helps consolidate free memory blocks and reduce external fragmentation over time. This approach aims to strike a balance between memory optimization and system performance by allowing compaction activities to occur during periods of reduced demand for system resources. However, periodic compaction may not be as responsive to dynamic changes in memory usage and may not prevent fragmentation from impacting system performance in real-time.

In addition to the challenges associated with external fragmentation, memory compaction strategies must also contend with the potential for increased overhead and computational complexity. Compacting memory involves scanning and rearranging memory blocks, which can be resource-intensive, especially in systems with large memory capacities. The computational cost of compaction activities may impact overall system performance and responsiveness, making it essential to carefully balance the benefits of reduced fragmentation with the overhead introduced by compaction processes.

Furthermore, compaction strategies may face challenges in scenarios where processes have stringent timing requirements or real-time constraints. Real-time systems, such as those used in critical applications like aerospace or medical devices, demand predictable and deterministic behavior. Memory compaction activities, especially those performed synchronously with memory allocation, may introduce unpredictable delays, potentially violating real-time constraints. Balancing the need for reduced fragmentation with the imperative of meeting real-time requirements becomes a critical consideration in the design and implementation of memory compaction strategies for such systems.

The choice of compaction strategy is influenced by various factors, including the nature of the system, the characteristics of the workloads it handles, and the performance requirements. In systems with dynamic workloads and varying memory demands, adaptive compaction strategies may be employed. These strategies dynamically adjust compaction activities based on the system's current state and workload characteristics. Adaptive compaction aims to optimize memory usage without imposing unnecessary overhead during periods of low fragmentation or low demand for memory resources.

Despite the challenges, effective memory compaction is crucial for maintaining the long-term performance and stability of computer systems, particularly those with dynamic workloads and varying memory demands. Compaction strategies must strike a delicate balance between reducing fragmentation, minimizing overhead, and ensuring compatibility with the specific requirements of the system. As technology continues to advance, the development of intelligent and adaptive compaction techniques, coupled with advancements in hardware support, will contribute to addressing the challenges posed by fragmented memory and optimizing memory utilization in diverse computing environments.

Synchronization challenges in managing memory for concurrent processes.

Synchronization challenges in managing memory for concurrent processes represent a critical aspect of operating system design, requiring careful consideration to ensure the orderly and reliable execution of multiple processes sharing the same memory space. In a multitasking environment, where multiple processes run concurrently, each process requires access to memory resources for the execution of its instructions and storage of data. However, the simultaneous execution of processes introduces complexities related to the coordination and synchronization of memory access, leading to challenges that impact system performance, reliability, and data consistency.

One of the primary synchronization challenges stems from the potential for race conditions, where the outcome of memory operations depends on the specific timing of their execution by different processes. Race conditions arise when two or more processes attempt to access or modify shared memory locations simultaneously, leading to unpredictable and unintended results. For example, if two processes read and modify the same variable concurrently without proper synchronization, the final value of the variable may be inconsistent or unexpected. Race conditions introduce non-deterministic behavior and pose a serious threat to the correctness and reliability of concurrent programs.

To mitigate race conditions and ensure the consistency of shared data, synchronization mechanisms such as locks, semaphores, and mutexes are employed. These synchronization primitives provide a means for processes to coordinate their access to shared resources, preventing concurrent access that could lead to race conditions. However, the use of locks introduces its own set of challenges, including the potential for deadlocks and contention. A deadlock occurs when multiple processes are blocked, each waiting for a resource held by another process, leading to a state where no progress can be made. Contention arises when multiple processes compete for the same resource, resulting in delays and decreased system efficiency.

Another synchronization challenge in memory management for concurrent processes is the need for atomicity in certain operations. Atomicity ensures that an operation is executed as a single, indivisible unit, without interference from other concurrent operations. For example, in the context of updating shared variables, atomicity is crucial to prevent race conditions and ensure that the variable is modified in a consistent manner. Achieving atomicity often involves using atomic instructions or hardware-supported mechanisms, such as compare-and-swap (CAS) operations. Ensuring atomicity is essential for maintaining data integrity and preventing scenarios where partial updates or interleaved operations lead to incorrect results.

The management of dynamic memory, including memory allocation and deallocation, introduces additional synchronization challenges in concurrent systems. When multiple processes share a common heap for dynamic memory allocation, issues such as memory leaks, data corruption, and resource contention become prominent. Memory leaks can occur when processes allocate memory dynamically but fail to deallocate it, leading to a gradual exhaustion of available memory. Concurrent deallocation introduces challenges related to freeing memory that may still be in use by other processes. Implementing a robust memory allocation and deallocation strategy that considers the complexities of concurrent access is essential for preventing memory-related issues and ensuring the efficient use of system resources.

Moreover, synchronization challenges extend to the realm of memory consistency models, which define the order in which memory operations become visible to different processes. In a multiprocessor system, each processor or core may have its own cache, leading to the possibility of inconsistent views of shared memory among processors. Memory consistency models, such as sequential consistency or relaxed consistency models, dictate the rules governing the order of memory operations and the visibility of changes across different processors. Coordinating memory consistency in a concurrent environment involves addressing issues such as cache coherence, ensuring that updates made by one processor become visible to others in a predictable and synchronized manner.

Concurrency control mechanisms in databases, a critical application of memory management, introduce synchronization challenges as well. In database systems, multiple transactions may concurrently read and modify shared data, necessitating mechanisms to ensure the isolation and consistency of transactions. Techniques such as locking, optimistic concurrency control, and transaction isolation levels are employed to coordinate access to shared database resources and prevent conflicts that could lead to data corruption or inconsistencies. Balancing the trade-off between concurrency and consistency in database systems requires careful consideration of the synchronization mechanisms and isolation levels employed.

The implementation of memory management for concurrent processes is also influenced by the choice of memory allocation algorithms. Dynamic memory allocation algorithms, such as those used in heap management, must contend with the challenges of fragmentation, contention, and scalability in a concurrent environment. The traditional memory allocation algorithms, like those based on segregated free lists or buddy systems, may need to be adapted or augmented to address the synchronization requirements of concurrent systems. Modern memory allocators often incorporate techniques such as thread-specific arenas or lock-free data structures to enhance scalability and reduce contention in the face of concurrent memory allocation and deallocation operations.

Furthermore, the emergence of multicore and multiprocessor systems has intensified the synchronization challenges in memory management. Concurrent access to shared resources, including memory, introduces the potential for increased contention and requires sophisticated synchronization mechanisms to maintain system efficiency. Techniques like lock-free and wait-free algorithms aim to minimize contention and ensure progress in the presence of concurrent operations. However, designing and implementing lock-free algorithms demands a deep understanding of concurrency, memory ordering, and low-level hardware considerations.

In summary, synchronization challenges in managing memory for concurrent processes represent a multifaceted and intricate aspect of operating system design. Addressing these challenges requires the careful consideration of race conditions, atomicity, memory consistency, concurrency control in databases, and memory allocation algorithms. The use of synchronization primitives, locks, and other coordination mechanisms introduces potential issues such as deadlocks and contention, necessitating thoughtful design and careful implementation. As computer systems continue to evolve with increasing levels of concurrency and parallelism, ongoing research and development efforts aim to devise innovative synchronization strategies that balance the demands of performance, reliability, and data consistency in the realm of memory management for concurrent processes.

Chapter 6: I/O Management: Enhancing System Interactions

Defining I/O management and its role in facilitating communication between the system and external devices.

I/O (Input/Output) management is a fundamental component of operating systems that plays a pivotal role in facilitating communication between the system and external devices. In the context of computing, I/O refers to the interaction between a computer system and the external world, encompassing the flow of data into and out of the system. External devices, such as keyboards, mice, storage devices, printers, and network interfaces, serve as the conduits through which information is exchanged between the computer and its environment. I/O management encompasses a set of functionalities and mechanisms designed to efficiently handle these interactions, ensuring the seamless flow of data between the system's internal components and the diverse array of external peripherals.

The role of I/O management becomes particularly crucial due to the heterogeneous nature of external devices, each with its own characteristics, communication protocols, and data transfer speeds. The challenge lies in providing a unified and standardized interface to abstract the complexities of interacting with diverse peripherals, allowing application programs and the operating system to communicate with external devices in a consistent manner. This abstraction shields higher-level software from the intricacies of individual devices, promoting portability and ease of development across a wide range of hardware configurations.

A fundamental aspect of I/O management is the concept of device drivers. Device drivers serve as intermediary software components that facilitate communication between the operating system and specific hardware devices. They encapsulate the details of device-specific operations, allowing the operating system to interact with the device using a standardized interface. Device drivers abstract the low-level hardware interactions, enabling applications and the operating system kernel to issue I/O requests without needing to understand the intricacies of the underlying hardware. This abstraction layer provided by device drivers contributes to the modularity and maintainability of the operating system.

The I/O management subsystem is responsible for handling various types of I/O operations, including input operations (reading data from external devices) and output operations (sending data to external devices). It coordinates the movement of data between the system's memory and external devices, ensuring efficient and reliable data transfer. The operating system's I/O management must contend with diverse challenges, including data buffering, error handling, and asynchronous I/O, to provide a robust and responsive I/O subsystem.

Data buffering is a critical aspect of I/O management, involving the use of memory buffers to temporarily store data during the transfer between the system and external devices. Buffers facilitate the decoupling of the often disparate speeds at which the CPU and external devices operate. They allow data to be transferred in blocks or chunks, reducing the frequency of direct interactions between the CPU and devices and improving overall system performance. Buffers also play a role in mitigating the impact of latency and variability in device response times, ensuring a smoother and more predictable data flow.

Effective error handling is another essential component of I/O management. External devices may encounter various issues during operation, such as communication errors, timeouts, or hardware failures. The I/O management subsystem is responsible for detecting and managing these errors, providing mechanisms for reporting errors to the application layer or taking corrective actions when possible. Proper error handling is crucial for maintaining the reliability and stability of the system, preventing catastrophic failures due to misbehaving or malfunctioning devices.

Asynchronous I/O, or non-blocking I/O, is a feature of I/O management that allows processes to initiate I/O operations and continue their execution without waiting for the completion of the operation. This asynchronous behavior enables more efficient utilization of system resources, as processes can overlap computation with I/O activities. The operating system's I/O management must provide appropriate mechanisms, such as asynchronous system calls or event-driven programming interfaces, to support non-blocking I/O and allow applications to achieve high levels of concurrency and responsiveness.

In the realm of storage devices, I/O management extends to disk I/O operations, which involve reading from and writing to storage devices such as hard drives or solid-state drives. Disk I/O management is critical for file systems and data storage, where efficient access to persistent data is essential. Caching mechanisms, read-ahead strategies, and disk scheduling algorithms are integral components of disk I/O management, optimizing the retrieval and storage of data from and to secondary storage devices.

Furthermore, networking I/O management is crucial for handling communication between a computer system and external networks. Network interfaces, routers, and other networking devices require specialized I/O management to handle data transmission over various network protocols. The I/O subsystem is responsible for managing network sockets, supporting communication protocols such as TCP/IP or UDP, and ensuring reliable and efficient data exchange between the system and remote hosts. Network I/O management is fundamental for applications that rely on network connectivity, including web browsers, email clients, and networked server applications.

Real-time systems introduce additional challenges to I/O management, as they often have stringent timing requirements and demand predictable and deterministic behavior. In real-time systems, the I/O management subsystem must ensure that I/O operations meet specified deadlines, allowing for the precise control of external devices in time-critical applications such as industrial control systems, medical devices, or embedded systems. Meeting real-time constraints involves minimizing I/O latencies, prioritizing I/O operations, and providing mechanisms for precise timing control.

The design and implementation of I/O management strategies are influenced by the evolving landscape of computing architectures, including the transition to multicore and many-core systems. The increasing parallelism in modern processors introduces new challenges and opportunities for I/O management, requiring synchronization mechanisms, efficient data movement across cores, and strategies for load balancing in I/O-intensive applications. As hardware architectures continue to advance, I/O management must adapt to leverage emerging technologies such as non-volatile memory, high-speed interconnects, and specialized accelerators to meet the growing demands of data-intensive workloads.

In conclusion, I/O management is a foundational aspect of operating systems, serving as the bridge between the computer system and a diverse array of external devices. Its role encompasses the abstraction of hardware intricacies through device drivers, the coordination of data movement between the system and peripherals, and the provision of a standardized interface for application programs. I/O management addresses challenges related to data buffering, error handling, asynchronous I/O, storage devices, networking, and real-time requirements. The effectiveness of I/O management directly impacts system performance, reliability, and the seamless integration of computing systems into the broader external environment. As technology continues to advance, the evolution of I/O management strategies remains integral to the development of efficient, scalable, and responsive computing systems.

Overview of different I/O devices and their controllers.

The landscape of I/O devices is diverse and encompasses a wide array of peripherals that facilitate communication between computer systems and the external world. Each I/O device serves a specific purpose and requires a dedicated controller to manage its interactions with the system. This overview delves into various I/O devices and their corresponding controllers, shedding light on the intricate mechanisms that enable seamless data exchange between the computer and its peripherals.

One of the most ubiquitous I/O devices is the keyboard, an essential input device for user interaction. Keyboards typically use a controller to manage the communication between individual keys and the computer system. Keyboards often employ a matrix arrangement of switches, and the controller is responsible for scanning the matrix, detecting key presses, and transmitting corresponding codes to the system. The communication protocol, such as PS/2 or USB, and the controller's ability to handle simultaneous key presses contribute to the responsiveness and functionality of modern keyboards.

Mice and other pointing devices represent another category of input devices, providing intuitive ways for users to interact with graphical user interfaces. These devices use controllers to track movement, clicks, and additional features like scroll wheels. Optical and laser sensors, along with the associated controller algorithms, enable precise tracking of the device's movement. The communication between the mouse and the system is often facilitated through USB or other standardized interfaces.

Storage devices, including hard disk drives (HDDs) and solid-state drives (SSDs), are crucial I/O devices for data storage and retrieval. These devices have their own controllers responsible for managing data read and write operations, error correction, and wear leveling (in the case of SSDs). The controller interacts with the system through interfaces such as SATA, PCIe, or NVMe. The evolution of storage device controllers has played a significant role in advancing data transfer speeds, improving reliability, and enhancing storage capacities in modern computing systems.

Printers and scanners represent essential output and input devices, respectively, in office and home environments. Printer controllers manage the translation of digital data into physical prints, interpreting print commands, and controlling the printing mechanisms. On the other hand, scanner controllers interpret input from image sensors, converting scanned images into digital data for processing by the computer system. These devices often use interfaces like USB or network protocols for communication.

Graphics processing units (GPUs) serve as specialized I/O devices designed to accelerate graphics rendering tasks. GPUs have evolved beyond their initial focus on graphics to become powerful parallel processors used in various computing applications, including scientific simulations and machine learning. GPU controllers manage the parallel execution of tasks and the efficient processing of graphics data. Modern GPUs are equipped with sophisticated controllers that support programmability, enabling developers to harness the computational power for a wide range of applications.

Network interface cards (NICs) are pivotal I/O devices for connecting computers within a network. NICs employ controllers to manage the transmission and reception of data packets, ensuring efficient communication between devices. These controllers implement network protocols such as Ethernet, Wi-Fi, or Bluetooth, and their performance directly impacts the speed and reliability of network connections. Advanced NIC controllers may support features like offloading, which offloads certain networking tasks from the main CPU to enhance overall system performance.

Audio devices, including sound cards and speakers, contribute to the multimedia experience of computer users. Sound card controllers manage the conversion of digital audio signals into analog signals for playback through speakers or headphones. These controllers also handle tasks such as audio processing, mixing, and providing support for various audio formats. The communication between the sound card and the system typically occurs through interfaces like PCI Express or USB.

Universal Serial Bus (USB) has emerged as a versatile interface connecting a multitude of I/O devices to computers. USB controllers are integrated into devices such as external storage drives, cameras, and input devices. The USB protocol allows for plug-and-play functionality, supporting the hot-swapping of devices without the need for system restarts. USB controllers manage data transfer rates, power delivery, and the negotiation of communication between the computer and connected devices.

Display controllers are instrumental in managing the output of visual information to monitors and displays. These controllers interpret graphical data from the system and generate signals to drive the display's pixels. They support display interfaces such as HDMI, DisplayPort, or VGA, providing resolutions, refresh rates, and color depths that contribute to the quality of visual output. Graphics cards often integrate powerful display controllers to handle the demands of modern graphics-intensive applications and gaming.

Storage controllers, separate from the devices themselves, play a pivotal role in managing access to storage devices and ensuring data integrity. RAID controllers, for example, enable the implementation of redundant arrays of independent disks for improved performance, fault tolerance, and data protection. Storage controllers may be integrated into the motherboard or exist as separate expansion cards, with interfaces like SATA or SAS connecting to HDDs, SSDs, or other storage media.

I/O controllers for buses and bridges are critical components that facilitate communication between various subsystems within a computer. Memory controllers manage access to the system's RAM, coordinating read and write operations between the CPU and memory modules. PCI Express controllers handle the high-speed data transfer between components, such as GPUs, storage devices, and networking interfaces. These controllers ensure efficient communication and data exchange among different subsystems, contributing to overall system performance.

In conclusion, the diverse landscape of I/O devices, each with its specific functionality, necessitates dedicated controllers to enable seamless communication with computer systems. From input devices like keyboards and mice to storage devices, graphics cards, and network interfaces, the role of I/O controllers is integral to the proper functioning of modern computing systems. These controllers abstract the intricacies of device-specific operations, allowing for standardized communication interfaces and ensuring compatibility across a broad spectrum of hardware configurations. As technology continues to advance, the evolution of I/O devices and controllers remains at the forefront of enhancing system capabilities, responsiveness, and the overall user experience.

Understanding the role of device drivers in mediating communication between the operating system and hardware.

The role of device drivers in mediating communication between the operating system and hardware is paramount in ensuring the seamless integration and functionality of diverse hardware components within a computer system. Device drivers serve as a crucial interface layer between the high-level software, including the operating system and applications, and the low-level hardware components such as peripheral devices, storage devices, and communication interfaces. The complexity and diversity of hardware architectures necessitate a standardized and abstracted way for the operating system to interact with a multitude of devices, and device drivers fulfill this critical role by providing a uniform interface and managing the intricacies of individual hardware implementations.

Device drivers act as specialized software modules that enable the operating system to understand and control the specific functionalities of hardware devices connected to the system. These drivers encapsulate the details of hardware-specific operations, allowing the operating system to issue commands, receive data, and manage the interactions with hardware devices without requiring an in-depth understanding of the intricacies of each device. The abstraction provided by device drivers shields higher-level software, including applications and the operating system kernel, from the complexities of low-level hardware communication, promoting portability and ease of development across a wide range of hardware configurations.

One of the primary functions of device drivers is to interpret high-level commands and requests from the operating system into a format that the corresponding hardware can understand and execute. For instance, when an application requests to print a document, the operating system communicates with the printer device driver, which, in turn, converts the print command into a series of low-level instructions that the printer hardware can process. This translation layer ensures that different devices, even within the same category, can be utilized interchangeably, provided they have compatible device drivers.

Device drivers also play a crucial role in managing the configuration and initialization of hardware devices during the system's boot-up process. As the operating system initializes, it relies on device drivers to identify connected hardware components, allocate resources such as memory addresses and interrupt lines, and establish the necessary communication pathways between the operating system and the hardware. This initialization process ensures that the hardware components are properly configured and ready for interaction, laying the foundation for their seamless integration into the overall system architecture.

Furthermore, device drivers are responsible for handling interrupts and events generated by hardware devices. When a hardware device requires attention or has completed a task, it often triggers an interrupt to notify the operating system. Device drivers manage these interrupts, ensuring that the appropriate actions are taken in response to hardware events. For example, a network interface card may generate an interrupt when it receives data, prompting the corresponding device driver to handle the reception of data and pass it to the operating system for further processing.

Efficient memory management is another critical aspect of device drivers. These drivers allocate and deallocate memory regions for data buffers and control structures used in communication between the operating system and hardware devices. Proper memory management by device drivers helps prevent issues such as memory leaks and ensures that the system's memory resources are used efficiently. The ability of device drivers to manage memory is particularly crucial in scenarios involving large data transfers, such as those with storage devices or high-speed communication interfaces.

Device drivers must also handle errors and exceptions that may occur during the interaction with hardware. Hardware components may encounter various issues, including communication errors, device malfunctions, or unexpected conditions. Device drivers are equipped with error-handling mechanisms to detect, report, and manage these issues. Proper error handling by device drivers contributes to the robustness and stability of the system, preventing catastrophic failures and providing the necessary feedback to the operating system or applications when hardware-related problems arise.

The modular nature of device drivers allows for easy extensibility and adaptability to changing hardware landscapes. When new hardware devices are introduced to the market, or existing devices undergo updates, device manufacturers can provide updated or new device drivers to ensure compatibility with the latest operating systems. This modular approach allows the operating system to support a wide range of hardware without requiring a complete overhaul, making it easier for users to integrate new devices into their systems and ensuring that the operating system remains versatile and forward-compatible.

In the context of plug-and-play functionality, device drivers play a pivotal role in enabling the seamless connection and recognition of new hardware devices without requiring manual intervention. Plug-and-play support relies on device drivers to dynamically recognize, configure, and initialize newly connected hardware components, allowing users to add or remove devices without restarting the system. This feature enhances the user experience, simplifying the process of integrating and using diverse hardware peripherals without the need for extensive manual configuration.

Moreover, device drivers contribute to the overall stability and security of the operating system by isolating the interactions with hardware. The operating system kernel, responsible for core system functionalities, relies on device drivers to interact with hardware devices in user space. This separation ensures that issues or errors in device drivers do not compromise the stability or security of the entire operating system. Additionally, modern operating systems implement various security measures, such as driver signing, to verify the authenticity and integrity of device drivers, mitigating the risk of malicious or unauthorized drivers compromising system security.

In the realm of real-time systems, where precise timing and deterministic behavior are essential, device drivers must adhere to stringent requirements. Real-time device drivers are designed to minimize interrupt latencies, ensuring timely responses to hardware events. These drivers often prioritize time-sensitive tasks, such as control systems in industrial automation or medical devices, to meet strict timing constraints and maintain the reliability of real-time operations.

In conclusion, device drivers play a multifaceted and indispensable role in mediating communication between the operating system and hardware. These software modules serve as the linchpin that enables the operating system to interact seamlessly with a myriad of hardware devices, abstracting the intricacies of low-level hardware communication and providing a standardized interface for applications. Device drivers manage device configuration, handle interrupts and events, support plug-and-play functionality, and contribute to system stability and security. Their modular and extensible nature ensures adaptability to evolving hardware landscapes, while their role in real-time systems underscores their significance in critical applications where timing precision is paramount. The effectiveness and reliability of device drivers are integral to the overall performance and functionality of modern computing systems.

The importance of I/O scheduling in optimizing data transfer between devices and the system.

The importance of I/O scheduling in optimizing data transfer between devices and the system lies at the heart of achieving efficient and responsive performance in computing environments. I/O scheduling refers to the strategy employed by the operating system to manage the order and timing of data transfers between storage devices and the system's memory. Given the intrinsic differences in speeds and characteristics between the CPU, memory, and various storage devices, effective I/O scheduling becomes paramount to mitigate bottlenecks, reduce latency, and ensure the optimal utilization of system resources.

One of the primary challenges addressed by I/O scheduling is the variance in access times among different storage devices. Traditional hard disk drives (HDDs), for instance, have mechanical components, leading to higher access times compared to solid-state drives (SSDs) with no moving parts. Additionally, within HDDs, seeking data on different tracks incurs varying latencies. I/O scheduling algorithms aim to minimize these latencies by strategically ordering and prioritizing I/O requests, allowing the operating system to schedule reads and writes in a manner that minimizes the physical movement of read/write heads and optimizes data retrieval. By intelligently managing the sequence of I/O operations, I/O scheduling contributes to enhancing overall system responsiveness and reducing the time required to complete data transfers.

In the context of multitasking and concurrent execution, where multiple processes may be contending for access to storage devices, I/O scheduling becomes crucial for fair and efficient resource allocation. The operating system must prioritize and arbitrate between competing I/O requests to prevent resource contention, ensure equitable access to storage devices, and avoid scenarios where certain processes monopolize I/O resources at the expense of others. Fairness in I/O scheduling becomes particularly relevant in scenarios involving real-time or interactive applications, where timely data access is critical for user experience and system responsiveness.

Furthermore, I/O scheduling plays a pivotal role in addressing the phenomenon of I/O starvation, wherein certain processes or applications may be consistently deprioritized in the queue of I/O requests. I/O starvation can lead to prolonged waiting times for critical tasks, adversely impacting the overall performance of the system. I/O scheduling algorithms must strike a balance between fairness and prioritization, ensuring that critical and time-sensitive I/O operations are not indefinitely delayed, while still providing equitable access to storage resources for all processes.

To tackle the challenges posed by the disparity in access times between storage devices, modern I/O scheduling algorithms leverage sophisticated techniques and heuristics. The concept of elevator algorithms, such as the SCAN (elevator) and C-SCAN, involves scanning the pending I/O requests in a manner similar to an elevator moving up and down a building. This approach minimizes seek times by grouping requests in a way that reduces the physical movement of the read/write heads. Additionally, anticipatory scheduling algorithms aim to predict future I/O requests based on historical patterns, allowing the operating system to proactively schedule data transfers and reduce latency.

In scenarios involving solid-state drives (SSDs), I/O scheduling faces different challenges. Unlike HDDs, SSDs do not have mechanical components, resulting in negligible seek times. However, SSDs have their own set of characteristics, such as wear leveling and block erase operations, that require specialized consideration in I/O scheduling. Algorithms like the Least Recently Used (LRU) and Multi-Queue I/O Schedulers (MQ) have been designed to optimize data placement on SSDs, considering factors such as wear leveling and minimizing write amplification, to prolong the lifespan and enhance the performance of SSDs.

Real-time systems introduce additional complexity to I/O scheduling requirements. In applications where timing constraints are stringent, such as industrial control systems or medical devices, the operating system must adhere to precise deadlines for I/O operations. Real-time I/O scheduling algorithms prioritize tasks with time-critical requirements, ensuring that data transfers occur within specified time bounds. These algorithms consider factors such as deadlines, priorities, and task characteristics to meet the stringent timing constraints imposed by real-time applications, where missed deadlines could have severe consequences.

Moreover, I/O scheduling plays a vital role in power management strategies, especially in mobile devices and laptops where battery life is a critical consideration. Energy-efficient I/O scheduling aims to minimize unnecessary wake-ups of storage devices, reducing power consumption during periods of low activity. By intelligently scheduling I/O operations and leveraging techniques like batch scheduling or opportunistic scheduling, the operating system can optimize power usage without compromising overall system responsiveness.

The adoption of I/O scheduling policies is often influenced by the specific characteristics of workloads and usage patterns. Different scenarios, such as database workloads, multimedia streaming, or file-sharing applications, may benefit from tailored I/O scheduling approaches. Adaptive algorithms, capable of dynamically adjusting to changing workloads, seek to optimize performance across diverse usage patterns. Machine learning techniques are also being explored to develop I/O scheduling algorithms that can adapt and learn from historical patterns to enhance future decision-making.

In conclusion, the importance of I/O scheduling in optimizing data transfer between devices and the system is evident in its multifaceted role addressing challenges related to storage device characteristics, resource contention, fairness, real-time constraints, power management, and evolving workload patterns. I/O scheduling algorithms aim to strike a delicate balance between minimizing access times, ensuring fairness in resource allocation, meeting real-time constraints, and optimizing power efficiency. As computing environments continue to evolve with advancements in storage technologies, heterogeneous architectures, and diverse usage scenarios, the ongoing research and development of sophisticated I/O scheduling strategies will remain instrumental in achieving efficient, responsive, and adaptive I/O operations that contribute to the overall performance and user experience of modern computing systems.

Exploring buffering mechanisms to enhance data transfer efficiency.

Exploring buffering mechanisms to enhance data transfer efficiency is a fundamental aspect of optimizing communication between various components in a computing system. Buffering involves the temporary storage of data in a designated area, known as a buffer, to facilitate the smooth and efficient transfer of information between devices operating at different speeds or with asynchronous communication patterns. Buffering mechanisms play a pivotal role in mitigating the impact of disparities in data transfer rates, reducing latency, and improving overall system performance.

One of the primary purposes of buffering mechanisms is to decouple the rates at which data is produced and consumed by different components in a system. In scenarios where the rate of data production exceeds the rate at which the data can be processed or consumed, buffering provides a crucial temporal cushion. For instance, in the context of input and output operations, a buffer can temporarily store data that is read or written at a different speed than the processing unit or storage device, preventing data loss and ensuring a continuous flow of information.

The concept of buffering is particularly significant in the context of I/O operations involving storage devices, network interfaces, and other peripherals. Disk buffering, for example, is employed in storage systems to smooth out the discrepancies between the relatively slow access times of traditional hard disk drives (HDDs) and the faster data transfer rates required by the CPU or memory. Buffers temporarily store data in transit, allowing the system to continue processing or generating data without being directly affected by the slower speed of certain I/O devices.

Network buffering is essential in networking scenarios where data is transmitted between systems over varying network speeds. Network interfaces utilize buffers to temporarily store incoming and outgoing data, compensating for network latency and jitter. Buffers provide a mechanism for handling bursts of data and accommodating the variable nature of network traffic, contributing to the stability and efficiency of data transfers in communication protocols such as Transmission Control Protocol (TCP).

Moreover, buffering mechanisms are integral to addressing the challenges posed by the asynchronous nature of communication between different components in a system. In scenarios where a sender and a receiver operate at different speeds or have varying processing capabilities, buffering acts as a synchronization mechanism. The buffer absorbs variations in the rate of data production and consumption, allowing the sender and receiver to operate independently, reducing the likelihood of data loss, and providing a mechanism to manage the flow of information seamlessly.

The size of the buffer is a critical parameter in buffering mechanisms, influencing the trade-off between latency and throughput. A larger buffer size can accommodate a greater volume of data, reducing the frequency of interruptions caused by data transfers. However, a larger buffer may introduce additional latency due to the time it takes to fill or drain the buffer completely. On the other hand, a smaller buffer size may result in lower latency but could lead to more frequent interruptions and reduced throughput. Striking the right balance in buffer size is a crucial consideration in optimizing data transfer efficiency, requiring careful analysis of the specific requirements and characteristics of the application or system.

Caching is a form of buffering that is widely used to enhance data transfer efficiency by storing frequently accessed data in a high-speed, temporary storage location. Caches act as intermediate buffers situated closer to the processing unit, reducing the time it takes to retrieve frequently accessed data. In the context of memory hierarchy, caches at different levels (L1, L2, and L3 caches) store copies of data to reduce the time taken to access frequently used instructions and data. This form of buffering exploits temporal and spatial locality in data access patterns, significantly improving the overall performance of processors and memory systems.

Buffering mechanisms are also crucial in scenarios involving multimedia streaming, where the timely delivery of data is essential for uninterrupted playback. Video and audio streaming services utilize buffers to store a certain amount of content in advance, allowing for variations in network conditions and minimizing the impact of momentary disruptions. Buffers provide a buffer of time, ensuring that the playback device has a continuous stream of data to render, even if there are temporary fluctuations or delays in the network.

In the context of interprocess communication within a computer system, buffering mechanisms are employed to facilitate efficient data exchange between different software components or processes. Shared memory buffers, message queues, and pipes are examples of buffering mechanisms used to pass data between processes. These mechanisms allow processes to operate asynchronously, decoupling the production and consumption of data, and enhancing overall system concurrency and responsiveness.

Buffering is not only limited to the physical storage of data but extends to the realm of software-based buffering mechanisms, including write-ahead logging in databases. Write-ahead logging ensures durability and consistency in database systems by buffering changes to the database in a log before the actual modifications are applied. This buffering strategy ensures that, even in the event of a system crash or failure, the database can be recovered to a consistent state by replaying the logged changes.

While buffering mechanisms provide significant benefits in terms of data transfer efficiency, they also introduce considerations related to data integrity and synchronization. Buffers must be managed carefully to prevent data corruption or loss in case of unexpected system failures. Techniques such as double buffering, checksums, and error-checking mechanisms are employed to ensure the integrity of data stored in buffers. Additionally, synchronization mechanisms are necessary to coordinate the interactions between producers and consumers of data in buffered systems, preventing issues such as race conditions and ensuring the orderly processing of information.

In conclusion, exploring buffering mechanisms to enhance data transfer efficiency is a multifaceted endeavor integral to the optimization of communication within computing systems. Buffers provide a crucial temporal and spatial cushion, addressing challenges related to disparate data transfer rates, asynchronous communication, and variations in processing capabilities. Whether applied to storage devices, network interfaces, interprocess communication, or multimedia streaming, buffering mechanisms play a central role in mitigating latency, improving throughput, and contributing to the overall responsiveness and efficiency of modern computing systems. The careful design and implementation of buffering strategies are essential considerations in achieving the delicate balance between minimizing data transfer delays and ensuring the integrity and reliability of information exchange within complex computing environments.

Strategies for managing interrupts generated by I/O devices.

Strategies for managing interrupts generated by I/O devices are essential in the realm of computing, where the efficient handling of input and output operations is paramount to overall system performance. Interrupts serve as a mechanism by which I/O devices signal the CPU to initiate specific actions, such as handling incoming data or signaling the completion of a data transfer. Effective interrupt management is crucial for ensuring timely responses to these events, minimizing processing overhead, and optimizing the coordination between the CPU and I/O devices.

One key strategy in interrupt management is the use of interrupt service routines (ISRs), which are specialized segments of code designed to handle specific interrupt conditions. When an I/O device generates an interrupt, the CPU transfers control to the corresponding ISR, allowing the system to promptly respond to the event. ISRs are designed to execute quickly and efficiently, addressing the immediate requirements of the interrupting device. Their swift execution is vital for minimizing the impact on overall system responsiveness and ensuring timely processing of incoming data or completion signals.

Another important consideration in interrupt management is the prioritization of interrupts. Not all interrupts have the same level of urgency or significance. Prioritizing interrupts allows the system to allocate resources and respond to higher-priority events first. This strategy ensures that critical operations, such as real-time tasks or time-sensitive I/O operations, receive immediate attention, preventing delays that could impact system functionality. Prioritization is often implemented using an interrupt controller, which categorizes interrupts based on their priority levels and sequences them accordingly for processing.

Interrupt masking is a technique employed to control the flow of interrupts during specific periods of program execution. Maskable interrupts can be temporarily disabled or enabled by the CPU, allowing the system to manage the timing of interrupt processing. Masking interrupts can be useful in scenarios where the CPU needs to focus on critical tasks or perform operations that should not be interrupted. However, careful consideration must be given to the duration for which interrupts are masked, as prolonged interruptions may lead to missed events or degraded system performance.

Additionally, nested interrupt handling is a strategy that allows the system to handle interrupts while another interrupt is already being processed. In a multitasking environment, where multiple processes or threads may generate interrupts simultaneously, nested interrupt handling ensures that the CPU can respond to higher-priority interrupts even if a lower-priority interrupt is currently being processed. This approach enhances the flexibility and responsiveness of the system, preventing potential bottlenecks that could arise from a strict, sequential handling of interrupts.

Interrupt coalescing is a technique used to optimize interrupt processing by consolidating multiple interrupts into a single, more efficient operation. In scenarios where a high-frequency stream of interrupts is generated by an I/O device, coalescing allows the system to group these interrupts and process them in a batch. This reduces the overhead associated with handling individual interrupts, minimizing the impact on CPU resources and enhancing overall system efficiency. Coalescing is particularly beneficial in networking environments, where it can improve the handling of data packets and reduce interrupt processing overhead.

Furthermore, edge-triggered and level-triggered interrupts represent two distinct strategies for managing interrupt signals. In edge-triggered interrupts, the interrupt is triggered by a specific change in the signal, such as a rising or falling edge. This strategy is effective for handling discrete events, ensuring that the interrupt is only triggered when the signal transitions between specific states. On the other hand, level-triggered interrupts remain active as long as the interrupt signal is in a particular state. Level-triggered interrupts are suitable for scenarios where the interrupt condition persists, such as continuous data availability. The choice between edge-triggered and level-triggered interrupts depends on the nature of the I/O device and the events being signaled.

In scenarios involving multiple CPUs or processor cores, interrupt affinity is a strategy that assigns specific interrupts to particular processors. This ensures that each processor handles a designated set of interrupts, preventing unnecessary contention and enhancing parallelism in interrupt processing. Interrupt affinity is particularly relevant in multicore systems, where efficient distribution of interrupt handling tasks contributes to overall system scalability and performance.

Another strategy for managing interrupts involves the use of deferred interrupt handling or bottom halves. In this approach, time-consuming or non-time-critical portions of interrupt processing are deferred to a later point in the execution flow, allowing the CPU to quickly acknowledge and respond to the interrupt while postponing resource-intensive tasks. Deferred interrupt handling enhances the responsiveness of the system, ensuring that critical operations are addressed promptly while providing flexibility in managing additional processing tasks associated with the interrupt.

Moreover, interrupt preemption is a technique that allows higher-priority interrupts to interrupt the processing of lower-priority interrupts. This strategy ensures that time-sensitive or critical interrupt conditions take precedence over less urgent events, preventing delays in responding to important system events. Interrupt preemption enhances the real-time capabilities of the system, enabling it to promptly address high-priority interrupts without waiting for the completion of lower-priority interrupt processing.

In networking environments, interrupt moderation is a strategy aimed at reducing the rate at which interrupts are generated by network interfaces. This technique involves aggregating multiple network events into a single interrupt, reducing the frequency of interrupt service routine invocations. Interrupt moderation minimizes the overhead associated with interrupt handling in networking scenarios, where high-frequency interrupts can impact overall system efficiency. It strikes a balance between timely response to network events and optimizing CPU utilization.

Furthermore, adaptive interrupt moderation or dynamic interrupt moderation adjusts the level of moderation based on system conditions and workloads. This strategy allows the system to dynamically adapt to varying levels of network activity, ensuring that interrupt moderation is tuned to the current requirements of the system. Adaptive interrupt moderation contributes to the efficient utilization of system resources, aligning interrupt processing with the dynamically changing demands of network communication.

In conclusion, strategies for managing interrupts generated by I/O devices are diverse and tailored to address the specific requirements of modern computing systems. Whether through the use of interrupt service routines, prioritization, masking, nested interrupt handling, interrupt coalescing, or other techniques, effective interrupt management is crucial for optimizing system responsiveness, handling diverse workloads, and ensuring the seamless coordination between the CPU and I/O devices. The choice of a particular strategy depends on the nature of the I/O devices, the real-time requirements of the system, and the overall goals of achieving efficient interrupt handling in the dynamic landscape of contemporary computing architectures.

The role of DMA in improving data transfer speed between devices and memory.

The role of Direct Memory Access (DMA) in improving data transfer speed between devices and memory is a fundamental aspect of optimizing the efficiency and performance of modern computer systems. DMA serves as a mechanism that allows peripheral devices to directly access the system's memory without involving the central processing unit (CPU) in every data transfer operation. This offloading of memory access tasks to dedicated DMA controllers significantly enhances data transfer rates, reduces CPU involvement, and contributes to overall system responsiveness.

Traditionally, data transfer between devices and memory required the intervention of the CPU. When a peripheral device, such as a hard disk drive or network interface, needed to read or write data to memory, the CPU had to initiate and oversee the entire process. This involvement of the CPU not only introduced processing overhead but also limited the overall speed of data transfers, as the CPU had competing demands from other tasks and processes.

DMA addresses this limitation by introducing a dedicated DMA controller that acts as an intermediary between devices and memory. When a peripheral device initiates a data transfer, the DMA controller takes charge of the operation, independently managing the movement of data between the device and memory without direct CPU involvement. This parallel processing capability significantly accelerates data transfer speeds, as the CPU is free to focus on other tasks while the DMA controller efficiently handles the movement of data.

One of the key advantages of DMA is its ability to perform block transfers of data. Rather than transferring data one byte or word at a time, DMA controllers can move entire blocks or chunks of data in a single operation. This block transfer capability minimizes the overhead associated with initiating and completing individual data transfers, further enhancing the efficiency of data movement between devices and memory. Block transfers are particularly advantageous in scenarios involving large datasets, such as file transfers or multimedia streaming, where high-speed, sequential data access is essential.

Moreover, DMA plays a crucial role in improving system multitasking capabilities. In a multitasking environment, where multiple processes or applications may be simultaneously accessing data from peripheral devices, efficient data transfer mechanisms are vital. DMA allows for concurrent data transfers between devices and memory, enabling multiple processes to access data without causing contention for the CPU's attention. This concurrent data transfer capability enhances system responsiveness and ensures that the performance of one task does not unduly impact the execution of others.

The concept of scatter-gather is another significant feature of DMA that contributes to improved data transfer efficiency. Scatter-gather allows DMA controllers to handle non-contiguous blocks of data, scattered across different memory locations, as a single logical unit. This capability is particularly valuable in scenarios involving fragmented data or scenarios where data is stored in a dispersed manner in memory. Scatter-gather enables DMA controllers to efficiently gather data from disparate locations or scatter data to various destinations, providing a flexible and streamlined approach to managing data transfers.

In the context of storage devices, such as hard disk drives (HDDs) and solid-state drives (SSDs), DMA significantly impacts read and write operations. When a storage device needs to read or write a large amount of data to or from memory, the DMA controller takes charge of the process. This allows for high-speed, direct transfers between the storage device and memory, reducing latency and enhancing the overall throughput of storage operations. As storage devices continue to evolve with higher data transfer rates, DMA becomes increasingly crucial in maximizing the performance potential of these devices.

DMA's role in networking is also pivotal, particularly in the context of network interface controllers (NICs). When data is received or needs to be transmitted over a network, the DMA controller manages the movement of data between the NIC and memory. This direct transfer capability is essential for achieving efficient data rates in networking scenarios, where timely processing of incoming or outgoing data packets is critical. DMA enables network communication to occur independently of the CPU, allowing for uninterrupted data transfer operations and ensuring optimal network performance.

In addition to improving data transfer speed, DMA contributes to the overall energy efficiency of computer systems. By offloading data transfer tasks from the CPU, DMA controllers enable the CPU to enter lower power states when it is not actively involved in processing data transfers. This power management capability is particularly relevant in scenarios where devices operate intermittently or have periods of inactivity. DMA's role in optimizing power usage aligns with broader efforts in modern computing to enhance energy efficiency and reduce overall system power consumption.

The integration of DMA is a foundational aspect of the modern computer architecture, and its impact extends beyond data transfer speed improvements. System designers and developers leverage DMA's capabilities to enhance the performance of diverse applications and workloads. In scenarios involving multimedia processing, for example, DMA accelerates the movement of large datasets, such as video or audio streams, between storage devices and memory, ensuring smooth playback and responsiveness.

Furthermore, the use of DMA is instrumental in real-time systems, where precise timing and low-latency data access are paramount. DMA controllers are designed to operate with minimal latency, ensuring that time-sensitive data transfers occur promptly. This real-time capability is crucial in applications such as industrial automation, medical devices, and control systems, where the timely processing of data is essential for maintaining system reliability and performance.

While DMA offers numerous advantages in terms of data transfer speed and system efficiency, its implementation requires careful consideration of potential challenges. Coordinating data transfers between DMA controllers and other system components necessitates robust synchronization mechanisms to avoid conflicts and ensure data integrity. System designers must carefully manage shared resources, such as memory, to prevent contention between DMA operations and other CPU-centric tasks.

In conclusion, the role of DMA in improving data transfer speed between devices and memory is pivotal in shaping the performance landscape of modern computer systems. DMA's ability to offload memory access tasks from the CPU, perform block transfers, handle scatter-gather operations, and facilitate concurrent data transfers enhances system responsiveness, throughput, and multitasking capabilities. Whether applied to storage devices, networking scenarios, multimedia processing, or real-time systems, DMA stands as a cornerstone technology that contributes to the efficiency, scalability, and energy efficiency of contemporary computing architectures. As the demands for higher data transfer rates and more sophisticated applications continue to evolve, DMA remains a critical element in meeting these challenges and advancing the capabilities of computing systems.

Identifying common errors in I/O operations and strategies for error detection and recovery.

Identifying common errors in Input/Output (I/O) operations and implementing effective strategies for error detection and recovery is integral to ensuring the reliability, integrity, and robustness of computer systems. I/O operations involve the transfer of data between the system and external devices, including storage devices, network interfaces, and various peripherals. Errors in these operations can stem from a multitude of factors, such as hardware malfunctions, communication issues, or software bugs, and addressing them necessitates a comprehensive approach that encompasses both error detection and recovery mechanisms.

One common error in I/O operations is the occurrence of read or write errors on storage devices, which can lead to data corruption or loss. Strategies for error detection in storage I/O involve the use of checksums or cyclic redundancy checks (CRC) to verify the integrity of transferred data. By attaching a checksum or CRC value to the data, the system can later compare this value with the recalculated checksum or CRC at the destination, identifying any discrepancies that may indicate errors. This form of error detection is widely employed in file systems, disk controllers, and storage protocols to ensure the accuracy of data transfers.

Communication errors in networking I/O operations pose another significant challenge, with issues such as packet loss, corruption, or network congestion affecting data integrity. Error detection strategies in networking involve the use of protocols like Transmission Control Protocol (TCP), which employs sequence numbers, acknowledgments, and checksums to ensure reliable and error-free data transmission. TCP's acknowledgment mechanism allows the sender to detect and recover from lost or corrupted packets by retransmitting them. Additionally, error detection codes, such as the Internet Control Message Protocol (ICMP) checksum, are utilized to verify the integrity of network packets, enabling the identification of errors and facilitating recovery mechanisms.

In the realm of multimedia I/O operations, where real-time data streams are prevalent, errors such as jitter, packet loss, or latency can severely impact the quality of audio or video playback. Error detection strategies in multimedia applications often involve the use of buffering and synchronization mechanisms. Buffers can temporarily store incoming data, allowing the system to absorb variations in data arrival times and compensate for jitter. Synchronization mechanisms, such as timestamping, enable the alignment of audio and video components, ensuring a seamless playback experience even in the presence of minor errors or delays.

Furthermore, device-specific errors in I/O operations, such as those involving printers, scanners, or input devices, require tailored error detection and recovery strategies. For example, in printing operations, where paper jams or communication errors may occur, sensors and feedback mechanisms are employed to detect issues. The printer may pause, alert the user, or attempt to recover by reattempting the print job. In the case of input devices, error detection may involve validating the input data against predefined criteria to identify anomalies or inconsistencies, preventing erroneous commands or data from impacting the system.

Effective error recovery strategies in I/O operations often hinge on the concept of redundancy. Redundancy involves duplicating or adding extra information to data to facilitate error recovery. In storage systems, redundant arrays of independent disks (RAID) are widely used for fault tolerance. RAID configurations, such as RAID 1 (mirroring) or RAID 5 (parity), provide the ability to recover from disk failures by leveraging redundant copies of data or parity information. This redundancy ensures that even if a disk fails, the system can reconstruct the lost data using the available redundant information.

In networking, forward error correction (FEC) is a prevalent technique for error recovery. FEC involves adding redundant information to transmitted data, allowing the receiver to correct errors without the need for retransmission. This is particularly beneficial in scenarios where low-latency communication is crucial, as it mitigates the impact of errors without incurring the delay associated with retransmission. Reed-Solomon codes, convolutional codes, and Turbo codes are examples of FEC algorithms employed in various communication protocols to enhance error recovery capabilities.

The role of error detection and recovery in database I/O operations is paramount, given the critical nature of data integrity. Database management systems (DBMS) employ transactional processing and logging mechanisms to ensure the atomicity, consistency, isolation, and durability (ACID) properties of transactions. In the event of a failure, such as a system crash or power outage, the DBMS uses transaction logs to recover the database to a consistent state. Checkpoints, a form of error recovery strategy, involve periodically saving a snapshot of the database's state, enabling quicker recovery by reducing the amount of data that needs to be processed during the restoration process.

Moreover, in file systems, journaling is a prevalent error recovery technique. Journaling involves maintaining a log or journal of changes to the file system. Before modifying critical data structures, such as the file allocation table (FAT) or inode, the file system first records the intended changes in the journal. In the event of a system crash or unexpected shutdown, the file system can use the journal to replay the recorded changes, ensuring that the file system remains consistent and recoverable.

In the context of I/O operations involving external storage devices, unplanned removal or disconnection can lead to errors and data corruption. Error detection mechanisms in these scenarios often involve the use of hot-plug detection and removal notifications. Hot-plug detection allows the system to identify when a device has been connected or disconnected, triggering appropriate error recovery procedures. Operating systems and file systems may implement mechanisms to gracefully handle the sudden removal of external devices, such as flushing write buffers and unmounting file systems to prevent data corruption.

Furthermore, error recovery in I/O operations may require the implementation of retry mechanisms. When an error is detected, the system can attempt to recover by retrying the operation, whether it be a read, write, or communication attempt. This approach is particularly useful for transient errors that may be resolved with a subsequent attempt. Retry mechanisms are commonly employed in storage systems, network protocols, and communication interfaces to enhance the robustness of I/O operations in the face of intermittent issues.

In the event of persistent or catastrophic errors, I/O operations may need to resort to error reporting and logging. Error reporting mechanisms notify system administrators or users of detected errors, providing information about the nature and source of the problem. Error logs capture detailed information about errors, aiding in postmortem analysis and diagnostics. Effective error reporting and logging contribute to proactive error management, allowing system administrators to address issues promptly and prevent potential data loss or service disruptions.

In conclusion, identifying common errors in I/O operations and implementing robust strategies for error detection and recovery are essential elements of maintaining the stability, integrity, and reliability of computer systems. Whether addressing errors in storage, networking, multimedia, databases, or external devices, a multifaceted approach is necessary. Techniques such as checksums, redundancy, hot-plug detection, retry mechanisms, and error reporting collectively contribute to a resilient framework for managing errors and ensuring the continued functionality and data integrity of diverse I/O operations. As computing systems continue to evolve in complexity and scale, the ongoing refinement of error detection and recovery strategies remains a critical focus in the pursuit of building robust and reliable computing environments.

Challenges and strategies in managing I/O in distributed and networked systems.

Challenges and strategies in managing Input/Output (I/O) operations in distributed and networked systems constitute a complex landscape where data transfer efficiency, reliability, and coordination across diverse components are paramount considerations. Distributed systems, characterized by the presence of interconnected nodes or processors, and networked systems, where devices communicate over networks, introduce unique challenges that necessitate specialized strategies for effective I/O management.

One of the primary challenges in distributed and networked systems is the variability in latency and bandwidth across the network. Unlike local I/O operations where data transfers occur within the confines of a single machine, distributed systems must contend with the unpredictable delays introduced by network communication. Strategies to mitigate these challenges involve optimizing data transfer protocols and employing techniques like compression and caching. By minimizing the amount of data transmitted and utilizing efficient compression algorithms, the impact of network latency can be reduced. Additionally, caching frequently accessed data locally can help alleviate the need for repeated network round-trips, enhancing overall system performance.

The issue of reliability is particularly pronounced in networked environments, where the likelihood of packet loss, corruption, or network failures is higher compared to local I/O operations. Error detection and recovery mechanisms play a crucial role in managing I/O in distributed systems. Protocols like Transmission Control Protocol (TCP) incorporate mechanisms such as checksums and acknowledgments to ensure reliable data transmission. Furthermore, strategies like redundancy and replication, such as in distributed databases or storage systems, provide fault tolerance by maintaining multiple copies of data across different nodes, allowing for recovery in the event of node failures or data corruption during network transfers.

Coordinating concurrent I/O operations across distributed or networked nodes introduces synchronization challenges. Concurrent access to shared resources, such as files or databases, requires strategies to prevent conflicts and ensure data consistency. Locking mechanisms, distributed transaction protocols, and coordination frameworks like Two-Phase Commit (2PC) are employed to maintain consistency and prevent data corruption. However, these strategies often introduce trade-offs in terms of performance and scalability, requiring careful consideration in the design of distributed systems.

Scalability is a central concern in managing I/O operations in distributed systems, especially as the number of nodes and the volume of data increase. Strategies for scalable I/O management involve the use of distributed file systems, parallel processing, and sharding techniques. Distributed file systems, such as the Google File System (GFS) or the Hadoop Distributed File System (HDFS), distribute data across multiple nodes, enabling parallel access and enhancing scalability. Parallel processing frameworks, like Apache Spark, leverage distributed computing capabilities to perform I/O operations concurrently on large datasets, further enhancing scalability.

Moreover, the heterogeneity of devices and communication protocols in networked systems adds complexity to I/O management. Interfacing with diverse devices, such as printers, sensors, or IoT devices, requires standardized communication protocols and device drivers. Universal Plug and Play (UPnP), Message Queuing Telemetry Transport (MQTT), and Common Object Request Broker Architecture (CORBA) are examples of protocols and middleware that facilitate communication between heterogeneous devices. Additionally, employing abstraction layers and standardized APIs helps in creating a uniform interface for I/O operations, irrespective of the underlying device or communication protocol.

In the context of distributed databases and storage systems, the challenge of maintaining data consistency across multiple nodes while ensuring high availability is addressed through the use of distributed consensus algorithms. Strategies such as the Paxos algorithm and the Raft consensus protocol provide a framework for achieving consensus among distributed nodes, enabling them to agree on the state of shared data. These consensus mechanisms play a pivotal role in ensuring that I/O operations on distributed databases are coordinated and result in consistent and coherent outcomes.

Security concerns in networked and distributed systems introduce additional challenges to I/O management. Data transmission over networks is susceptible to eavesdropping, unauthorized access, and other security threats. Strategies for secure I/O operations involve the use of encryption, secure communication protocols (e.g.,

HTTPS), and access control mechanisms. Encrypting data during transmission safeguards against unauthorized interception, and access control ensures that only authorized entities can initiate or access specific I/O operations. Additionally, securing the communication channels through techniques like Virtual Private Networks (VPNs) or Secure Socket Layer (SSL) further enhances the overall security posture of networked and distributed systems.

The dynamic nature of networked and distributed environments necessitates adaptive strategies for managing I/O operations. Adaptive I/O management involves dynamically adjusting to changing network conditions, workload patterns, and resource availability. Techniques such as Quality of Service (QoS) mechanisms allow the system to prioritize I/O operations based on their importance or criticality. Additionally, load balancing algorithms distribute I/O requests evenly across nodes, preventing resource bottlenecks and optimizing overall system performance.

The trade-off between consistency and availability, often referred to as the CAP theorem, poses a fundamental challenge in distributed systems. The CAP theorem asserts that it is impossible for a distributed system to simultaneously provide Consistency, Availability, and Partition Tolerance. Strategies for managing I/O operations in distributed systems involve carefully navigating this trade-off. Systems can be designed to prioritize either consistency or availability, depending on the specific requirements of the application or use case. For example, NoSQL databases like Apache Cassandra prioritize availability and partition tolerance over strict consistency, making them well-suited for certain distributed applications.

Furthermore, managing I/O operations in distributed and networked systems requires addressing the challenge of data locality. Data locality refers to the proximity of data to the processing unit or node that needs it. Strategies such as data partitioning, colocation of data and computation, and leveraging distributed caching mechanisms help optimize data locality. Colocating computation and data within the same node or partitioning data based on access patterns reduces the need for extensive data transfers across the network, improving I/O performance in distributed environments.

In the context of cloud computing, the virtualized and shared nature of resources introduces challenges related to I/O performance isolation and resource contention. Strategies for managing I/O in cloud environments involve leveraging resource isolation mechanisms, such as virtualization and containerization. Virtual machines and containers encapsulate applications and their dependencies, providing a degree of isolation that prevents resource contention. Additionally, cloud providers offer scalable storage solutions and network configurations to accommodate the diverse I/O needs of applications running in distributed and cloud environments.

In conclusion, the challenges and strategies in managing I/O operations in distributed and networked systems constitute a multifaceted landscape that demands careful consideration of factors such as latency, reliability, synchronization, scalability, security, adaptability, and data locality. Addressing these challenges involves the judicious application of various strategies, including error detection and recovery mechanisms, redundancy, consensus algorithms, adaptive management techniques, and considerations of the CAP theorem trade-offs. As distributed and networked systems continue to evolve to meet the demands of modern computing, ongoing research and innovation in I/O management strategies remain crucial to ensuring the efficiency, reliability, and scalability of these complex computing environments.

Analyzing instances where effective I/O management contributed to enhanced system performance.

Effective Input/Output (I/O) management plays a pivotal role in enhancing system performance across diverse computing environments, ranging from individual devices to large-scale distributed systems. One notable instance where I/O management significantly contributes to improved system performance is in the context of storage subsystems. Modern storage devices, such as hard disk drives (HDDs) and solid-state drives (SSDs), exhibit substantial variations in access times, throughput, and latency. I/O management strategies, including intelligent caching mechanisms, prefetching, and I/O scheduling algorithms, are employed to optimize data retrieval and storage. Caching, for instance, involves temporarily storing frequently accessed data in fast-access memory, reducing the need for time-consuming disk reads and enhancing overall system responsiveness. Prefetching anticipates the need for specific data and proactively loads it into memory, mitigating the impact of storage latencies. Moreover, I/O scheduling algorithms prioritize and order pending I/O requests, minimizing seek times and maximizing disk throughput. In storage subsystems, effective I/O management not only accelerates data access but also prolongs the lifespan of SSDs by minimizing unnecessary write operations, contributing to a more efficient and reliable system.

Networking scenarios represent another domain where effective I/O management profoundly influences system performance. The efficient transfer of data over networks is crucial for diverse applications, including web browsing, file transfers, and real-time communication. In this context, the Transmission Control Protocol (TCP) exemplifies the impact of sophisticated I/O management. TCP employs congestion control mechanisms, flow control, and error recovery strategies to ensure reliable and efficient data transmission. Congestion control mechanisms adjust the rate of data transmission based on network conditions, preventing network congestion and optimizing overall throughput. Flow control regulates the pace of data exchange between sender and receiver, preventing overwhelmment and ensuring a balanced transmission. Additionally, error recovery mechanisms, such as acknowledgments and retransmission, contribute to the reliability of data delivery. The effective I/O management embedded in TCP enables robust and efficient communication over networks, addressing challenges related to variable latency, packet loss, and bandwidth fluctuations.

In the realm of databases, where I/O operations are intrinsic to data retrieval and storage, well-designed I/O management significantly influences system performance. Database systems often employ indexing structures, query optimization, and buffer pools to enhance I/O efficiency. Indexing structures, such as B-trees, facilitate rapid data retrieval by organizing and optimizing the storage of key-value pairs. Query optimization involves selecting the most efficient execution plans for database queries, minimizing I/O overhead and computational costs. Buffer pools act as caches for frequently accessed data pages, reducing the need for repeated disk reads and enhancing response times. Furthermore, database systems leverage I/O parallelism to execute multiple I/O operations concurrently, taking advantage of the parallel processing capabilities of modern storage devices. By implementing these I/O management strategies, database systems achieve improved query performance, reduced access times, and enhanced overall system efficiency.

Real-time systems, where timely and predictable responses are critical, illustrate another domain where effective I/O management is paramount. Industries such as aviation, healthcare, and industrial automation rely on real-time systems to guarantee precise control and monitoring. In these environments, I/O operations must occur within specified time constraints to maintain system integrity and safety. Real-time operating systems (RTOS) employ specialized I/O management techniques, including priority scheduling, deterministic scheduling algorithms, and interrupt handling mechanisms. Priority scheduling ensures that high-priority I/O tasks are given precedence, meeting stringent deadlines and guaranteeing timely responses. Deterministic scheduling algorithms, such as Rate Monotonic

Scheduling (RMS) or Earliest Deadline First (EDF), further enhance predictability by allocating resources based on task deadlines. Additionally, efficient interrupt handling ensures that time-critical I/O events are promptly processed, minimizing latency and contributing to the reliability of real-time systems.

In the context of multimedia applications, effective I/O management plays a crucial role in delivering seamless and high-quality user experiences. Video streaming services, for instance, require efficient data retrieval and processing to ensure uninterrupted playback. Buffering mechanisms, adaptive streaming, and content delivery networks (CDNs) exemplify I/O management strategies in multimedia applications. Buffers temporarily store video segments, allowing the system to overcome variations in network bandwidth and prevent interruptions in playback. Adaptive streaming adjusts the quality of video content based on available bandwidth, optimizing playback performance and reducing buffering delays. CDNs distribute multimedia content across geographically dispersed servers, minimizing the distance between users and content sources, thereby reducing latency and improving overall streaming performance. The effective management of I/O operations in multimedia applications results in smoother playback, reduced latency, and an enhanced user experience.

Furthermore, the realm of scientific computing showcases instances where efficient I/O management is integral to achieving optimal performance. High-performance computing (HPC) environments, utilized in scientific simulations and data-intensive applications, demand careful orchestration of I/O operations to prevent bottlenecks and ensure computational efficiency. Parallel file systems, data staging, and asynchronous I/O are examples of strategies employed in HPC environments. Parallel file systems distribute data across multiple storage devices, enabling concurrent access and enhancing overall I/O throughput. Data staging involves strategically preloading data onto computing nodes before it is required, reducing the impact of I/O delays during computation. Asynchronous I/O allows multiple I/O operations to proceed concurrently without blocking the execution of computational tasks. These I/O management strategies contribute to the scalability and efficiency of scientific computing applications, enabling researchers to perform complex simulations and analyses with optimal performance.

In the context of cloud computing, effective I/O management is fundamental to ensuring the responsiveness and scalability of applications hosted in cloud environments. Cloud providers offer scalable storage solutions, Content Delivery Networks (CDNs), and distributed file systems to optimize I/O performance. Scalable storage solutions, such as Amazon S3 or Google Cloud Storage, allow applications to dynamically scale their storage needs based on demand. CDNs distribute content to edge servers, reducing latency and improving the retrieval speed of data for end-users. Distributed file systems, such as Hadoop Distributed File System (HDFS) in cloud-based big data analytics, enable efficient storage and retrieval of large datasets across distributed clusters. By leveraging these I/O management capabilities in cloud environments, applications benefit from increased agility, reduced latency, and improved overall system performance.

Moreover, the deployment of I/O management strategies is evident in the optimization of gaming systems, where responsive and immersive user experiences are paramount. In gaming environments, efficient I/O operations are crucial for loading game assets, textures, and levels in real-time. Caching mechanisms, asset streaming, and parallel I/O are among the strategies employed. Caching stores frequently used game assets in memory, minimizing load times and enhancing the responsiveness of in-game actions. Asset streaming dynamically loads game assets during gameplay, reducing the need for large upfront data loads and enabling seamless transitions between game levels. Parallel I/O takes advantage of multi-core processors to execute I/O operations concurrently, accelerating data transfers and optimizing overall gaming performance. The effective management of I/O operations in gaming systems contributes to reduced load times, improved rendering, and an immersive gaming experience.

In conclusion, instances abound across various computing domains where effective I/O management significantly contributes to enhanced system performance. From storage subsystems and networking scenarios to databases, real-time systems, multimedia applications, scientific computing, cloud environments, and gaming systems, the careful orchestration of I/O operations is fundamental to achieving optimal responsiveness, reliability, and scalability. The strategies employed, including caching, parallelism, prefetching, and adaptive mechanisms, reflect the diverse and dynamic nature of contemporary computing. As technology continues to advance, the ongoing refinement of I/O management techniques remains pivotal for meeting the evolving demands of modern computing environments and delivering optimal user experiences.

Chapter 7: Error Handling and Fault Tolerance

D efining the importance of error handling in maintaining system stability.

Error handling is a critical aspect of maintaining system stability in the ever-evolving landscape of computer systems and software applications. At its core, error handling is the systematic process of identifying, reporting, and responding to unexpected or erroneous conditions that may arise during the execution of a program or the operation of a system. The importance of robust error handling cannot be overstated, as it directly influences the reliability, integrity, and resilience of a system across a myriad of scenarios and use cases.

One fundamental role of error handling lies in preventing system failures and crashes that can result from unforeseen circumstances or erroneous inputs. Software applications, operating systems, and other complex systems are designed to execute a multitude of tasks, often involving interactions with external resources, user inputs, or other software components. Errors can manifest in various forms, including invalid inputs, resource unavailability, network failures, or unexpected changes in the system state. Without effective error handling mechanisms, a single error could potentially propagate, triggering a cascade of failures and compromising the stability of the entire system. Robust error handling acts as a safeguard, intercepting errors as they occur, and providing the system with the means to gracefully recover or terminate in a controlled manner, preventing catastrophic failures and ensuring system stability.

Moreover, error handling is essential for maintaining data integrity and consistency within a system. In data-centric applications, errors during input validation, storage, retrieval, or processing can lead to corrupted or inconsistent data. For instance, in database systems, errors during data transactions or storage operations can compromise the reliability of the stored information. Effective error handling ensures that such issues are detected, reported, and appropriately addressed, preventing the propagation of inaccurate or incomplete data throughout the system. This is particularly crucial in domains where data accuracy is paramount, such as financial systems, healthcare applications, or any environment where the integrity of information is foundational to the system's purpose.

In the context of user-facing applications, error handling is pivotal for providing a positive user experience and maintaining user trust. When errors occur, whether due to user inputs, system malfunctions, or external factors, users need clear and meaningful feedback to understand what went wrong and how to proceed. A well-designed error handling system communicates errors in a user-friendly manner, avoiding technical jargon and providing actionable information or guidance. This not only aids users in resolving issues but also enhances the overall usability of the system. On the contrary, a lack of or inadequate error handling can result in cryptic error messages, confusing user interfaces, and frustration, ultimately diminishing user confidence and satisfaction with the system.

Effective error handling is also integral to security considerations within a system. Security vulnerabilities often arise from unexpected or malicious inputs, and without proper error handling, these inputs may go unnoticed, exposing the system to potential exploits. For instance, input validation errors can lead to injection attacks, buffer overflows, or other security breaches. Robust error handling includes mechanisms for validating and sanitizing inputs, detecting and logging suspicious activities, and responding to potential security threats in a proactive manner. In this way, error handling becomes an essential component of a comprehensive security strategy, contributing to the overall resilience of the system against both accidental and intentional threats.

In distributed systems and networked environments, error handling is crucial for maintaining the stability of communication and data exchange. The complexities introduced by network delays, packet loss, or service unavailability necessitate a robust approach to error detection and recovery. Protocols like Transmission Control Protocol (TCP) incorporate sophisticated error handling mechanisms, including checksums, acknowledgments, and retransmission, to ensure reliable data transfer over networks. In distributed systems, where components may communicate asynchronously, error handling becomes a means of maintaining consistency and preventing data corruption. Well-designed error handling strategies enable systems to gracefully handle network failures, recover from communication errors, and adapt to the dynamic nature of distributed environments, contributing to the overall stability of interconnected systems.

Furthermore, error handling is instrumental in supporting the maintainability and troubleshooting efforts throughout the lifecycle of a system. Comprehensive error reporting and logging mechanisms provide valuable diagnostic information that aids developers, system administrators, and support teams in identifying the root causes of issues. Error logs, stack traces, and detailed error messages empower those responsible for maintaining the system to quickly pinpoint and address problems, reducing downtime and streamlining the debugging process. This becomes particularly crucial in large-scale systems, where identifying and resolving errors promptly is essential for ensuring continuous operation and minimizing disruptions.

In regulated industries and mission-critical systems, error handling is often a compliance requirement. Regulations and standards, such as those in healthcare, finance, or aviation, mandate robust error handling practices to ensure the safety, accuracy, and reliability of systems. Compliance with these standards not only helps organizations meet legal and regulatory obligations but also underscores the importance of error handling in scenarios where system failures can have severe consequences. The implementation of comprehensive error handling mechanisms becomes a key factor in achieving and maintaining compliance, demonstrating a commitment to quality, accountability, and the well-being of users or stakeholders.

As systems evolve, undergo updates, or integrate with third-party services, effective error handling becomes a crucial component for future-proofing and adaptability. Changes in system configurations, dependencies, or external APIs may introduce new sources of errors or modify the behavior of existing ones. A robust error handling strategy allows a system to gracefully adapt to changes, accommodating unforeseen scenarios and ensuring that errors are promptly identified, reported, and addressed. This adaptability is essential for the long-term stability and sustainability of systems as they evolve over time.

In conclusion, the importance of error handling in maintaining system stability is multi-faceted and foundational to the design, operation, and evolution of computer systems. Robust error handling mechanisms prevent catastrophic failures, preserve data integrity, enhance user experiences, bolster security, support troubleshooting efforts, and ensure compliance with regulatory standards. As systems continue to grow in complexity and interconnectivity, effective error handling remains an indispensable aspect of software engineering and system design, contributing to the overall reliability, resilience, and trustworthiness of modern computing environments.

Identification and classification of common errors in operating systems.

Identifying and classifying common errors in operating systems is crucial for understanding and addressing the diverse challenges that may arise during the execution and management of system resources. One prevalent category of errors pertains to hardware-related issues, where the operating system encounters errors stemming from faulty components or communication breakdowns. Hardware errors can manifest as memory errors, disk failures, or issues with peripheral devices, disrupting the normal operation of the system. For instance, memory errors may result in application crashes or system instability, while disk failures can lead to data corruption or loss. Identification of these hardware-related errors often involves diagnostic tools, system logs, and error messages that provide insights into the specific components or devices experiencing issues.

Another significant class of errors in operating systems involves software-related issues, ranging from programming errors in applications to compatibility problems between software components or between the software and the operating system itself. Software errors can lead to application crashes, system instability, or unexpected behaviors. Common examples include segmentation faults, null pointer dereferences, or logic errors in application code. Compatibility issues may arise when software components make assumptions about the underlying operating system that prove incorrect, resulting in errors during execution. Robust error handling mechanisms, debugging tools, and application logs are employed to identify and diagnose software-related errors, enabling developers to rectify issues and improve the overall stability of the system.

Kernel errors represent a critical category of errors that directly impact the core of the operating system. The kernel serves as the central component responsible for managing system resources, handling interrupts, and ensuring overall system stability. Kernel errors can manifest as kernel panics, system freezes, or unexpected reboots. These errors often arise from issues such as faulty device drivers, memory corruption, or conflicts in resource allocation. Kernel debugging tools and crash dump analysis are employed to identify the root causes of kernel errors, allowing developers to address issues within the core of the operating system and enhance its reliability.

File system errors constitute another common class of errors, affecting the organization and storage of data on disk drives. File system errors can arise from power outages, improper shutdowns, or hardware failures, leading to data corruption, lost files, or degraded performance. The operating system employs file system check tools (such as fsck in Unix-based systems) to identify and repair errors in the file system structure. Journaling file systems, like those used in modern operating systems, maintain logs of file system transactions to facilitate error recovery and maintain data consistency in the event of unexpected shutdowns or errors.

Network-related errors pose a significant challenge in operating systems, particularly in environments where systems communicate over networks. Connectivity issues, packet loss, and network congestion can lead to errors in data transmission, affecting the reliability and performance of networked systems. Error detection and correction mechanisms, such as those employed by the Transmission Control Protocol (TCP), aim to ensure the integrity of data transmitted over networks. Network monitoring tools, logs, and diagnostic utilities assist in identifying and troubleshooting network-related errors, enabling administrators to optimize network performance and address connectivity issues.

Security-related errors represent a critical and often sensitive class of errors that can compromise the integrity, confidentiality, and availability of system resources. Security vulnerabilities, misconfigurations, or inadequate access controls may lead to unauthorized access, data breaches, or malicious activities within the operating system. Common security errors include buffer overflows, privilege escalation vulnerabilities, or inadequate encryption practices. Security auditing tools, intrusion detection systems, and log analysis play a vital role in identifying and classifying security-related errors. Prompt remediation of these errors is essential to fortify the operating system against potential threats and safeguard sensitive data.

Memory management errors pose significant challenges in operating systems, particularly in scenarios where inefficient memory allocation, deallocation, or corruption occurs. Memory leaks, where applications fail to release allocated memory, can lead to gradual degradation of system performance and eventual exhaustion of available memory. Buffer overflows, a common type of memory management error, can result in the corruption of adjacent memory regions, potentially leading to system crashes or security vulnerabilities. Memory debugging tools and profiling utilities assist in identifying memory-related errors, allowing developers to optimize memory usage, prevent leaks, and enhance the overall efficiency of the operating system.

Concurrency and synchronization errors arise in multi-tasking or multi-threaded environments, where multiple processes or threads concurrently access shared resources. Race conditions, deadlocks, or improper synchronization can lead to unpredictable behaviors, system hangs, or data corruption. Identifying and addressing concurrency errors require careful analysis of program logic, utilization of synchronization mechanisms (such as locks or semaphores), and debugging tools that highlight potential race conditions or deadlocks. Effective concurrency control is essential for maintaining the stability and reliability of the operating system, particularly in environments with high levels of parallelism.

User-related errors, stemming from actions taken by system users, represent a common source of challenges for operating systems. These errors may include unintentional deletions of critical files, misconfigurations, or attempts to execute unauthorized operations. User authentication errors, such as incorrect login credentials, can impact system accessibility and security. Auditing tools, access controls, and user privilege management are employed to identify and mitigate user-related errors. Effective user education and awareness programs also play a role in reducing the occurrence of errors initiated by system users, contributing to a more secure and stable operating environment.

Environmental errors encompass issues that arise due to external factors, such as power fluctuations, temperature extremes, or physical damage to hardware components. Power outages, for instance, can lead to abrupt system shutdowns, potentially resulting in file system errors or data loss. Environmental monitoring tools and uninterruptible power supply (UPS) systems are employed to detect and mitigate the impact of environmental errors. Redundancy and failover mechanisms may also be implemented to ensure system resilience in the face of unforeseen environmental challenges.

In conclusion, the identification and classification of common errors in operating systems span a wide array of challenges, from hardware and software issues to kernel errors, file system errors, network-related errors, security vulnerabilities, memory management errors, concurrency issues, user-related errors, and environmental challenges. Each category presents unique complexities and requires specific tools, methodologies, and best practices for detection, diagnosis, and resolution. A comprehensive understanding of these common errors is essential for system administrators, developers, and users to effectively manage, troubleshoot, and enhance the stability and reliability of operating systems across diverse computing environments.

Exploring techniques for detecting errors in processes, memory, and I/O operations.

Exploring techniques for detecting errors in processes, memory, and Input/Output (I/O) operations is essential for ensuring the reliability, stability, and security of computer systems. In the realm of processes, error detection techniques often revolve around monitoring the execution of programs and identifying anomalies that may indicate potential issues. Anomaly detection algorithms analyze process behavior, resource utilization, and system calls to detect deviations from expected patterns. Additionally, watchdog timers are employed to monitor the responsiveness of processes, triggering alerts or corrective actions if a process becomes unresponsive or enters an infinite loop. Comprehensive logging and auditing mechanisms capture events related to process execution, facilitating post-mortem analysis and error diagnosis. Furthermore, techniques such as checksums or hash functions may be applied to critical process data to detect corruption and unauthorized modifications.

Memory errors, including issues such as memory leaks, buffer overflows, and corruption, are critical concerns that can lead to system instability and security vulnerabilities. Memory debugging tools, such as AddressSanitizer and Valgrind, play a pivotal role in identifying memory-related errors during program development and testing. These tools employ techniques like instrumentation and dynamic analysis to detect memory leaks, access violations, and illegal memory operations. Additionally, static code analysis tools examine source code for potential memory issues before the program is even executed. Memory protection mechanisms, such as Data Execution Prevention (DEP) and Address Space Layout Randomization (ASLR), contribute to error prevention by making it harder for attackers to exploit memory vulnerabilities. Moreover, runtime checks and guards, like canaries placed around critical data structures, assist in detecting and preventing buffer overflows, enhancing the overall robustness of memory management.

In the domain of I/O operations, error detection techniques are crucial for ensuring the integrity and reliability of data transfers between the system and external devices. Redundancy and error-checking codes, such as cyclic redundancy checks (CRC) or checksums, are commonly employed to verify the accuracy of transmitted data. These codes generate a checksum or hash value based on the transmitted data, which the recipient can use to verify whether the data was received without errors. Error detection and correction protocols, like those implemented in Transmission Control Protocol (TCP), provide mechanisms for detecting and recovering from errors during data transmission over networks. I/O operation monitoring tools, network analyzers, and logging mechanisms capture and analyze I/O-related events, facilitating the identification of errors and performance bottlenecks. Furthermore, parity checking and error correction codes in storage systems, such as RAID configurations, contribute to error detection and recovery in the event of disk failures.

In the context of process execution, system calls play a central role in interacting with the operating system kernel and managing resources. Monitoring system calls is a powerful technique for detecting errors and unauthorized activities. System call auditing tools, like Auditd on Linux systems, enable the logging and analysis of system calls made by processes. Anomalies in system call patterns, unexpected privilege escalations, or attempts to access restricted resources can be indicative of errors or security breaches. Additionally, system call interposition techniques, such as the use of dynamic link libraries (DLL) in Windows or the LD_PRELOAD mechanism in Unix-like systems, allow for the interception and modification of system calls, enabling the implementation of custom error detection logic.

Concurrency errors, arising from the simultaneous execution of multiple threads or processes, present unique challenges for error detection. Techniques such as static analysis and model checking are employed to identify potential race conditions, deadlocks, and data races during the development phase. These tools analyze the source code or executable and explore possible execution paths to detect concurrency-related errors. Runtime verification, using tools like ThreadSanitizer or Helgrind, dynamically monitors program execution to identify concurrency issues, such as data races or synchronization errors. Lock analysis techniques, including lock usage profiling and deadlock detection, contribute to identifying and preventing errors related to the coordination of concurrent activities. Additionally, transactional memory systems offer a higher-level abstraction for concurrent programming, reducing the likelihood of errors by providing atomicity and isolation guarantees.

Error detection in networked environments involves a multifaceted approach to ensuring the reliability and security of data exchange. Cryptographic techniques, including digital signatures and message authentication codes (MACs), authenticate the origin and integrity of transmitted data. Secure communication protocols, such as Transport Layer Security (TLS) or Secure Sockets Layer (SSL), encrypt data during transmission, preventing eavesdropping and tampering. Network intrusion detection and prevention systems (IDS/IPS) analyze network traffic for patterns indicative of malicious activities or security threats. Packet inspection tools and network analyzers monitor the integrity of transmitted data, identifying errors or anomalies that may arise during network communication. Additionally, error detection in network protocols is often built into the protocol design, such as in TCP, where acknowledgments and sequence numbers are used to confirm the successful transmission of data and detect errors in the order or loss of packets.

Environmental errors, stemming from external factors like power fluctuations or physical damage, require specialized techniques for detection and mitigation. Environmental monitoring systems, equipped with sensors for temperature, humidity, and power supply, detect variations outside acceptable thresholds. Uninterruptible power supply (UPS) systems provide a buffer against power fluctuations and ensure a graceful shutdown in the event of power outages. Redundant hardware configurations, including mirrored disks and hot-swappable components, contribute to error resilience by mitigating the impact of hardware failures resulting from environmental factors. Error detection in environmental conditions is often integrated into system health monitoring tools, alerting administrators to potential issues before they lead to system failures.

In conclusion, exploring techniques for detecting errors in processes, memory, and I/O operations involves a comprehensive set of strategies spanning hardware, software, and network aspects of computing systems. Anomaly detection, watchdog timers, memory debugging tools, checksums, cryptographic techniques, system call monitoring, concurrency analysis, and environmental monitoring collectively contribute to the identification and prevention of errors. As computing systems continue to evolve in complexity and scale, the development and application of robust error detection techniques remain pivotal for ensuring the reliability, security, and performance of modern computing environments.

Strategies for recovering from errors and restoring system functionality.

Strategies for recovering from errors and restoring system functionality are essential components of robust and resilient computing environments. When errors occur, whether due to hardware failures, software bugs, or external factors, the ability to swiftly and effectively recover is paramount for minimizing downtime and maintaining the integrity of system operations. One fundamental strategy involves implementing comprehensive backup and restoration mechanisms. Regularly backing up critical data, system configurations, and application settings enables organizations to recover from various errors, including data corruption, accidental deletions, or system failures. Automated backup solutions, such as incremental or differential backups, streamline the process by capturing only changes since the last backup, reducing both storage requirements and the time needed for recovery. By maintaining reliable and up-to-date backups, organizations can restore systems to a known and functional state in the event of errors, ensuring business continuity and data integrity.

In the context of software errors, particularly those affecting application functionality, the implementation of transactional mechanisms provides a powerful strategy for recovery. Transactional systems ensure that a series of operations are either completed successfully or rolled back entirely in the face of errors, preserving the consistency and integrity of data. Database management systems, for example, often use transactions to guarantee atomicity, consistency, isolation, and durability (ACID properties). If an error occurs during the execution of a transaction, the system can roll back to the previous state, preventing partial or inconsistent changes. Transactional approaches extend beyond databases and are increasingly applied to distributed systems and microservices architectures, providing a foundation for error recovery and ensuring that the system remains in a coherent state.

In the realm of memory errors, where issues like memory leaks or corruption may compromise system stability, employing effective garbage collection mechanisms becomes crucial for recovery. Garbage collection, a memory management strategy, automatically identifies and reclaims memory occupied by objects that are no longer in use, preventing memory leaks. In languages with garbage collection support, such as Java or C#, automatic memory reclamation helps mitigate the impact of memory-related errors. Additionally, memory protection mechanisms, such as segmentation fault handling in operating systems, contribute to error recovery by isolating faulty processes and preventing them from causing cascading failures. For large-scale distributed systems, strategies like replicating critical components or employing containers with resource limits can help isolate and recover from memory-related errors in a distributed and resilient manner.

Concurrency errors, arising from simultaneous execution of multiple threads or processes, necessitate strategies for detection and recovery. Rollback mechanisms, such as those in database systems or distributed transactional models, allow systems to revert to a previous consistent state in the face of concurrency-related errors. Checkpointing, a technique employed in high-performance computing and parallel processing, involves saving the current state of a computation periodically. In the event of an error or failure, the system can restart from the last checkpoint, minimizing the impact of errors and ensuring progress is not lost. Additionally, deadlock detection and resolution strategies contribute to recovery from concurrency errors. Deadlocks, where multiple processes are blocked waiting for each other to release resources, can be resolved by rolling back transactions, releasing locks, or employing algorithms that preemptively break deadlocks.

Network-related errors, which may result from issues such as packet loss, latency, or communication failures, demand strategies for error detection and recovery to ensure the reliability of distributed systems. Reliable communication protocols, like those implemented in Transmission Control Protocol (TCP), use acknowledgment mechanisms and retransmission strategies to recover from packet loss or errors during data transmission. Application-layer protocols, such as Hypertext Transfer Protocol (HTTP), often leverage mechanisms like retrying failed requests or employing exponential backoff strategies to recover from transient network errors. Redundancy and failover mechanisms, such as those in distributed systems or cloud architectures, contribute to error recovery by redirecting traffic to alternative nodes or servers in the event of a network-related failure. Load balancers and content delivery networks (CDNs) play a crucial role in distributing traffic across multiple servers, enhancing reliability and enabling recovery from network-related errors.

Environmental errors, stemming from external factors like power outages, temperature extremes, or physical damage, necessitate strategies to ensure system resilience and recovery. Uninterruptible power supply (UPS) systems, equipped with battery backups, provide a temporary power source during outages, allowing systems to shut down gracefully or continue operation until power is restored. Redundant power supplies and generators offer additional layers of protection against power-related errors, ensuring continuous operation in critical environments. System health monitoring tools, integrated with environmental sensors, can detect variations in temperature, humidity, or other environmental conditions, triggering alerts or corrective actions to prevent errors caused by adverse environmental factors. Additionally, physical security measures, such as securing server rooms or data centers against unauthorized access, contribute to error prevention and recovery by minimizing the risk of intentional or accidental damage.

Security-related errors, which may result from unauthorized access, data breaches, or exploitation of vulnerabilities, demand specialized strategies for detection and recovery. Intrusion detection and prevention systems (IDS/IPS) play a pivotal role in identifying security incidents by monitoring network traffic, system logs, and application behavior for patterns indicative of malicious activities. When a security breach is detected, automated responses or incident response teams can implement strategies for recovery, such as isolating compromised systems, revoking unauthorized access, and restoring affected data from secure backups. Patch management and vulnerability scanning tools contribute to error prevention by identifying and addressing security vulnerabilities before they can be exploited. Additionally, encryption and access controls help protect sensitive data, limiting the impact of security-related errors and providing a foundation for recovery.

In scenarios where errors lead to data corruption, file system errors, or unexpected system crashes, employing file system check tools becomes essential for recovery. Tools like fsck (File System Consistency Check) on Unix-based systems or chkdsk (Check Disk) on Windows systems analyze and repair file system inconsistencies, recovering data and restoring the integrity of file structures. Journaling file systems, such as ext4 or NTFS, maintain logs of file system transactions, enabling recovery from unexpected shutdowns or errors. Redundant array of independent disks (RAID) configurations, utilizing parity or mirroring, contribute to error recovery by allowing systems to continue operation even in the presence of disk failures. Data redundancy and backup strategies, combined with file system check tools, offer a comprehensive approach to recovering from errors affecting data integrity and file systems.

In conclusion, strategies for recovering from errors and restoring system functionality encompass a diverse set of approaches tailored to address specific challenges in different domains of computing. Backup and restoration mechanisms, transactional models, garbage collection, checkpointing, and redundancy contribute to recovery strategies, ensuring systems can swiftly recover from hardware failures, software bugs, and environmental or security-related errors. As technology continues to advance, the development and refinement of recovery strategies remain crucial for maintaining the resilience, reliability, and continuity of modern computing environments.

The concept of fault tolerance and its significance in critical systems.

The concept of fault tolerance represents a cornerstone in the design and operation of critical systems, playing a pivotal role in ensuring the reliability, availability, and continuous functionality of systems operating in demanding or mission-critical environments. At its core, fault tolerance refers to a system's ability to maintain or recover its normal operations despite the occurrence of faults or failures.

In the context of critical systems, which are deployed in sectors such as aerospace, healthcare, transportation, and energy, the significance of fault tolerance cannot be overstated. The key objective is to minimize the impact of faults, which can range from hardware malfunctions and software errors to environmental challenges, and to enable the system to continue providing its essential services without compromising safety, security, or performance.

In critical systems, where the consequences of failures can be severe, the pursuit of fault tolerance starts with the recognition that faults are inevitable. Hardware components may degrade over time, software may contain bugs or vulnerabilities, and external factors such as power outages or environmental conditions may introduce uncertainties. As a result, fault tolerance strategies are integrated into the system architecture, encompassing a spectrum of techniques that collectively enhance the system's ability to detect, isolate, and recover from faults. One fundamental approach involves redundancy, where critical components or subsystems are duplicated to ensure that if one part fails, a backup can seamlessly take over. This redundancy can be implemented at various levels, including hardware redundancy with duplicated processors or storage devices, software redundancy through parallel processing or error-correcting codes, and data redundancy through mirroring or replication.

Redundancy alone, however, is not sufficient to achieve comprehensive fault tolerance. Detection mechanisms are equally crucial in identifying faults promptly and accurately. Real-time monitoring, sensors, and diagnostic tools continuously assess the health and performance of system components. Anomalies or deviations from expected behavior trigger alarms or corrective actions. For example, in avionics systems, sensors continuously monitor critical parameters such as engine performance or aircraft attitude. If deviations beyond predetermined thresholds are detected, the system can initiate corrective measures, ranging from adjusting control surfaces to activating redundant systems. Advanced monitoring may also involve predictive analytics, machine learning algorithms, or artificial intelligence to anticipate faults based on historical data or evolving patterns, providing a proactive approach to fault detection.

Isolation mechanisms further enhance fault tolerance by containing the impact of faults and preventing them from propagating throughout the entire system. For instance, in distributed computing environments, the isolation of faulty nodes or components prevents a localized fault from affecting the entire system. Virtualization technologies, such as hypervisors, contribute to isolation by encapsulating software components within virtual machines, ensuring that a failure in one virtualized instance does not compromise others. In safety-critical systems like nuclear power plants or autonomous vehicles, isolation strategies are meticulously designed to confine faults to specific subsystems or components, maintaining the overall system's operational integrity.

Recovery strategies constitute the final pillar of fault tolerance, focusing on the system's ability to recover from faults and resume normal operations swiftly. These strategies often involve automated processes that restore functionality, switch to redundant components, or transition to backup systems. In the event of a hardware failure, failover mechanisms redirect traffic or processing to redundant components seamlessly, minimizing downtime. Software-based recovery strategies may include graceful degradation, where the system continues to operate with reduced functionality in the presence of faults, allowing critical services to persist even under suboptimal conditions. Moreover, rollback mechanisms, transactional models, and checkpointing strategies contribute to recovering from software errors or data corruption, ensuring the system remains in a consistent and reliable state.

The significance of fault tolerance in critical systems is particularly evident in applications where the consequences of failures extend beyond inconvenience to potential harm, loss of life, or extensive economic impact. In the aerospace industry, for example, where avionics systems control the flight of aircraft, fault tolerance is a non-negotiable aspect of design. Redundant flight control computers, multiple sensors, and sophisticated fault detection algorithms are implemented to ensure the continuous safety of passengers and crew. Similarly, in healthcare, where medical devices and systems are integral to patient care, fault tolerance is paramount. Infusion pumps, ventilators, and diagnostic equipment incorporate redundant components and rigorous testing to withstand faults and continue functioning reliably in critical medical scenarios.

Transportation systems, including autonomous vehicles and railway signaling systems, heavily rely on fault tolerance to prevent accidents and ensure the safety of passengers and cargo. Redundant sensors, fail-safe braking systems, and sophisticated control algorithms contribute to the fault tolerance of these systems, providing layers of protection against unexpected events. In energy infrastructure, where power grids and nuclear plants operate continuously to meet the demands of society, fault tolerance is essential. Redundant power lines, backup generators, and automated control systems enable the energy sector to respond to faults, such as equipment failures or fluctuations in demand, without compromising the reliability of power supply.

The field of telecommunications also underscores the importance of fault tolerance, where network reliability is paramount for global connectivity. Telecommunication networks employ redundant communication links, load balancing, and rapid rerouting strategies to maintain connectivity even in the face of network failures or disruptions. Data centers, which house critical computing resources for various industries, implement fault tolerance at multiple levels, including redundant power supplies, cooling systems, and server configurations. The cloud computing paradigm further extends fault tolerance by distributing applications across multiple geographically dispersed data centers, ensuring resilience against regional outages or disasters.

The military and defense sectors place a premium on fault tolerance in their systems, where mission-critical operations demand continuous functionality despite potential adversarial actions or unforeseen circumstances. Redundant communication channels, navigation systems, and failover mechanisms contribute to the fault tolerance of military hardware and command and control systems. Additionally, space exploration missions, where communication delays and harsh environmental conditions are prevalent, leverage fault tolerance strategies to ensure the success of missions. Redundant systems, fault-tolerant software, and autonomous decision-making capabilities enable spacecraft to navigate, communicate, and conduct scientific experiments even in the harsh conditions of space.

In conclusion, the concept of fault tolerance is not merely a technical consideration but a fundamental necessity in critical systems that operate in environments where the consequences of failures are significant. The integration of redundancy, detection, isolation, and recovery mechanisms collectively empowers critical systems to withstand faults and continue delivering essential services. The significance of fault tolerance is deeply rooted in safeguarding human lives, ensuring the stability of infrastructure, and mitigating the impact of unforeseen events. As technology advances and critical systems become increasingly complex, fault tolerance remains an indispensable aspect of design and operation, embodying a commitment to resilience, safety, and unwavering performance in the face of challenges.

Implementing redundancy through backup systems and data replication.

Implementing redundancy through backup systems and data replication is a foundational strategy in the realm of information technology, critical infrastructure, and various applications where continuous availability and fault tolerance are imperative. The essence of redundancy lies in the creation of duplicates or backups of essential components, systems, or data to ensure seamless operations in the face of failures, errors, or unforeseen events. In the context of backup systems, the primary objective is to create copies of critical data, applications, or configurations, providing a safety net against data loss, corruption, or system failures. These backup systems serve as a form of insurance, enabling organizations to recover swiftly and reliably from events that may compromise the integrity or availability of their primary systems.

One of the fundamental aspects of implementing redundancy through backup systems involves the development and execution of robust backup strategies. Organizations meticulously design these strategies based on their specific needs, considering factors such as data volume, frequency of changes, recovery time objectives (RTO), and recovery point objectives (RPO). Differential, incremental, and full backups are common methodologies used to capture changes in data over time, optimizing storage efficiency and minimizing the time required for data restoration. Backup systems often utilize a combination of onsite and offsite storage to mitigate risks associated with local disasters, theft, or other localized incidents. Additionally, the choice between physical and cloud-based backups introduces flexibility and scalability, allowing organizations to tailor their backup systems to meet evolving business requirements.

In critical infrastructure, such as financial institutions, healthcare systems, and government agencies, where data integrity and availability are paramount, backup systems are integral components of the overall disaster recovery and business continuity planning. Regularly scheduled backups, complemented by rigorous testing and validation procedures, ensure that organizations can restore critical systems and data efficiently in the event of hardware failures, software glitches, or even malicious attacks. For instance, financial institutions employ redundant data centers with synchronized backups to maintain continuous banking services, protecting against disruptions caused by hardware failures, cyber threats, or natural disasters. Healthcare systems, reliant on electronic health records and medical imaging data, implement redundant backup systems to safeguard patient information and ensure uninterrupted healthcare delivery.

Data replication, as a complementary strategy to backup systems, extends redundancy to real-time or near-real-time duplication of data across multiple locations or systems. While backup systems are often employed for periodic snapshots or point-in-time copies, data replication operates continuously, synchronizing changes made to the primary data with mirrored copies in real-time. This dynamic replication ensures that redundant systems maintain an up-to-date and consistent representation of the primary data, minimizing the risk of data loss or inconsistencies in the event of a failure. In scenarios where downtime is not acceptable, such as in online transaction processing (OLTP) systems or critical infrastructure, data replication is a fundamental mechanism for achieving high availability.

Database systems, a critical component in various applications, often leverage data replication to enhance fault tolerance and performance. In a replicated database architecture, changes made to the primary database are immediately propagated to one or more replica databases. This not only provides redundancy for data preservation but also enables load balancing and scalability by distributing read queries across multiple replicas. Synchronous replication ensures that changes are mirrored in real-time, providing a high level of data consistency but potentially introducing latency. Asynchronous replication, on the other hand, allows for a slight delay in data synchronization, offering improved performance at the cost of potential data lag during a failure event.

In cloud computing environments, data replication is a fundamental mechanism for ensuring reliability, scalability, and disaster recovery. Cloud service providers offer geographically distributed data centers, enabling organizations to replicate their data and applications across multiple regions. This geographic redundancy enhances availability and resilience, allowing organizations to maintain operations even in the face of regional outages or disruptions. Cloud-based replication services often provide flexibility in choosing replication models, such as master-slave replication, multi-master replication, or hub-and-spoke replication, catering to diverse application requirements. Additionally, cloud providers integrate automated backup and snapshot features, further enhancing redundancy and facilitating data recovery.

The e-commerce sector, characterized by high transaction volumes and continuous customer interactions, heavily relies on redundancy through data replication to ensure uninterrupted service. Redundant databases and application servers, distributed across geographically diverse locations, enable e-commerce platforms to withstand surges in traffic, hardware failures, or even deliberate attacks. Data consistency is maintained through synchronous or asynchronous replication, allowing organizations to balance the trade-off between consistency and performance based on their specific needs. The redundancy provided by data replication aligns with the expectation of users for seamless and reliable online shopping experiences, even in the face of unforeseen events.

In the field of telecommunications, where network reliability is paramount for global connectivity, data replication strategies are employed to ensure continuous operations. Telecommunication networks implement redundant systems and data replication to cope with failures, such as hardware malfunctions, fiber cuts, or other disruptions. Dynamic rerouting of network traffic, facilitated by real-time data replication, helps maintain connectivity and minimizes service interruptions. Furthermore, data replication contributes to load balancing and efficient resource utilization, allowing telecommunication providers to optimize their network infrastructure for resilience and performance.

The implementation of redundancy through backup systems and data replication extends to critical infrastructure in the energy sector, where power grids and utility systems require continuous operations for societal well-being. Redundant control systems, synchronized through data replication, enable utilities to monitor and manage power distribution reliably. Backup systems for supervisory control and data acquisition (SCADA) systems ensure that operators can restore control quickly in the event of failures. Similarly, in the oil and gas industry, where data integrity and real-time monitoring are crucial, redundancy through data replication enhances the reliability of exploration and production operations.

While redundancy through backup systems and data replication provides resilience against various failures, it is essential to consider the associated challenges and trade-offs. Storage costs, network bandwidth requirements, and complexities in managing replicated systems demand careful planning and resource allocation. Organizations must strike a balance between the level of redundancy required and the resources available to maintain it. Additionally, considerations for data consistency, latency, and synchronization modes in replicated environments require a nuanced approach tailored to the specific needs of applications and systems.

In conclusion, implementing redundancy through backup systems and data replication is a multifaceted strategy that addresses the diverse challenges of ensuring continuous availability, fault tolerance, and data integrity. From critical infrastructure to cloud-based services, redundancy plays a pivotal role in safeguarding against hardware failures, software errors, and unforeseen events. Backup systems provide periodic snapshots for data recovery, while data replication operates in real-time to maintain consistency and availability. The dynamic interplay between these strategies aligns with the evolving landscape of information technology, underscoring the importance of redundancy in achieving resilience, performance, and reliability across diverse applications and industries.

Techniques for rolling back processes and recovering from system failures.

Techniques for rolling back processes and recovering from system failures constitute a critical aspect of modern computing, ensuring the resilience and stability of applications and infrastructure. The concept of rolling back processes involves reverting the state of a system or application to a previous, known-good state after a failure, error, or unexpected event. This rollback mechanism is designed to undo changes made during the execution of a process, mitigating the impact of faults and facilitating the restoration of normal operations. The need for robust rollback techniques arises from the inherent complexity and unpredictability of computing environments, where hardware failures, software bugs, or external disruptions can jeopardize the integrity and functionality of systems.

One fundamental approach to rolling back processes involves the implementation of transactional models, particularly in the context of database management systems (DBMS). Transactions, which represent a sequence of operations that must be executed atomically, either fully succeed or fail as a unit. If a failure occurs during the execution of a transaction, the system can automatically roll back the transaction to its initial state, ensuring data consistency and integrity. This atomicity property, a key aspect of the ACID (Atomicity, Consistency, Isolation, Durability) model, ensures that database transactions are either completed successfully or leave no trace of their execution in the event of a failure, preventing partial or inconsistent updates to the data.

In distributed computing environments, where processes may span multiple nodes or systems, rolling back processes involves sophisticated coordination mechanisms to maintain consistency. Two-phase commit protocols, such as the Two-Phase Commit (2PC) and Three-Phase Commit (3PC), are employed to ensure that distributed transactions either commit or roll back consistently across all participating nodes. These protocols involve a coordinator and multiple participants, ensuring that all nodes agree on whether to commit or roll back a transaction. In the event of a failure or disagreement, the system can initiate a rollback to maintain a consistent state across the distributed environment, preventing data inconsistencies.

Checkpointing is another prominent technique for rolling back processes and recovering from system failures, especially in high-performance computing (HPC) and long-running applications. Checkpointing involves saving the current state of a process periodically, creating checkpoints that represent stable points in the execution. In the event of a failure, the system can roll back the process to the most recent checkpoint, minimizing the amount of work that needs to be redone. Checkpointing strategies can be either process-level, where individual processes save their state, or system-level, where the entire system's state is saved. Checkpointing introduces a trade-off between the frequency of checkpoints and the overhead of saving and restoring states, with more frequent checkpoints reducing potential data loss but increasing the computational overhead.

Rollback and recovery mechanisms extend beyond individual processes to encompass entire systems and applications. In the realm of operating systems, where stability is paramount, techniques like system restore points or snapshots enable users to roll back the entire system to a previous state. System restore points capture the system's configuration and state at specific moments, allowing users to revert the system to a state where it was functioning correctly. Virtualization technologies, such as hypervisors, leverage snapshotting to capture the state of virtual machines at a given point in time. These snapshots enable administrators to roll back virtual machines to a known-good state in the event of failures or system errors, providing a powerful tool for system recovery.

In cloud computing environments, where the distributed nature and scale of infrastructure present unique challenges, rollback techniques are fundamental for ensuring continuous operations. Cloud providers offer services like AWS Elastic Beanstalk or Kubernetes, which facilitate the deployment and management of applications. These services often integrate rolling back capabilities, allowing users to revert to a previous version or configuration of their applications in case of issues introduced by updates or changes. Additionally, cloud-based databases often provide point-in-time recovery features, enabling users to roll back the database to a specific timestamp, mitigating the impact of data corruption or erroneous updates.

In microservices architectures, where applications are composed of small, independent services, rollback techniques are essential for maintaining system stability and reliability. Canary deployments, a strategy where a new version of a service is gradually rolled out to a subset of users, provide a controlled environment for monitoring the impact of changes. If issues or failures are detected, the deployment can be rolled back before affecting the entire user base. Feature toggles or feature flags are employed to enable or disable specific features within a service dynamically. In the event of a failure or unexpected behavior, features can be toggled off to revert to a stable state, minimizing the impact on users.

The orchestration and management of containerized applications, facilitated by platforms like Docker and Kubernetes, introduce additional considerations for rolling back processes. Container orchestration tools often provide versioning and rollback features, allowing users to deploy specific versions of containerized applications and roll back to previous versions if issues arise. Kubernetes, for example, supports rolling updates and rollbacks, enabling users to update or revert the deployment of applications seamlessly. Container images, encapsulating the application and its dependencies, contribute to a consistent and reproducible environment, simplifying the rollback process by reverting to a known image state.

Real-time systems, particularly those in safety-critical domains such as avionics or healthcare, demand advanced rollback techniques to ensure continuous and predictable operation. In these environments, where failures can have severe consequences, techniques such as triple modular redundancy (TMR) are employed. TMR involves triplicating critical components and comparing their outputs in real-time. If a discrepancy or failure is detected, the system can roll back to the majority-voted correct output, maintaining system integrity and preventing errors from propagating.

Recovery strategies after a rollback play a crucial role in resuming normal operations and preventing the recurrence of failures. Redundancy, as seen in the use of backup systems and data replication, contributes to recovery by providing alternative resources or configurations. Automated error recovery mechanisms, often integrated into system monitoring tools, can identify the cause of a failure, initiate the rollback process, and apply corrective actions to restore normal operations. Additionally, logging and auditing mechanisms capture information about the events leading to a failure, facilitating postmortem analysis and helping administrators understand the root cause of the issue.

In conclusion, techniques for rolling back processes and recovering from system failures are integral components of the resilience and reliability of computing systems across diverse domains. From databases and distributed computing to virtualization, cloud environments, and microservices architectures, the ability to rollback processes ensures that unexpected events or errors do not compromise the integrity or availability of systems. The choice of rollback techniques depends on the specific requirements of applications and the criticality of the systems in which they operate. As computing environments continue to evolve, the refinement and adaptation of rollback strategies remain crucial for maintaining the stability and functionality of modern computing systems.

Importance of maintaining error logs for diagnostic purposes.

The importance of maintaining error logs for diagnostic purposes is a fundamental aspect of effective system administration, software development, and overall information technology management. Error logs serve as invaluable repositories of information, capturing details about unexpected events, anomalies, or faults that occur within a system or application. These logs play a multifaceted role in enhancing the diagnostic capabilities of IT professionals, offering insights into the root causes of issues, facilitating troubleshooting processes, and contributing to the overall reliability and performance of computing systems.

In the realm of system administration, error logs provide a real-time and historical record of system activities, enabling administrators to monitor the health and status of servers, networks, and applications. By diligently recording errors, warnings, and informational messages, these logs become a dynamic tool for proactively identifying and addressing potential issues before they escalate. System administrators leverage error logs to track resource utilization, identify performance bottlenecks, and detect patterns indicative of impending failures. Regularly reviewing error logs empowers administrators to make informed decisions about system maintenance, upgrades, or optimizations, ensuring the continuous and optimal operation of IT infrastructure.

In software development, error logs are indispensable tools for diagnosing and rectifying issues during the development life cycle and post-deployment phases. When applications encounter errors or unexpected behaviors, detailed error logs provide developers with contextual information, including stack traces, error codes, and time-stamps. This wealth of information significantly accelerates the debugging process, allowing developers to pinpoint the exact location and nature of errors. Moreover, error logs aid in reproducing and testing reported issues, providing a solid foundation for implementing effective solutions. By maintaining comprehensive error logs, software development teams foster a culture of accountability and transparency, facilitating collaboration and knowledge transfer among team members.

Diagnostic purposes extend beyond routine troubleshooting, making error logs a critical component in incident response and security analysis. In the context of cybersecurity, error logs serve as a valuable source of information for detecting and investigating security incidents. Unusual or suspicious patterns, anomalies, or unauthorized access attempts are often revealed in error logs, enabling security professionals to identify potential threats and implement timely countermeasures. By analyzing error logs, security teams can trace the steps of malicious activities, understand attack vectors, and fortify defenses against recurring threats. This proactive use of error logs is instrumental in maintaining the integrity and confidentiality of sensitive data, safeguarding organizations from cyber threats.

Furthermore, error logs play a pivotal role in meeting compliance and auditing requirements across various industries. Regulatory standards, such as the Health Insurance Portability and Accountability Act (HIPAA) in healthcare or the Payment Card Industry Data Security Standard (PCI DSS) in finance, often mandate the logging and monitoring of system activities. Error logs serve as crucial documentation, providing evidence of compliance with data protection and security regulations. In the event of an audit or investigation, organizations can rely on error logs to demonstrate adherence to industry-specific standards, showcase due diligence in protecting sensitive information, and facilitate the resolution of any non-compliance issues.

The diagnostic significance of error logs becomes even more apparent in complex and distributed computing environments, including cloud infrastructures and microservices architectures. In these environments, where numerous interconnected components collaborate to deliver services, the potential for errors and failures increases exponentially. Error logs act as a unified source of truth, aggregating information from various components and services. They enable DevOps teams to gain a holistic view of system behavior, troubleshoot issues across distributed systems, and orchestrate seamless incident response. By centralizing error logs, organizations enhance their ability to monitor, diagnose, and optimize the performance of intricate computing ecosystems.

In the context of web applications and e-commerce platforms, maintaining error logs is paramount for delivering a positive user experience. Errors affecting user interactions, such as failed transactions, page load errors, or authentication issues, are logged to provide developers and support teams with immediate visibility into user-reported problems. Error logs become an integral part of customer support workflows, guiding support personnel in diagnosing user-reported issues, reproducing errors, and swiftly implementing resolutions. This proactive approach not only minimizes the impact on users but also fosters customer trust by demonstrating a commitment to addressing and resolving issues in a timely manner.

In the healthcare sector, where the reliability and accuracy of medical information systems are critical, error logs play a vital role in ensuring patient safety and regulatory compliance. Electronic health record (EHR) systems, diagnostic equipment, and communication platforms generate extensive error logs that capture events ranging from system errors to user access attempts. Healthcare organizations leverage error logs to monitor the integrity of patient data, detect anomalies in medical device communications, and ensure compliance with privacy regulations. The ability to trace and diagnose errors in healthcare systems directly contributes to the quality of patient care, clinical decision-making, and the overall effectiveness of healthcare IT infrastructure.

Educational institutions and e-learning platforms also recognize the importance of error logs in maintaining the functionality and accessibility of online learning environments. In virtual classrooms and learning management systems, error logs provide administrators and educators with insights into issues such as user authentication failures, content delivery errors, or platform downtime. These logs empower educational institutions to swiftly address technical glitches, optimize the user experience, and ensure uninterrupted access to educational resources. By leveraging error logs, educational organizations enhance the reliability of digital learning ecosystems, enabling students and educators to focus on the learning experience without disruptions.

The efficient utilization of error logs is closely tied to the implementation of effective log management practices. Log management solutions aggregate, analyze, and visualize error logs, offering centralized visibility into system behavior and performance. These solutions provide search and filtering capabilities, allowing administrators, developers, and security professionals to extract relevant information quickly. Additionally, log management tools often support alerting mechanisms, enabling real-time notification of critical events or patterns, further enhancing the proactive use of error logs for diagnostics.

Despite the undeniable advantages of error logs, organizations must also address challenges associated with log volume, storage, and privacy considerations. High-volume environments generate vast amounts of log data, requiring scalable log management solutions and storage infrastructure. Retention policies must balance the need for historical log data with storage costs and compliance requirements. Moreover, organizations must implement robust security measures to protect sensitive information contained in error logs, ensuring that privacy and confidentiality standards are upheld.

In conclusion, the importance of maintaining error logs for diagnostic purposes permeates virtually every facet of information technology, from system administration and software development to cybersecurity, compliance, and user support. Error logs serve as the eyes and ears of computing systems, capturing the nuances of system behavior, revealing anomalies, and guiding IT professionals in diagnosing and resolving issues. Whether in traditional data centers, cloud environments, or complex distributed architectures, the conscientious use of error logs contributes to the resilience, reliability, and security of computing ecosystems. As organizations continue to navigate the complexities of modern IT landscapes, error logs remain indispensable tools for fortifying their ability to monitor, diagnose, and optimize system performance.

Methods for predicting potential errors before they occur.

Methods for predicting potential errors before they occur constitute a proactive approach to ensuring the reliability, stability, and optimal performance of systems and applications. Anticipating and addressing potential errors before they manifest is essential in preventing service disruptions, minimizing downtime, and enhancing overall user experience. This predictive approach leverages a combination of techniques, including proactive monitoring, anomaly detection, statistical analysis, machine learning, and comprehensive testing methodologies.

Proactive monitoring plays a foundational role in predicting potential errors by continuously observing system metrics, performance indicators, and resource utilization. Through the use of monitoring tools and instrumentation, administrators gain real-time insights into the health and behavior of servers, networks, and applications.

Anomalies in system behavior, such as sudden spikes in resource usage or deviations from expected patterns, can be indicative of underlying issues that may lead to errors. By establishing baseline performance metrics and thresholds, administrators can configure monitoring systems to trigger alerts when deviations occur, allowing them to investigate and address potential problems before they impact users.

Anomaly detection, often integrated into proactive monitoring solutions, involves the identification of abnormal patterns or behaviors that may precede errors. Machine learning algorithms, statistical models, and pattern recognition techniques contribute to the automated detection of anomalies in large datasets. These algorithms learn from historical data, establishing normal behavior and identifying deviations that may signal impending issues. Anomaly detection extends beyond simple threshold-based alerts, providing a sophisticated means of predicting potential errors based on complex relationships and patterns within the monitored environment.

Statistical analysis complements proactive monitoring and anomaly detection by applying mathematical models to historical data, enabling the identification of trends, patterns, and correlations. Time-series analysis, regression models, and correlation analysis help uncover relationships between different variables and provide a quantitative understanding of system behavior. By identifying statistical anomalies or trends that may indicate an increased likelihood of errors, administrators can take preemptive actions, such as adjusting system configurations, optimizing resource allocation, or deploying additional infrastructure to mitigate potential issues.

Machine learning algorithms play a pivotal role in predicting potential errors by leveraging the power of artificial intelligence to analyze vast amounts of data and identify complex patterns. Supervised learning models, trained on labeled datasets containing examples of normal and erroneous behavior, can classify new data instances and predict the likelihood of errors based on learned patterns. Unsupervised learning techniques, such as clustering or dimensionality reduction, enable the discovery of hidden structures within data, aiding in the identification of outliers or unusual patterns that may precede errors. The application of machine learning for predictive analytics empowers organizations to move beyond reactive approaches, fostering a proactive stance in managing system reliability and performance.

Comprehensive testing methodologies contribute to error prediction by systematically evaluating the robustness and resilience of software applications and systems under various conditions. This includes unit testing, integration testing, system testing, and performance testing. By simulating real-world scenarios and subjecting applications to varying workloads, organizations can uncover potential vulnerabilities, bottlenecks, or code defects that may lead to errors in production. Load testing, stress testing, and scalability testing are particularly crucial for identifying performance limitations and predicting how the system will behave under heavy usage or adverse conditions. Addressing issues uncovered during testing phases enables organizations to preemptively resolve potential errors before they impact end-users.

The concept of chaos engineering introduces a proactive approach to predicting potential errors by deliberately introducing controlled chaos into a system to uncover weaknesses and vulnerabilities. Chaos experiments involve injecting faults, disruptions, or unexpected conditions into a running system to observe how it responds. By simulating real-world failures, organizations gain insights into the system's resiliency and can identify potential weak points that might lead to errors in production. The chaos engineering approach aligns with the philosophy that systems should be designed not just to function under normal conditions but to gracefully handle unexpected and challenging scenarios, ultimately enhancing the system's predictability and reliability.

In the realm of cybersecurity, threat intelligence and proactive vulnerability assessments contribute to predicting potential errors related to security breaches and data compromises. Continuous monitoring of emerging threats, vulnerabilities, and attack vectors allows security professionals to anticipate and address potential security incidents before they occur. Penetration testing and ethical hacking methodologies simulate cyber-attacks to identify vulnerabilities and weaknesses in a system's defenses. Predicting potential errors in the form of security breaches involves staying ahead of evolving threats, promptly applying security patches, and implementing proactive security measures to fortify the overall resilience of information systems.

Predictive maintenance strategies, often applied in industrial settings, extend the concept of error prediction to physical systems and equipment. By leveraging sensor data, telemetry, and historical performance information, organizations can anticipate equipment failures and schedule maintenance activities proactively. Condition monitoring, predictive analytics, and machine learning models can predict when machinery or components are likely to experience issues, allowing organizations to replace or repair them before failures occur. This approach minimizes downtime, reduces operational costs, and enhances the reliability of critical infrastructure in sectors such as manufacturing, energy, and transportation.

In cloud computing environments, predictive scaling emerges as a technique for anticipating changes in workload and resource requirements. By analyzing historical usage patterns, seasonal trends, and application performance metrics, cloud service providers and administrators can predict when additional resources will be needed to accommodate increased demand. Proactively adjusting the number of virtual instances, scaling infrastructure horizontally or vertically, and optimizing resource allocation contribute to preventing performance degradation or outages that might result from inadequate capacity planning.

The adoption of predictive analytics in business intelligence extends the predictive capabilities beyond technical domains to strategic decision-making. Organizations leverage predictive models and data-driven insights to anticipate market trends, customer behaviors, and competitive dynamics. Predictive analytics empowers businesses to identify potential challenges, capitalize on emerging opportunities, and make informed decisions based on a proactive understanding of the factors that may impact performance and outcomes.

In conclusion, methods for predicting potential errors before they occur embody a proactive and strategic approach to managing the reliability, resilience, and performance of systems and applications. Through the integration of proactive monitoring, anomaly detection, statistical analysis, machine learning, comprehensive testing methodologies, chaos engineering, cybersecurity practices, and predictive maintenance, organizations can anticipate and address potential issues before they manifest in production environments. This proactive stance not only minimizes the impact of errors on end-users but also fosters a culture of continuous improvement and optimization across diverse domains of information technology and beyond. As technology evolves, the refinement and integration of these predictive methods remain crucial for organizations striving to stay ahead of challenges, mitigate risks, and deliver consistent and reliable services.

Analyzing historical instances where effective error handling and fault tolerance saved critical systems.

Analyzing historical instances where effective error handling and fault tolerance saved critical systems unveils a rich tapestry of real-world scenarios where resilient systems, designed with foresight and robust mechanisms, averted potential disasters and maintained operational continuity. One notable case is the story of the Mars Pathfinder mission in 1997. The Pathfinder spacecraft, tasked with landing the Sojourner rover on Mars, faced the challenges of entering the Martian atmosphere and executing a complex descent. The mission planners implemented a meticulous error handling and fault tolerance strategy. During the descent, the spacecraft's onboard computer detected an anomaly in the inertial measurement unit readings. The fault tolerance system, equipped with redundant sensors and control systems, autonomously corrected the discrepancy. This quick and automated response ensured the successful landing of the Pathfinder and the deployment of the Sojourner rover, marking a pivotal moment in space exploration.

In the realm of financial systems, the story of the Knight Capital Group in 2012 serves as a cautionary tale about the importance of effective error handling. Knight Capital, a prominent algorithmic trading firm, suffered a catastrophic system failure due to a faulty software update. The erroneous update triggered a flood of unintended orders, resulting in significant financial losses within a matter of minutes. However, the fault tolerance mechanisms of the broader financial ecosystem played a crucial role in mitigating the impact. Stock exchanges swiftly identified the abnormal trading activity, halted Knight Capital's trades, and rolled back the erroneous transactions. The incident underscored the significance of robust error handling practices in high-frequency trading environments and prompted industry-wide reassessments of risk management protocols.

In the aviation sector, the Gimli Glider incident of 1983 stands out as a testament to effective error handling and fault tolerance in the face of unexpected challenges. Air Canada Flight 143, a Boeing 767, experienced a fuel miscalculation that resulted in both engines losing power at 41,000 feet. The flight crew, guided by Captain Robert Pearson and First Officer Maurice Quintal, navigated the powerless aircraft using their airmanship skills. The fault tolerance of the aircraft's avionics systems allowed for a limited restoration of power, enabling the crew to execute a successful emergency landing in Gimli, Manitoba. The incident showcased the importance of human-machine collaboration and the resilience of aviation systems in the presence of unforeseen errors.

The healthcare industry has witnessed instances where effective error handling and fault tolerance played a crucial role in preserving patient safety. In 1985, the Therac-25 medical accelerator, designed for radiation therapy, experienced a series of catastrophic failures due to software-related errors. These errors led to patients receiving massive overdoses of radiation, resulting in injuries and fatalities. The incident prompted a reevaluation of safety practices in medical device development. Subsequent advancements in error handling and fault tolerance, along with rigorous testing and regulatory measures, have contributed to the development of safer medical technologies, emphasizing the critical role of resilience in healthcare systems.

The resilience of communication networks was put to the test during the Internet worm incident of 1988. Designed by Robert Tappan Morris, the worm was intended to gauge the size of the internet but ended up causing widespread disruptions. The incident demonstrated the importance of fault tolerance in the early internet architecture. While the worm exploited vulnerabilities in Unix systems, the distributed and decentralized nature of the internet allowed unaffected portions to continue operating. This incident prompted the development of better security practices and the recognition of the need for fault tolerance in networked systems, contributing to the evolution of internet infrastructure.

In the context of e-commerce and online services, Amazon's experience on Christmas Eve in 2012 provides insights into the significance of robust error handling mechanisms. An influx of traffic and last-minute shoppers overwhelmed Amazon's cloud services, leading to widespread service outages. However, the fault tolerance built into Amazon's infrastructure allowed the system to recover gradually. Automated error handling mechanisms identified bottlenecks, rerouted traffic, and scaled resources dynamically to accommodate the surge in demand. This incident highlighted the importance of anticipating peak loads, implementing redundancy, and prioritizing fault tolerance to ensure continuous service delivery during critical periods.

The Fukushima Daiichi nuclear disaster in 2011 exemplifies the importance of error handling and fault tolerance in critical infrastructure. Following a massive earthquake and tsunami, the Fukushima nuclear power plant faced a series of failures, including the loss of power, cooling system malfunctions, and subsequent meltdowns. The plant's design incorporated multiple layers of fault tolerance, such as backup generators and emergency cooling systems. While the disaster exposed shortcomings in the overall safety design, the presence of fault-tolerant features played a role in mitigating the extent of the catastrophe. This incident underscored the critical need for continuous improvement in safety engineering and disaster preparedness for complex systems.

In the realm of transportation, the safe landing of US Airways Flight 1549 on the Hudson River in 2009 serves as a remarkable example of effective error handling and fault tolerance. After both engines suffered bird strikes and lost power shortly after takeoff, Captain Chesley "Sully" Sullenberger and First Officer Jeffrey Skiles successfully executed an emergency landing on the river. The fault tolerance of the Airbus A320's systems, coupled with the skill and experience of the flight crew, played a pivotal role in the successful outcome. The incident showcased the importance of human factors, training, and resilient aircraft systems in averting disaster during critical moments.

In the domain of power systems, the Northeast blackout of 2003 illustrates the cascading impact of errors and the importance of fault tolerance in preventing widespread disruptions. Triggered by a software bug in an energy management system, the blackout affected a vast region of North America. However, the fault tolerance of the power grid prevented a complete and prolonged blackout. Automatic error handling mechanisms isolated affected areas, rerouted power, and initiated recovery procedures. The incident led to significant improvements in the reliability and monitoring of power systems, emphasizing the role of fault tolerance in ensuring the resilience of critical infrastructure.

The financial crisis of 2008 revealed the interconnectedness of global financial systems and highlighted the need for effective error handling and fault tolerance in the banking sector. The collapse of Lehman Brothers and subsequent turmoil exposed vulnerabilities in risk management, regulatory oversight, and financial instrument complexity. Central banks and regulatory bodies stepped in to stabilize the financial system, demonstrating a form of fault tolerance at the macroeconomic level. Subsequent reforms focused on enhancing transparency, stress testing, and error recovery mechanisms to fortify the financial system against future crises.

The Deepwater Horizon oil spill in 2010 showcased the importance of error handling and fault tolerance in preventing and responding to catastrophic failures in complex engineering systems. The blowout preventer, a critical safety device, failed to activate and contain the well, resulting in one of the largest environmental disasters in history. The incident highlighted the need for robust error detection, emergency shutdown mechanisms, and fail-safe designs in offshore drilling operations. Post-incident investigations underscored the importance of proactive risk management and fault tolerance in preventing systemic failures with far-reaching consequences.

In the dynamic field of space exploration, the Apollo 13 mission in 1970 exemplifies the effectiveness of error handling and fault tolerance in the face of unexpected challenges. After an oxygen tank explosion jeopardized the mission, the crew and ground control collaborated to overcome numerous obstacles. The fault tolerance of the spacecraft's systems allowed for creative problem-solving, improvised solutions, and successful mission re-entry. The incident underscored the importance of adaptability, teamwork, and resilient spacecraft design in ensuring the safety of astronauts during space missions.

The examples across diverse domains underscore the critical role of effective error handling and fault tolerance in preserving the functionality, safety, and reliability of critical systems. Whether in the realms of space exploration, finance, healthcare, transportation, or energy, these instances demonstrate that anticipating and mitigating errors is paramount for preventing catastrophic failures. These historical narratives serve as valuable lessons, emphasizing the ongoing need for robust engineering, proactive risk management, and continuous improvement in the face of evolving challenges in complex systems.

Chapter 8: Future Trends in Operating System Process Management

S etting the stage for exploring emerging trends in operating system process management.

Setting the stage for exploring emerging trends in operating system process management requires a comprehensive understanding of the historical evolution and the foundational principles that have shaped the landscape of process management within operating systems. Since the inception of computing, operating systems have played a central role in coordinating and optimizing the execution of processes. Early systems, like the batch processing systems of the 1950s, focused on efficiently running a sequence of predefined jobs without user interaction. The evolution continued with the advent of time-sharing systems, introducing the concept of multiple users sharing the same computing resources concurrently. The evolution of process management mirrored the broader trends in computing, responding to the increasing demand for efficiency, responsiveness, and resource utilization.

As computing technologies progressed, so did the intricacy of applications and the diversity of computing platforms. The emergence of distributed systems, client-server architectures, and the transition to the internet era marked significant shifts in the operating environment. These changes necessitated a reevaluation of process management strategies to accommodate the challenges of parallelism, scalability, and resource sharing across networked environments. The client-server model, prevalent in the late 20th century, introduced new considerations for managing processes across different tiers of a distributed system. Operating systems had to adapt to facilitate communication and coordination between client and server processes, often relying on inter-process communication (IPC) mechanisms to enable seamless collaboration.

The rise of personal computing in the 1980s and 1990s brought a shift toward graphical user interfaces (GUIs) and the demand for more interactive and user-friendly systems. Operating systems like Microsoft Windows and Apple's macOS became dominant players, introducing a new paradigm for process management. Graphical interfaces allowed users to interact with processes visually, launching applications, managing files, and multitasking with greater ease. The operating system had to evolve to handle the complexities of managing a multitude of graphical processes while providing a responsive and intuitive user experience. This era witnessed innovations in process scheduling algorithms, memory management, and user interface design, setting the stage for a user-centric approach to process management.

The turn of the century brought about the proliferation of mobile computing and the advent of smartphones, leading to yet another transformation in operating system process management. Mobile operating systems, such as Android and iOS, had to address the unique challenges posed by resource-constrained devices, diverse hardware architectures, and the need for energy-efficient operation. Process management in mobile environments emphasized power efficiency, responsiveness, and seamless task switching to accommodate the on-the-go nature of mobile usage. Additionally, the introduction of app stores and the sandboxing of applications for security and stability necessitated a rethinking of how processes were isolated and managed within the operating system.

In recent years, the landscape of computing has witnessed the ascendance of cloud computing, edge computing, and the proliferation of Internet of Things (IoT) devices. These trends have ushered in a new era for operating system process management, characterized by the need for dynamic scalability, resource orchestration, and efficient handling of distributed workloads. Cloud-based operating systems, exemplified by platforms like Amazon Web Services (AWS) and Microsoft Azure, prioritize the efficient allocation and de-allocation of resources in response to changing demand. Edge computing environments, which bring computational capabilities closer to the data source, require operating systems to manage processes in a decentralized and geographically distributed fashion, optimizing for low latency and high availability.

The increasing prevalence of containerization and container orchestration tools, such as Docker and Kubernetes, represents a significant shift in how processes are managed within modern operating systems. Containers encapsulate applications and their dependencies, providing a lightweight and consistent environment across different infrastructure. Container orchestration platforms enable the efficient deployment, scaling, and management of containerized applications, fostering a more agile and scalable approach to process management. Operating systems are adapting to support container runtimes, integrate with orchestration platforms, and provide the necessary isolation and resource allocation mechanisms to ensure the effective coexistence of containerized processes.

The advent of serverless computing introduces another layer of abstraction in process management, shifting the focus from managing traditional long-running processes to handling ephemeral and event-triggered functions. Serverless platforms, such as AWS Lambda and Azure Functions, abstract away the underlying infrastructure, allowing developers to focus on writing functions that respond to specific events. Operating systems in serverless environments must efficiently instantiate, execute, and scale functions in a stateless manner, redefining the traditional notions of persistent processes and resource management.

Artificial intelligence (AI) and machine learning (ML) are also influencing the landscape of operating system process management. The integration of AI into operating systems can enhance process scheduling, resource allocation, and predictive maintenance. AI-driven algorithms can learn from historical patterns, user behaviors, and system dynamics to make intelligent decisions in real-time, optimizing the performance and efficiency of process management. Moreover, the advent of edge AI, where AI models are deployed directly on edge devices, necessitates operating systems to manage the execution of AI workloads while considering resource constraints and latency requirements.

Security considerations play an increasingly critical role in shaping the future of process management within operating systems. With the growing sophistication of cyber threats, operating systems must implement robust mechanisms for isolating processes, ensuring data privacy, and preventing unauthorized access. The rise of hardware-based security features, such as Trusted Execution Environments (TEEs) and secure enclaves, introduces new possibilities for enhancing the security of processes. Operating systems are incorporating these features to provide a trusted execution environment where sensitive processes can run securely, shielded from potential attacks.

Looking ahead, the exploration of emerging trends in operating system process management will continue to be influenced by the evolving landscape of computing. Quantum computing, with its potential to revolutionize processing power, poses challenges and opportunities for rethinking process management at a fundamental level. As quantum computing matures, operating systems will need to adapt to harness the unique capabilities of quantum processors while maintaining compatibility with classical computing architectures. Quantum-safe algorithms, quantum process scheduling, and the integration of quantum and classical computing are areas that will shape the future of process management in quantum computing environments.

In conclusion, exploring emerging trends in operating system process management necessitates a holistic perspective that spans the historical evolution of computing paradigms to the current state of diverse and distributed computing environments. The challenges and opportunities presented by mobile computing, cloud computing, containerization, serverless computing, AI, edge computing, security considerations, and the potential impact of quantum computing collectively shape the trajectory of how operating systems manage processes. As technology continues to advance, operating systems will play a pivotal role in orchestrating and optimizing the execution of processes, ensuring efficiency, security, and adaptability in an ever-changing computing landscape.

Examining the role of AI in optimizing process management.

Examining the role of Artificial Intelligence (AI) in optimizing process management unveils a transformative paradigm where intelligent algorithms and machine learning techniques revolutionize the way computing systems orchestrate and streamline workflows. At the core of this evolution lies the fusion of AI capabilities with traditional process management principles, creating a symbiotic relationship that enhances efficiency, adaptability, and responsiveness across diverse domains. One pivotal aspect is the application of AI in process scheduling, where dynamic and adaptive algorithms leverage predictive analytics to allocate resources efficiently. Traditional scheduling mechanisms, based on static rules or priorities, are eclipsed by AI-driven schedulers that analyze historical patterns, workload fluctuations, and system dynamics to make real-time decisions. This AI-driven approach enables systems to optimize task execution, minimize latency, and adapt to changing workloads, leading to enhanced overall system performance.

Furthermore, AI plays a crucial role in resource allocation, a cornerstone of effective process management. Through machine learning models and algorithms, systems can learn from historical usage patterns and dynamically allocate resources based on real-time demands. This adaptability ensures that processes receive the necessary computing resources to execute efficiently, avoiding bottlenecks and optimizing overall resource utilization. AI-driven resource allocation is particularly valuable in cloud computing environments, where the demand for resources fluctuates dynamically. The ability to predict resource needs and scale infrastructure accordingly contributes to cost efficiency, scalability, and the seamless operation of applications, marking a departure from static resource allocation strategies.

In the realm of adaptive load balancing, AI demonstrates its prowess in enhancing process management. Traditional load balancing mechanisms often rely on predefined rules or heuristics, but AI introduces a level of intelligence that enables systems to dynamically distribute workloads based on current conditions and predicted trends. Machine learning algorithms can analyze performance metrics, user behaviors, and system health to make informed decisions about load distribution, preventing overloading of specific nodes and optimizing response times. This dynamic load balancing approach ensures that computing resources are distributed efficiently, leading to improved system stability and the ability to handle varying levels of demand.

Moreover, AI contributes significantly to fault tolerance and error handling within process management. Machine learning algorithms can be trained to recognize patterns indicative of potential failures or anomalies in system behavior. By continuously monitoring and analyzing system metrics, AI-driven error detection mechanisms can identify irregularities that may precede failures. This proactive approach to fault tolerance allows systems to take corrective actions or initiate graceful degradation before errors escalate, thereby minimizing downtime and improving the overall reliability of the process management infrastructure.

In the context of process optimization, AI-powered predictive analytics emerges as a game-changer. By leveraging historical data, AI models can forecast future trends, anticipate peak workloads, and predict potential performance bottlenecks. This predictive capability enables proactive decision-making in process management, allowing systems to preemptively allocate resources, adjust scheduling priorities, and optimize configurations to meet anticipated demands. Predictive analytics also empowers administrators to plan for system upgrades, maintenance, or scaling based on data-driven insights, contributing to a more efficient and resilient computing environment.

Furthermore, the integration of AI into process management extends its impact to user-centric experiences. AI-driven personalization and adaptive user interfaces tailor the computing experience based on individual behaviors, preferences, and usage patterns. In the context of process management, this means that the operating system can intelligently adapt to user needs, optimize task prioritization, and predict user intentions. For instance, AI can anticipate commonly used applications, automate routine tasks, and dynamically adjust system settings to align with user preferences. This user-centric approach enhances productivity, streamlines workflows, and contributes to an overall smoother and more efficient computing experience.

In the domain of distributed systems, AI-driven coordination and communication mechanisms elevate the efficiency of process management across interconnected nodes. Decentralized AI algorithms facilitate autonomous decision-making at the edge, reducing the need for centralized control and minimizing communication overhead. This decentralized approach is particularly relevant in edge computing environments, where AI models can be deployed on edge devices to make local decisions based on real-time data. As a result, process management becomes more responsive, adaptable, and capable of handling distributed workloads with minimal latency.

Furthermore, the application of AI in process management extends to the domain of self-healing systems. AI-driven automation can detect and respond to anomalies, errors, or performance degradations autonomously. Self-healing mechanisms leverage machine learning to identify patterns associated with system failures, enabling automated remediation actions. This capability contributes to the overall resilience of the system, reducing the need for manual intervention in the face of common issues. The self-healing paradigm aligns with the broader trend of autonomous computing, where systems can adapt, optimize, and recover from adverse conditions without external intervention.

In the era of containerization and microservices architectures, AI plays a pivotal role in optimizing the deployment and scaling of containerized processes. Container orchestration platforms, such as Kubernetes, leverage AI-driven algorithms for efficient workload distribution, auto-scaling, and intelligent placement of containers. Machine learning models analyze historical performance data, predict future resource needs, and dynamically adjust the deployment of containers across clusters. This AI-driven orchestration ensures that containerized processes operate optimally, maximizing resource utilization and responsiveness in dynamic and rapidly changing environments.

Additionally, AI-driven cybersecurity measures have a direct impact on process management by enhancing security protocols, threat detection, and anomaly identification. Machine learning algorithms can analyze network traffic, system logs, and user behaviors to detect patterns indicative of potential security threats. By integrating AI-driven security measures into the fabric of process management, systems can respond proactively to security incidents, isolate compromised processes, and dynamically adjust access controls. This adaptive cybersecurity approach aligns with the evolving threat landscape, providing a more resilient defense against malicious activities that may target processes within the operating system.

The emergence of AI-driven edge computing introduces a novel dimension to process management, especially in scenarios where low-latency processing is crucial. Edge devices equipped with AI capabilities can locally process data, make intelligent decisions, and initiate actions without relying on centralized cloud resources. This distributed and AI-driven approach to process management is particularly relevant in applications such as real-time analytics, autonomous vehicles, and Industrial Internet of Things (IIoT) deployments. By pushing AI capabilities to the edge, process management becomes more responsive, scalable, and capable of meeting the stringent requirements of time-sensitive applications.

Looking ahead, the role of AI in optimizing process management is poised to continue evolving as new technologies, computing paradigms, and application domains emerge. Quantum computing introduces a new frontier where AI algorithms may harness the unique computational capabilities of quantum processors to solve complex optimization problems, further revolutionizing process management strategies. The fusion of AI with advancements in neuromorphic computing holds the potential to create intelligent systems that mimic human-like decision-making and adaptability. As AI-driven technologies continue to mature, the synergistic relationship between AI and process management will undoubtedly shape the future of computing, ushering in an era of intelligent, adaptive, and self-optimizing systems.

The influence of blockchain technology on distributed process management.

The influence of blockchain technology on distributed process management constitutes a revolutionary paradigm shift, reshaping how decentralized networks coordinate, validate, and secure processes across a multitude of participants. At its core, blockchain is a distributed ledger technology that enables the creation of tamper-resistant and transparent records of transactions, removing the need for a central authority and fostering trust among network participants. This foundational characteristic has profound implications for distributed process management, offering novel solutions to challenges related to transparency, security, and consensus in decentralized ecosystems.

One key aspect of blockchain's impact on distributed process management lies in its ability to provide a transparent and immutable record of transactions or events. In traditional distributed systems, establishing a single source of truth across multiple nodes can be challenging due to the absence of a centralized authority. Blockchain addresses this challenge by creating a decentralized and consensus-driven ledger that all participants can access and verify. This transparency ensures that all relevant parties within a distributed network share a common view of the processes and their chronological order, mitigating disputes and enabling a high degree of accountability.

Smart contracts, self-executing programs with predefined rules encoded on the blockchain, represent a pivotal advancement in the intersection of blockchain and distributed process management. These programmable contracts automate and enforce the execution of predefined rules and conditions without the need for intermediaries. In decentralized applications (dApps), smart contracts facilitate the coordination and execution of processes, ranging from financial transactions to complex business logic. This decentralized automation ensures that processes are executed transparently, autonomously, and with a high degree of reliability, as smart contracts operate based on predetermined and tamper-proof logic.

The consensus mechanisms inherent in blockchain contribute significantly to the reliability of distributed process management. Traditional distributed systems often rely on consensus algorithms to ensure agreement among nodes, but these mechanisms can face challenges related to trust and potential vulnerabilities. Blockchain introduces consensus mechanisms such as Proof of Work (PoW) and Proof of Stake (PoS), where participants reach agreement on the state of the blockchain through cryptographic processes. This consensus layer enhances the trustworthiness of distributed process management by providing a secure and decentralized method for validating transactions and ensuring the integrity of the shared ledger.

Blockchain technology's impact on data integrity and security is particularly noteworthy in the context of distributed process management. The use of cryptographic techniques, such as hashing and digital signatures, ensures the immutability of data recorded on the blockchain. Once a block is added to the chain, it becomes practically impossible to alter previous blocks, safeguarding the historical record of processes. This feature enhances the security and verifiability of distributed processes, reducing the risk of fraudulent activities and unauthorized alterations. In essence, blockchain acts as a secure and transparent layer for recording and verifying the outcomes of decentralized processes.

Decentralized Autonomous Organizations (DAOs), facilitated by blockchain, exemplify a novel approach to distributed process management where decision-making and governance are automated through smart contracts. DAOs operate on a consensus-driven model, allowing stakeholders to vote on proposals and collectively determine the direction of the organization. The transparent and auditable nature of blockchain ensures that decision-making processes within DAOs are open to scrutiny, promoting fairness and inclusivity. While DAOs have showcased the potential for decentralized governance, they also raise challenges related to security vulnerabilities and the need for resilient mechanisms to prevent exploitation.

The concept of tokenization, enabled by blockchain technology, introduces a novel incentive structure within distributed process management. Tokens represent digital assets on the blockchain, and their distribution can be tied to specific processes or contributions within a decentralized network. This tokenized incentive model aligns the interests of participants with the success of the network, fostering collaboration and innovation. In decentralized applications, tokens often serve as a means of accessing services, participating in governance, or even representing ownership rights. This token economy incentivizes users to contribute positively to the network, creating a dynamic and self-sustaining ecosystem.

Blockchain's impact on distributed process management extends beyond financial transactions, encompassing supply chain management as a prominent use case. The decentralized and transparent nature of blockchain facilitates the recording of every stage of the supply chain, from production to distribution. This transparency enhances traceability, reduces the risk of fraud, and ensures that stakeholders across the supply chain have access to accurate and real-time information. Smart contracts can automate various aspects of supply chain processes, such as triggering payments upon delivery or enforcing quality standards. This application of blockchain not only streamlines supply chain operations but also enhances overall trust and accountability in the global economy.

Interoperability and standardization are critical considerations in the realm of distributed process management, especially in environments where multiple blockchain networks coexist. The challenge lies in creating seamless communication and collaboration among diverse blockchains and their respective applications. Interoperability protocols, such as cross-chain communication standards and interoperability frameworks, aim to address this challenge by establishing common standards for data exchange and smart contract interactions. These initiatives are vital for creating a unified and interconnected ecosystem where processes can seamlessly traverse multiple blockchains, fostering a more inclusive and collaborative decentralized landscape.

Decentralized Identity (DID) solutions, enabled by blockchain, redefine how identity is managed and verified in distributed systems. Traditional identity management often relies on centralized authorities, raising concerns about privacy and security. Blockchain-based DID solutions empower individuals to control their own identities, reducing the reliance on centralized entities. By storing identity credentials on a blockchain and providing selective disclosure through zero-knowledge proofs, individuals can prove their identity without revealing unnecessary information. This decentralized approach to identity management enhances privacy, security, and user autonomy in the context of distributed processes.

Blockchain's impact on distributed process management is further exemplified in the context of decentralized finance (DeFi). DeFi platforms leverage blockchain technology to enable financial services, such as lending, borrowing, and trading, without the need for traditional intermediaries. Smart contracts govern the execution of financial processes, ensuring transparency, automation, and trust in a decentralized environment. DeFi has gained significant traction, showcasing the potential of blockchain to revolutionize traditional financial services and democratize access to global financial markets.

Challenges and considerations also accompany the integration of blockchain into distributed process management. Scalability remains a persistent challenge, particularly as blockchain networks strive to handle an increasing number of transactions and smart contract executions. High transaction fees and energy consumption, especially in Proof of Work blockchains, have prompted exploration of more sustainable consensus mechanisms. Additionally, regulatory considerations and the need for interoperability standards pose challenges to the widespread adoption of blockchain technology.

In conclusion, the influence of blockchain technology on distributed process management heralds a transformative era where decentralized networks operate with transparency, security, and autonomy. The tamper-resistant nature of blockchain, coupled with smart contracts, consensus mechanisms, and token economies, redefines how processes are coordinated, validated, and incentivized in decentralized ecosystems. From supply chain management to decentralized finance, the impact of blockchain is evident across diverse domains, shaping a future where distributed processes are not only efficient and secure but also inherently democratic and inclusive. As blockchain technology continues to evolve and address existing challenges, its role in optimizing distributed process management is likely to become increasingly integral to the fabric of the digital economy.

Evolving security measures to combat modern threats.

The evolving landscape of cybersecurity demands a dynamic and adaptive approach to security measures, as modern threats continue to outpace traditional defense mechanisms. In the digital age, where interconnected systems and ubiquitous connectivity prevail, the magnitude and sophistication of cyber threats pose significant challenges to the security of individuals, organizations, and nations. The paradigm shift from perimeter-based security to a more holistic and proactive cybersecurity strategy is evident in the multifaceted measures employed to combat these modern threats.

One of the fundamental shifts in cybersecurity is the recognition that a perimeter-centric approach is insufficient in the face of advanced and persistent threats. Traditional firewalls and antivirus solutions, while still essential components, are no longer the sole guardians of an organization's security. The rise of cloud computing, mobile devices, and remote work has expanded the attack surface, necessitating the adoption of a more comprehensive and adaptive security posture. Organizations now focus on a defense-in-depth strategy that involves layering security controls throughout the entire infrastructure, from endpoints to networks, and extending to cloud environments.

Endpoint security has evolved to address the increased sophistication of malware and ransomware attacks targeting individual devices. Traditional antivirus solutions have been augmented or replaced by advanced endpoint protection platforms that leverage machine learning, behavioral analysis, and threat intelligence to detect and respond to malicious activities in real-time. Endpoint detection and response (EDR) solutions play a crucial role in not only identifying threats but also providing the visibility and context needed for effective incident response. The integration of artificial intelligence and automation enhances the speed and accuracy of threat detection, enabling organizations to proactively defend against evolving threats.

The migration of infrastructure and services to the cloud has necessitated a paradigm shift in security measures. Cloud security focuses on protecting data, applications, and infrastructure in dynamic and scalable cloud environments. Cloud access security brokers (CASBs) have emerged as critical components, providing visibility into cloud usage, enforcing security policies, and protecting data as it moves between on-premises and cloud environments. Identity and access management (IAM) solutions are integral to cloud security, ensuring that only authorized users and devices can access cloud resources. As organizations embrace multi-cloud and hybrid cloud architectures, the need for cloud-native security solutions becomes paramount to ensure consistent protection across diverse environments.

The advent of DevOps practices, where development and operations teams collaborate closely to achieve continuous delivery, has led to the rise of DevSecOps. In this integrated approach, security is embedded into the development process from the outset rather than being treated as an afterthought. Automation plays a key role in DevSecOps, allowing security controls to be applied consistently and continuously throughout the software development lifecycle. Security-as-code practices enable the codification of security policies and configurations, ensuring that security is an integral part of the development pipeline. DevSecOps represents a cultural shift towards a more collaborative and proactive security mindset, aligning development and security objectives to deliver secure and resilient applications.

The proliferation of mobile devices in both personal and corporate contexts has introduced a new dimension of complexity to cybersecurity. Mobile security measures encompass not only the protection of the devices themselves but also the applications and data accessed from these devices. Mobile device management (MDM) and mobile application management (MAM) solutions enable organizations to enforce security policies, manage device configurations, and ensure the integrity of mobile applications. The concept of zero trust, which assumes that no user or device can be trusted by default, is increasingly applied to mobile security. Continuous authentication, device posture assessment, and mobile threat defense mechanisms contribute to a comprehensive mobile security strategy.

The interconnected nature of modern systems and the increasing reliance on third-party services have elevated the importance of supply chain security. Cyber adversaries recognize the potential vulnerabilities introduced through the supply chain and exploit them to infiltrate target organizations. Supply chain attacks, including software supply chain attacks and hardware compromises, have become prevalent and pose significant risks. Organizations are adopting measures such as supply chain risk assessments, vendor security evaluations, and the implementation of security controls at various stages of the supply chain. Enhanced due diligence and transparency in the supply chain are essential to identify and mitigate potential risks, ensuring the integrity and security of the products and services consumed.

Artificial intelligence (AI) and machine learning (ML) have become integral components in the evolution of security measures. Cybersecurity solutions leveraging AI and ML analyze vast amounts of data to identify patterns, detect anomalies, and predict potential threats. Behavioral analytics, powered by machine learning algorithms, enable the detection of abnormal user activities and deviations from established baselines. AI-driven threat intelligence platforms enhance the ability to correlate and contextualize threat data, providing security teams with actionable insights. Automation, facilitated by AI, is employed for tasks such as threat hunting, incident response, and the orchestration of security workflows, enabling organizations to respond rapidly to emerging threats.

As organizations embrace digital transformation and IoT (Internet of Things) technologies, the security of connected devices becomes paramount. The sheer proliferation of IoT devices, ranging from smart home devices to industrial sensors, introduces new attack vectors and challenges. Security measures for IoT encompass device authentication, encryption of communication, and the implementation of security-by-design principles. Network segmentation and monitoring are crucial to isolate and detect anomalous activities related to IoT devices. The integration of IoT security into broader cybersecurity frameworks ensures a holistic approach to protecting interconnected ecosystems.

Threat intelligence has evolved into a critical component of cybersecurity measures, providing organizations with timely and relevant information about potential threats and vulnerabilities. Open-source and commercial threat intelligence feeds aggregate data from various sources, including security researchers, government agencies, and industry collaborations. Threat intelligence platforms analyze and contextualize this data, enabling organizations to proactively defend against emerging threats. Threat hunting, a proactive and iterative search for threats within an organization's environment, leverages threat intelligence to identify and mitigate potential risks before they manifest into full-blown incidents.

The significance of user awareness and training in cybersecurity has grown exponentially, recognizing that human factors are often exploited in cyberattacks. Phishing attacks, social engineering, and credential compromises target users as the weakest link in the security chain. Security awareness programs educate users about common cyber threats, safe online practices, and the importance of reporting suspicious activities. Simulated phishing exercises help organizations assess the effectiveness of their training programs and identify areas for improvement. User-centric security measures aim to create a culture of cybersecurity awareness and responsibility, empowering individuals to contribute to the overall resilience of the organization.

Regulatory compliance has become a driving force in shaping cybersecurity measures, with various industries subject to specific regulations and standards. Compliance frameworks such as GDPR (General Data Protection Regulation), HIPAA (Health Insurance Portability and Accountability Act), and PCI DSS (Payment Card Industry Data Security Standard) mandate specific security controls to protect sensitive data and ensure privacy. Organizations are compelled to implement measures such as data encryption, access controls, and incident response plans to comply with regulatory requirements. The convergence of cybersecurity and compliance efforts facilitates a comprehensive approach to risk management, aligning security measures with legal and regulatory obligations.

The integration of threat detection and response capabilities has become a central focus in modern cybersecurity measures. Security information and event management (SIEM) solutions aggregate and analyze log data from various sources, enabling the detection of suspicious activities and security incidents. The evolution towards extended detection and response (XDR) platforms expands the scope beyond traditional SIEM, incorporating additional telemetry sources and facilitating a more holistic approach to threat detection. Automated response capabilities, such as threat containment and mitigation, enhance the speed and efficiency of incident response efforts. Threat intelligence feeds play a crucial role in enriching the context of detected threats, empowering security teams to make informed decisions in real-time.

The realization that cybersecurity is a continuous and evolving process has given rise to the concept of resilience. Cyber resilience encompasses the ability of an organization to anticipate, prepare for, respond to, and recover from cyber threats. It goes beyond traditional security measures to include incident response planning, business continuity, and disaster recovery. Cyber resilience acknowledges that security breaches are inevitable and focuses on minimizing the impact and downtime associated with security incidents. Regular assessments, tabletop exercises, and the integration of cyber resilience into overall risk management strategies ensure that organizations are well-prepared to navigate the evolving threat landscape.

In conclusion, the evolution of security measures to combat modern threats reflects the dynamic nature of the cybersecurity landscape. The integration of advanced technologies, proactive strategies, and a holistic approach to security underscores the need for adaptability and resilience. As cyber threats continue to evolve, organizations must remain vigilant, stay abreast of emerging technologies, and cultivate a culture of cybersecurity awareness. The synergy of people, processes, and technology is paramount in building robust defense mechanisms that can withstand the challenges posed by the ever-changing threat landscape.

Exploring the potential impact of quantum computing on process optimization.

Exploring the potential impact of quantum computing on process optimization unveils a transformative paradigm where the computational power of quantum systems has the potential to revolutionize how complex problems are solved and processes are optimized. Quantum computing harnesses the principles of quantum mechanics, leveraging qubits to exist in multiple states simultaneously, enabling parallel computations that traditional classical computers find challenging. One of the most anticipated applications of quantum computing lies in optimization problems, where finding the best solution among a vast number of possibilities is a computationally intensive task.

In the realm of process optimization, quantum computing holds the promise of solving complex optimization problems that classical computers struggle to address efficiently. Classical optimization algorithms, such as those based on gradient descent, become increasingly inefficient as the complexity of the problem grows. Quantum algorithms, on the other hand, exhibit an inherent advantage in exploring multiple solutions simultaneously, potentially leading to exponential speedup for certain optimization tasks. Quantum algorithms like the Quantum Approximate Optimization Algorithm (QAOA) and the Quantum Annealing Optimization Algorithm (QAOA) have been developed specifically to address optimization challenges across various domains.

One area where quantum computing is poised to make a significant impact on process optimization is in supply chain management. The optimization of supply chain processes involves intricate decisions related to inventory management, logistics, and resource allocation. Classical algorithms face challenges in handling the sheer complexity and combinatorial nature of these optimization problems. Quantum algorithms offer the potential to explore numerous combinations simultaneously, enabling faster and more efficient optimization of supply chain processes. This could lead to reduced costs, improved resource utilization, and enhanced overall efficiency in the management of supply chain networks.

Similarly, the field of logistics, which involves the efficient movement of goods and resources, stands to benefit from the quantum advantage in process optimization. Routing optimization, a fundamental challenge in logistics, involves determining the most efficient paths for vehicles, considering factors such as traffic conditions and delivery constraints. Quantum computing algorithms can explore multiple routing options simultaneously, providing the capability to find optimal solutions in a fraction of the time compared to classical methods. This quantum-driven efficiency in logistics optimization could lead to reduced transportation costs, minimized delivery times, and improved overall logistics performance.

In the financial sector, quantum computing holds the potential to revolutionize portfolio optimization, a complex problem involving the allocation of assets to achieve desired investment objectives while managing risk. Traditional portfolio optimization algorithms face limitations in handling the vast number of possible asset combinations and their associated risk-return profiles. Quantum algorithms, such as Variational Quantum Eigensolver (VQE) and Quantum Approximate Optimization Algorithm (QAOA), offer the capability to explore the solution space exponentially faster, allowing for more sophisticated and accurate portfolio optimization. This quantum-driven enhancement could lead to more robust investment strategies, improved risk management, and better returns for investors.

Optimizing complex manufacturing processes represents another domain where quantum computing could have a transformative impact. Manufacturing involves intricate decisions related to production schedules, resource allocation, and quality control. Classical optimization algorithms may struggle to find optimal solutions in real-time due to the sheer complexity of these processes. Quantum algorithms have the potential to address these challenges by exploring multiple optimization paths concurrently, offering a quantum advantage in optimizing manufacturing workflows. This quantum-driven efficiency could lead to improved production efficiency, reduced costs, and enhanced overall quality in manufacturing operations.

The energy sector, grappling with the optimization of power grid operations, is another domain where quantum computing could bring about significant advancements. Power grid optimization involves balancing supply and demand, managing grid stability, and minimizing energy losses. Classical optimization algorithms may face limitations in handling the complexity and dynamic nature of power grid operations. Quantum algorithms, equipped with the ability to explore numerous scenarios simultaneously, offer a promising avenue for more efficient power grid optimization. This quantum advantage could result in improved energy distribution, reduced environmental impact, and enhanced overall resilience of power grids.

Additionally, quantum computing's impact on process optimization extends to the realm of artificial intelligence (AI) and machine learning (ML). Training complex ML models involves optimizing numerous parameters to achieve accurate predictions. Classical optimization methods, while effective, can be computationally intensive and time-consuming. Quantum algorithms, such as Quantum Machine Learning (QML), have the potential to expedite the training process by exploring multiple parameter spaces simultaneously. This quantum-driven acceleration could lead to faster model training, enabling the development of more sophisticated and accurate AI and ML models across various applications.

Despite the immense potential, it's essential to acknowledge the challenges and considerations associated with the practical implementation of quantum computing for process optimization. Quantum computers are highly sensitive to environmental conditions and require extremely low temperatures to maintain qubit coherence. Furthermore, the current state of quantum hardware faces limitations in terms of error rates and scalability. Quantum error correction, a crucial component for building fault-tolerant quantum computers, is an ongoing area of research to address these challenges.

Another consideration is the need for quantum software development and algorithmic expertise. As quantum computers operate on fundamentally different principles than classical computers, the design and implementation of quantum algorithms require a specialized skill set. Quantum software development platforms and programming languages, such as Qiskit and Cirq, are emerging to facilitate the development of quantum applications. Bridging the gap between quantum hardware and algorithm development remains a critical aspect of realizing the full potential of quantum computing for process optimization.

Furthermore, the issue of quantum decoherence poses a challenge to the stability and reliability of quantum computations. Decoherence occurs when quantum states lose their coherence due to interactions with the external environment, leading to errors in quantum calculations. Mitigating decoherence and developing robust error-correction techniques are essential for harnessing the full potential of quantum computing in practical applications.

In conclusion, exploring the potential impact of quantum computing on process optimization reveals a promising frontier where quantum algorithms could provide unprecedented advantages in solving complex optimization problems across various domains. From supply chain management to logistics, finance, manufacturing, energy, and artificial intelligence, quantum computing has the potential to usher in a new era of efficiency, speed, and innovation. While challenges and considerations exist, ongoing advancements in quantum hardware, software, and algorithmic research indicate a trajectory towards unlocking the transformative power of quantum computing for optimizing intricate processes in ways previously deemed unattainable with classical computing paradigms. As the field continues to evolve, the integration of quantum computing into the optimization landscape holds the promise of reshaping industries and solving real-world challenges with unparalleled computational capabilities.

Strategies for designing energy-efficient operating systems.

Designing energy-efficient operating systems involves a multifaceted approach that encompasses various strategies addressing both hardware and software aspects. The quest for energy efficiency has gained prominence in response to the increasing demand for sustainability, coupled with the proliferation of battery-powered devices and the environmental impact of data centers. One fundamental strategy revolves around optimizing power management at the hardware level. This includes the development of low-power components, such as processors, memory modules, and peripherals, which consume less energy during operation. Advanced power gating techniques, dynamic voltage and frequency scaling (DVFS), and aggressive clock gating contribute to minimizing power consumption during periods of low activity, effectively aligning hardware performance with the demands of running applications.

At the heart of energy-efficient operating systems lies the importance of effective CPU scheduling. Schedulers play a crucial role in determining which processes or threads receive CPU time, influencing overall system power consumption. Dynamic Voltage and Frequency Scaling (DVFS) techniques come into play, allowing the operating system to dynamically adjust the CPU's voltage and clock frequency based on workload demands. By scaling down the CPU during periods of low activity, energy consumption is reduced, and battery life is extended in mobile devices. Implementing intelligent scheduling policies that consider workload characteristics and prioritize energy-efficient execution paths further enhances the efficiency of CPU usage.

In the context of energy efficiency, efficient memory management is a critical consideration. Memory hierarchy optimization, including the use of low-power RAM and intelligent caching strategies, contributes to reducing energy consumption. Operating systems can employ techniques such as memory compression and selective page swapping to minimize data movement between RAM and storage devices, thereby conserving energy. Additionally, optimizing algorithms for memory allocation and deallocation reduces unnecessary data movements and access, leading to lower power consumption. Effective memory management not only impacts energy efficiency but also contributes to improved overall system performance.

Another pivotal aspect of energy-efficient operating systems is the management of I/O devices. Techniques such as Device Power Management (DPM) enable the operating system to selectively power down or scale back the activity of I/O devices during periods of inactivity. By intelligently managing the power states of devices like network interfaces, storage devices, and peripherals, the operating system contributes to significant energy savings. Additionally, asynchronous I/O operations and batch processing of tasks enable the aggregation of device activities, reducing the frequency of device wake-ups and transitions between power states.

The incorporation of advanced power-aware algorithms and policies within the operating system's kernel is essential for achieving energy efficiency. Operating systems can utilize predictive models and heuristics to anticipate future workload patterns and adapt power management strategies accordingly. Machine learning techniques can be employed to analyze historical usage patterns and optimize power states dynamically. Moreover, the design of energy-aware scheduling policies, which consider the power consumption characteristics of different hardware components, contributes to a more fine-grained and responsive approach to power management.

The integration of energy-awareness into the file system is a crucial element of energy-efficient operating systems. File systems can leverage techniques such as delayed disk flushing and intelligent caching mechanisms to reduce the frequency of disk access and minimize power consumption. Furthermore, adopting energy-aware storage devices with low-power modes and optimizing data storage layouts can lead to more efficient use of storage resources. By aligning file system operations with power-efficient storage strategies, the operating system can contribute to overall energy savings in both desktop and server environments.

Virtualization technologies play a significant role in data centers and cloud computing environments, where optimizing energy consumption is a priority. Energy-efficient operating systems leverage techniques such as server consolidation, dynamic VM migration, and resource provisioning based on workload demand to achieve efficient utilization of hardware resources. Virtual machine (VM) management policies that consider both performance and energy efficiency contribute to maximizing the overall efficiency of data center operations. Additionally, advancements in containerization technologies offer lightweight and energy-efficient alternatives to traditional virtualization, further optimizing resource utilization.

Collaborative efforts between the operating system and application software are vital for achieving optimal energy efficiency. Application developers can adopt energy-efficient coding practices, such as minimizing unnecessary computations, optimizing data access patterns, and adopting concurrency models that align with energy-aware scheduling policies. At the same time, operating systems can provide programming interfaces and tools that enable developers to profile and optimize their applications for energy efficiency. Ensuring that applications gracefully handle power management events, such as CPU frequency changes and device power state transitions, contributes to a seamless integration of energy efficiency across the software stack.

Power-aware networking is a critical dimension of energy-efficient operating systems, particularly in the context of mobile devices and wireless communication. Wireless network interfaces consume a significant amount of energy, and optimizing their usage contributes to extended battery life. Operating systems can employ strategies such as adaptive transmission power control, intelligent network interface selection, and efficient data transfer protocols to minimize the energy consumption of network communications. Additionally, the integration of energy-efficient networking protocols and the ability to selectively power down networking components during idle periods further enhance overall energy efficiency.

Energy-efficient operating systems must also consider the impact of user interactions on system power consumption. User-centric power management involves dynamically adjusting system performance and power states based on user activity and preferences. Techniques such as adaptive screen brightness, intelligent keyboard backlight control, and fine-grained control over system sleep states contribute to a more responsive and energy-efficient user experience. Moreover, user-centric power management interfaces empower users to customize energy-saving settings based on their specific usage patterns and priorities, promoting a balance between energy efficiency and user satisfaction.

Security considerations are integral to energy-efficient operating systems, as certain security mechanisms can impact power consumption. For instance, advanced encryption algorithms used for securing data may introduce additional computational overhead and energy consumption. Energy-efficient operating systems must strike a balance between providing robust security measures and minimizing the impact on overall energy efficiency. Moreover, the integration of hardware-based security features, such as Trusted Platform Modules (TPMs) and secure enclaves, can enhance system security without compromising energy efficiency.

Ongoing research and development in the field of energy-efficient operating systems focus on emerging technologies and novel approaches to further optimize power management. The exploration of alternative computing architectures, such as neuromorphic and energy-efficient processors, presents new possibilities for achieving unprecedented levels of energy efficiency. Additionally, advancements in quantum computing may introduce unique opportunities for energy-efficient computation, although the practical implementation of quantum computing in operating systems remains a subject of ongoing exploration.

In conclusion, the design of energy-efficient operating systems encompasses a holistic and collaborative approach, addressing hardware and software components to optimize power consumption across diverse computing environments. From hardware-level power management to intelligent CPU scheduling, memory optimization, and I/O device management, each facet contributes to achieving energy efficiency. Collaboration between the operating system, applications, and user interactions further refines the energy-efficient design, offering a balance between power savings and system responsiveness. As technology continues to evolve, the pursuit of energy efficiency in operating systems remains a dynamic and critical endeavor, shaping the sustainability and performance of computing systems in a rapidly changing landscape.

The rise of edge computing and its implications for process management.

The rise of edge computing marks a transformative shift in the landscape of information technology, reshaping how data is processed, stored, and managed. Edge computing represents a departure from the traditional centralized cloud computing paradigm, bringing computational capabilities closer to the data source, often at the periphery or "edge" of the network. This distributed computing model holds profound implications for process management across various industries, introducing new opportunities and challenges that redefine the way organizations handle data, execute applications, and optimize workflows.

At the core of the shift towards edge computing is the recognition of the limitations of traditional cloud-centric approaches, especially in scenarios where low-latency, high-bandwidth, and real-time processing are paramount. In contrast to the latency introduced by sending data to distant cloud data centers, edge computing leverages localized processing power, enabling faster response times and improved performance for applications that require rapid decision-making. This proximity to data sources is particularly crucial in applications such as autonomous vehicles, industrial automation, and augmented reality, where split-second decisions can have significant consequences.

Edge computing's impact on process management is most prominently seen in the realm of data processing and analytics. By processing data closer to where it is generated, edge computing minimizes the need for extensive data transfers to centralized cloud servers. This not only reduces latency but also alleviates the strain on network bandwidth, making it more feasible to manage and analyze vast amounts of data in near real-time. Edge analytics enable organizations to extract valuable insights from data at the source, facilitating quicker and more informed decision-making without relying on round-trip communication to a distant cloud infrastructure.

Furthermore, the distributed nature of edge computing introduces a paradigm shift in how applications are deployed and managed. Edge devices, which range from IoT sensors to edge servers, become integral components of the computing ecosystem. This decentralized architecture enables the execution of applications directly at the edge, reducing the reliance on centralized cloud servers for every computational task. This distributed execution model has implications for process management as organizations need to adapt their strategies for deploying, monitoring, and updating applications across a geographically dispersed network of edge devices.

The proliferation of edge computing also reshapes the dynamics of network architectures, particularly in the context of edge-to-cloud integration. Hybrid architectures, combining edge and cloud resources, enable organizations to strike a balance between localized processing and the vast storage and computational capabilities offered by the cloud. Effective process management in such hybrid environments necessitates orchestration mechanisms that seamlessly coordinate tasks and data flows between edge devices and cloud services. This orchestration extends beyond traditional cloud-native solutions, requiring adaptability to diverse edge environments with varying compute and storage capacities.

Security considerations are paramount in the era of edge computing, introducing new challenges and considerations for process management. Edge devices, often deployed in uncontrolled or physically exposed environments, pose unique security risks. Securing the edge involves implementing robust authentication, encryption, and access control mechanisms to protect both data in transit and at rest. Process management strategies need to incorporate security measures that address the specific vulnerabilities associated with distributed edge environments, where physical security, device integrity, and network security become critical components of a comprehensive security posture.

In addition to security, the sheer diversity of edge devices presents challenges in terms of standardization and interoperability. Edge computing environments may encompass a wide array of devices with varying architectures, operating systems, and communication protocols. Effective process management in such heterogeneous environments requires standardized approaches for application development, deployment, and monitoring. The development of open standards and industry-wide collaborations becomes essential to foster a cohesive ecosystem where edge devices from different vendors can seamlessly interoperate.

The advent of edge computing is particularly transformative in industries where real-time decision-making is mission-critical. In healthcare, for example, edge computing facilitates the processing of patient data at the point of care, enabling quicker diagnostics, personalized treatment plans, and timely interventions. Edge-enabled medical devices and wearables collect and process health data in real-time, providing healthcare professionals with actionable insights without the need for centralized data processing. Process management in healthcare must adapt to this distributed model, ensuring that data privacy, security, and compliance standards are maintained while harnessing the benefits of edge computing for improved patient outcomes.

Similarly, in manufacturing and industrial automation, edge computing revolutionizes process management by bringing intelligence directly to the factory floor. Edge devices embedded in machinery and sensors enable real-time monitoring, predictive maintenance, and adaptive control of manufacturing processes. This localized decision-making capability enhances operational efficiency, reduces downtime, and optimizes resource utilization. Process management strategies in industrial settings must evolve to incorporate edge-based analytics, predictive algorithms, and adaptive control mechanisms, orchestrating a seamless integration between edge devices and central control systems.

The rise of edge computing also has profound implications for the Internet of Things (IoT), where the sheer volume of connected devices generates massive amounts of data. Edge computing alleviates the burden on centralized cloud servers by enabling on-device processing and filtering of IoT data at the edge. This not only conserves bandwidth but also enables more efficient use of cloud resources for higher-level analytics and decision-making. Process management in IoT scenarios involves handling the complexity of managing diverse edge devices, ensuring data integrity, and implementing scalable solutions for aggregating and analyzing data at both the edge and cloud levels.

While edge computing offers numerous advantages, it introduces complexities in managing the lifecycle of edge devices, particularly in remote or inaccessible locations. Edge devices may have limited processing power, storage, and connectivity, making traditional methods of device management challenging. Effective process management involves implementing decentralized device management solutions that can handle tasks such as software updates, configuration changes, and monitoring at the edge. Over-the-air updates, containerization, and edge-native management platforms become crucial components in ensuring the reliability and security of edge devices.

Edge computing's impact on process management extends to the domain of content delivery and streaming services. Content delivery networks (CDNs) leverage edge computing to cache and deliver content closer to end-users, reducing latency and enhancing the user experience. This decentralized content delivery model requires sophisticated process management strategies to dynamically allocate and distribute content across edge servers based on user demand, network conditions, and content popularity. Intelligent load balancing, content prefetching, and adaptive streaming algorithms become essential for optimizing content delivery in edge computing environments.

In the context of smart cities, edge computing emerges as a key enabler for managing diverse urban processes efficiently. Edge devices deployed throughout the city, including sensors, cameras, and intelligent infrastructure, contribute to real-time data collection and analysis. Edge computing facilitates localized decision-making for tasks such as traffic management, environmental monitoring, and public safety. Process management in smart cities involves orchestrating the interplay between edge devices, central command centers, and cloud services to ensure the seamless functioning of various urban processes.

The rise of edge computing introduces a new dimension to the evolving landscape of artificial intelligence (AI) and machine learning (ML). Edge-based AI and ML models enable localized inference, allowing devices to make intelligent decisions without relying on continuous connectivity to central cloud servers. This is particularly valuable in applications such as autonomous vehicles, drones, and robotics, where real-time decision-making is imperative. Process management in edge-driven AI involves deploying, updating, and monitoring machine learning models at the edge, considering factors such as model size, accuracy, and resource constraints.

In conclusion, the rise of edge computing signifies a paradigm shift with profound implications for process management across diverse industries. The move towards decentralized, edge-centric computing models transforms how data is processed, applications are deployed, and workflows are optimized. From healthcare to manufacturing, IoT to smart cities, edge computing introduces new opportunities for real-time decision-making, improved efficiency, and enhanced user experiences. However, this transformation also brings forth challenges related to security, standardization, device management, and interoperability. Effective process management in the era of edge computing requires adaptive strategies that embrace the distributed nature of computing, ensuring a seamless integration of edge and cloud resources to meet the demands of an increasingly connected and data-driven world.

The integration of human-centric design principles in process management.

The integration of human-centric design principles in process management represents a pivotal shift in the way organizations approach the development, optimization, and execution of processes. Rooted in the philosophy of placing human needs, behaviors, and experiences at the forefront of design, human-centric design seeks to create processes that are not only efficient and functional but also intuitive, meaningful, and aligned with the diverse needs of end-users. At its essence, this approach recognizes that the success of any process is intrinsically tied to how well it caters to the human element—considering user behaviors, preferences, and the overall user experience throughout the entire lifecycle of a process.

A fundamental aspect of human-centric design in process management is empathy, emphasizing a deep understanding of the people who interact with and are impacted by a process. By immersing designers, engineers, and stakeholders in the perspective of end-users, organizations gain valuable insights into their needs, pain points, and aspirations. This empathic understanding serves as the foundation for crafting processes that not only fulfill functional requirements but also resonate with the human aspects of the user experience. In essence, the process becomes a vehicle for enhancing the quality of human interactions, whether they involve employees, customers, or other stakeholders.

Human-centric design places a premium on user engagement, recognizing that processes are most effective when they actively involve and empower users. In process management, this translates into fostering collaboration, providing clear communication channels, and allowing users to contribute to the design and improvement of processes. Collaborative design workshops, user feedback sessions, and iterative prototyping become integral components of the process management lifecycle, ensuring that the final processes are not just imposed on users but co-created with them. This collaborative approach not only enhances the usability of processes but also cultivates a sense of ownership and engagement among users.

Usability and accessibility are core tenets of human-centric design, ensuring that processes are designed with a diverse user base in mind. This includes considerations for individuals with varying levels of expertise, physical abilities, and cultural backgrounds. Human-centric process management strives to eliminate barriers and friction points in the user journey, making processes accessible to everyone. This involves designing intuitive user interfaces, providing clear instructions, and accommodating different learning styles. Accessibility features, such as screen readers and language localization, are integrated seamlessly into processes to ensure inclusivity and equal access to information and services.

The iterative nature of human-centric design aligns well with the dynamic nature of process management. Continuous feedback loops, prototyping, and user testing are woven into the fabric of the design and optimization process. This iterative approach allows organizations to respond to changing user needs, technological advancements, and evolving business requirements. It also enables the identification and correction of issues early in the design phase, reducing the likelihood of costly rework and ensuring that the final processes are finely tuned to meet the ever-changing demands of the user landscape.

Embracing human-centric design principles in process management extends beyond the digital realm to encompass the physical and environmental aspects of the user experience. In manufacturing, for example, the design of production processes considers the ergonomics of workstations, the safety of operators, and the overall well-being of the workforce. Human-centric process management recognizes that the physical environment plays a crucial role in shaping user experiences and, consequently, the efficiency and effectiveness of processes. Ergonomic design, safety protocols, and attention to the overall work environment contribute to creating processes that not only drive operational excellence but also prioritize the health and satisfaction of those involved in the process.

The application of human-centric design principles in process management is particularly evident in customer-centric organizations, where the end-user experience is a central focus. Customer journey mapping, a key tool in human-centric design, becomes an essential practice in understanding and optimizing processes from the customer's perspective. It involves charting the entire customer interaction lifecycle, identifying touchpoints, pain points, and opportunities for improvement. This comprehensive view allows organizations to align processes with customer expectations, deliver personalized experiences, and foster long-term customer loyalty. Human-centric process management in customer-centric environments is a strategic imperative for organizations aiming to differentiate themselves through superior customer experiences.

The role of human-centric design extends to employee-centric processes, recognizing that the internal user experience is equally critical for organizational success. Employee journey mapping, analogous to customer journey mapping, becomes a tool for understanding the various touchpoints and interactions employees have with organizational processes. This includes onboarding processes, training modules, performance reviews, and day-to-day workflows. By applying human-centric principles to employee-centric processes, organizations can enhance employee satisfaction, productivity, and overall well-being, contributing to a positive workplace culture.

The integration of human-centric design principles also addresses the psychological and emotional aspects of the user experience. Emotional design, a concept within human-centric design, recognizes that user experiences evoke emotions that influence perceptions and behavior. In process management, this involves designing processes that not only meet functional needs but also evoke positive emotional responses. Whether it's the delight of a well-designed user interface, the satisfaction of a streamlined workflow, or the reassurance of clear communication during a complex process, emotions play a crucial role in shaping user perceptions and fostering a positive relationship with the process.

Human-centric design principles underscore the importance of transparency and ethical considerations in process management. Organizations are increasingly mindful of the ethical implications of their processes, particularly in areas such as data privacy, security, and algorithmic decision-making. Human-centric design ensures that processes are designed with transparency in mind, providing clear explanations of how data is used, ensuring informed consent, and avoiding hidden complexities that may erode user trust. Ethical considerations are woven into the fabric of the design process, aligning processes with societal values and regulatory requirements.

The integration of human-centric design principles in process management also involves a reevaluation of metrics for success. While traditional metrics such as efficiency and cost-effectiveness remain important, human-centric metrics gain prominence. Metrics related to user satisfaction, engagement, and overall experience become key indicators of the success of a process. Organizations adopting human-centric process management measure success not only in terms of operational excellence but also in the positive impact processes have on the lives and experiences of users, both internal and external.

In conclusion, the integration of human-centric design principles in process management represents a paradigm shift that places the human experience at the heart of organizational processes. It acknowledges that processes, whether they involve customers, employees, or other stakeholders, are fundamentally human interactions that should be designed with empathy, usability, and inclusivity in mind. By prioritizing user needs, fostering collaboration, and continuously iterating based on user feedback, human-centric process management not only enhances operational efficiency but also creates meaningful, engaging, and sustainable processes that contribute to the overall well-being and satisfaction of those interacting with them. This approach is not just a design philosophy; it is a strategic imperative for organizations seeking to thrive in an era where user experiences are central to competitive differentiation and organizational success.

Strategies for developing eco-friendly operating systems.

Developing eco-friendly operating systems is a multifaceted endeavor that encompasses a range of strategies aimed at minimizing environmental impact, reducing energy consumption, and promoting sustainability throughout the entire lifecycle of computing systems. At the core of eco-friendly operating system development lies the optimization of energy efficiency, acknowledging the significant role that computing infrastructure plays in global energy consumption. One fundamental strategy involves the implementation of advanced power management features at both the hardware and software levels. Operating systems can leverage techniques such as dynamic voltage and frequency scaling (DVFS), intelligent CPU scheduling, and device power management to dynamically adjust power states and optimize energy consumption based on workload demands. By efficiently managing the power states of processors, memory, and peripherals, eco-friendly operating systems contribute to substantial energy savings, particularly in scenarios where devices operate at varying levels of activity.

Furthermore, the integration of energy-aware algorithms and policies within the operating system kernel is pivotal for achieving a fine-grained and responsive approach to power management. These algorithms may incorporate predictive models, heuristics, and machine learning techniques to analyze historical usage patterns and dynamically adjust power management strategies. By understanding workload characteristics and adapting to changing conditions, eco-friendly operating systems can optimize energy consumption in real-time, aligning system performance with actual demand and minimizing unnecessary power consumption during periods of low activity. This proactive approach to energy management is essential for creating operating systems that not only prioritize performance but also demonstrate a commitment to environmental sustainability.

A key aspect of eco-friendly operating systems involves addressing the challenges posed by energy-intensive components, such as graphics processing units (GPUs) and data storage devices. Advanced graphics rendering techniques, when combined with energy-efficient GPU architectures, contribute to reduced power consumption during graphical tasks. Moreover, the integration of storage management policies, such as intelligent caching and selective data retrieval, minimizes energy usage in storage devices. Eco-friendly operating systems prioritize efficient data access patterns, minimizing unnecessary data movements and access operations, which not only conserves energy but also enhances overall system performance.

In addition to optimizing energy efficiency, eco-friendly operating systems focus on the responsible use of resources, including materials used in the production of hardware components. The concept of circular computing becomes crucial, emphasizing the need for operating systems that support the recycling and repurposing of electronic devices. Eco-friendly operating systems can facilitate the identification and separation of recyclable materials in electronic devices, contributing to more sustainable manufacturing and reducing electronic waste. Moreover, these operating systems can implement features that encourage users to extend the lifespan of their devices through software updates, security patches, and support for older hardware, thus reducing the frequency of hardware replacements and the associated environmental impact.

The eco-friendly approach extends beyond individual devices to embrace the principles of cloud computing and data centers. Operating systems play a vital role in optimizing resource utilization in cloud environments, ensuring that virtualized instances are dynamically scaled based on demand to prevent overprovisioning and reduce idle resource consumption. Moreover, eco-friendly operating systems can support workload migration and consolidation techniques, enabling data centers to operate at higher levels of efficiency by consolidating workloads onto fewer servers during periods of lower demand. These strategies contribute not only to energy savings but also to the overall sustainability of cloud computing infrastructure.

Eco-friendly operating systems also emphasize the importance of sustainable software development practices. Optimizing code for performance and efficiency not only enhances the user experience but also reduces the computational resources required to execute applications. The use of programming languages that prioritize efficiency and resource utilization, combined with effective code profiling and optimization tools, contributes to the development of eco-friendly software ecosystems. Additionally, eco-friendly operating systems can encourage the adoption of energy-efficient programming paradigms, such as event-driven architectures and asynchronous processing, which minimize unnecessary computational overhead and contribute to a more sustainable computing environment.

Addressing the environmental impact of electronic waste (e-waste) is a critical aspect of eco-friendly operating system development. Operating systems can incorporate features that promote responsible end-of-life management for electronic devices. This includes support for secure data erasure, facilitating the safe disposal and recycling of devices. Furthermore, eco-friendly operating systems can implement mechanisms for the efficient retrieval and reuse of electronic components, promoting a circular economy by extending the lifecycle of hardware components. Collaborative efforts between operating system developers, hardware manufacturers, and recycling facilities are essential to establish standardized processes for e-waste management and ensure that electronic devices are recycled responsibly.

The adoption of virtualization and containerization technologies is integral to eco-friendly operating systems, enabling the efficient use of hardware resources and reducing the need for physical infrastructure. Virtualization allows multiple virtual machines (VMs) to run on a single physical server, optimizing resource utilization and reducing the overall number of servers required. Containerization further streamlines resource usage by encapsulating applications and their dependencies into lightweight, portable containers. Eco-friendly operating systems support these virtualization and containerization technologies, fostering the creation of energy-efficient and scalable computing environments that align with sustainability goals.

Eco-friendly operating systems actively contribute to the reduction of electronic waste by promoting the reuse and repurposing of hardware. The adoption of modular hardware designs, where individual components can be easily replaced or upgraded, aligns with the principles of eco-friendly computing. Operating systems can support modular architectures by providing driver support for a wide range of hardware components and ensuring compatibility with interchangeable parts. Additionally, eco-friendly operating systems can facilitate the identification and utilization of reusable hardware components, extending the lifespan of electronic devices and minimizing the environmental impact associated with frequent hardware replacements.

Collaboration with hardware manufacturers and industry stakeholders is essential for the success of eco-friendly operating systems.

Operating system developers can work closely with hardware vendors to ensure seamless integration of energy-efficient features, such as hardware power management and optimized device drivers. By establishing industry standards for eco-friendly hardware design and compatibility, operating systems can play a pivotal role in driving the adoption of sustainable computing practices across the technology ecosystem. Joint initiatives can also focus on designing electronic components with extended lifespans, reducing the need for frequent hardware upgrades and aligning with the principles of eco-friendly computing.

The development of eco-friendly operating systems encompasses a commitment to open standards and interoperability. By adhering to open-source principles, operating systems encourage collaboration and knowledge sharing among developers, fostering the creation of energy-efficient software solutions. Open standards facilitate the integration of eco-friendly features across different platforms and hardware architectures, promoting a more inclusive and sustainable computing ecosystem. Operating systems that prioritize open standards also empower users to make informed choices about hardware and software, enabling them to select devices and applications that align with eco-friendly principles.

The integration of renewable energy sources into the operation of computing systems is a key strategy for eco-friendly operating systems. Operating systems can incorporate features that enable the seamless integration of renewable energy technologies, such as solar and wind power, into the overall energy infrastructure. This involves optimizing power management policies to align with the availability of renewable energy sources, allowing computing systems to prioritize the use of clean energy when it is most abundant. Additionally, eco-friendly operating systems can support the development of smart grids and energy storage solutions, enabling efficient energy distribution and consumption in line with sustainability goals.

Eco-friendly operating systems contribute to the reduction of electronic waste by promoting the use of refurbished and recycled hardware. Operating systems can support compatibility with a wide range of hardware configurations, making it easier for users to repurpose older devices and extend their lifespan. Moreover, eco-friendly operating systems can facilitate the identification and utilization of reusable hardware components, promoting a circular economy by minimizing the environmental impact associated with the disposal of electronic devices. Collaboration with recycling initiatives and refurbishment programs further strengthens the commitment to sustainable computing practices, ensuring that electronic devices are managed responsibly throughout their lifecycle.

In conclusion, the development of eco-friendly operating systems involves a holistic and collaborative approach to sustainability, encompassing strategies that optimize energy efficiency, reduce electronic waste, and promote responsible resource management. From power management and hardware compatibility to software design and end-of-life considerations, eco-friendly operating systems play a pivotal role in shaping the future of sustainable computing. By embracing renewable energy, supporting modular hardware designs, and fostering open standards, these operating systems contribute to a more environmentally conscious technology ecosystem. As a catalyst for change, eco-friendly operating systems set the stage for a future where computing aligns seamlessly with ecological responsibility, paving the way for a more sustainable and resilient digital landscape.

Encouraging readers to stay informed and adapt to the evolving landscape of computing.

Encouraging readers to stay informed and adapt to the evolving landscape of computing is not merely a suggestion but a fundamental necessity in our dynamic and rapidly changing technological era. The computing landscape is marked by constant innovation, breakthroughs, and paradigm shifts that shape the way we live, work, and interact with the world. Staying informed about these changes is not just about keeping pace with the latest gadgets or software updates; it is about cultivating a proactive mindset that enables individuals to harness the full potential of technology while navigating its challenges. This encouragement extends beyond passive consumption of information to an active engagement with the transformative forces at play in computing, fostering a mindset of continuous learning and adaptability that is crucial for personal and professional growth.

In the ever-evolving realm of computing, staying informed begins with a keen awareness of emerging technologies and their potential impact on various aspects of life. From artificial intelligence and machine learning to blockchain, quantum computing, and beyond, understanding the fundamental principles and applications of these technologies empowers individuals to make informed decisions and participate meaningfully in the digital age. The onus is on readers to delve into the intricacies of these technologies, not just at a surface level but with a depth of understanding that enables them to critically evaluate their implications for society, privacy, and ethics.

The importance of staying informed also extends to the evolving landscape of cybersecurity, where threats are becoming more sophisticated, and the need for robust defenses is paramount. Readers must cultivate a foundational understanding of cybersecurity principles, ranging from basic practices like strong password management to more advanced concepts such as encryption, network security, and threat intelligence. In an interconnected world where data breaches and cyberattacks are prevalent, being well-informed about cybersecurity measures is not just a matter of personal safety but a societal responsibility. This knowledge empowers individuals to protect their digital identities, contribute to a more secure online environment, and adapt to the evolving tactics employed by cyber adversaries.

Adaptability is a cornerstone of success in the computing landscape, and readers are encouraged to embrace a growth mindset that values continuous learning and skill development. The pace of technological change demands a proactive approach to acquiring new skills and staying relevant in the job market. Whether it's learning a new programming language, mastering cloud computing platforms, or acquiring proficiency in data analytics, individuals who prioritize ongoing education position themselves for success in a competitive and rapidly changing job market. The encouragement to adapt is not confined to technical skills alone; it extends to cultivating soft skills such as critical thinking, problem-solving, and effective communication, which are essential in navigating the complexities of the modern workplace.

Part of staying informed and adaptive involves actively engaging with the broader tech community. Readers are encouraged to participate in industry conferences, webinars, and meetups where they can interact with experts, share insights, and stay abreast of the latest developments. Networking within the tech community not only provides exposure to diverse perspectives but also opens doors to collaborative opportunities, mentorship, and the exchange of ideas. Actively seeking out and participating in such communities fosters a sense of belonging, encourages the cross-pollination of knowledge, and contributes to the collective growth of the tech ecosystem.

Moreover, readers are urged to explore interdisciplinary connections between computing and other domains, recognizing that the impact of technology transcends traditional boundaries. The intersection of technology with fields like healthcare, finance, education, and sustainability presents exciting opportunities for innovation. Staying informed about these interdisciplinary connections allows individuals to contribute meaningfully to solving real-world challenges and encourages a holistic understanding of the societal implications of technological advancements. Whether it's exploring the role of artificial intelligence in healthcare or leveraging blockchain for sustainable practices, the encouragement is to think beyond siloed perspectives and embrace the interdisciplinary nature of modern computing.

In the age of information, readers are encouraged to be discerning consumers of content, distinguishing between reliable sources and misinformation. Developing digital literacy skills is essential for critically evaluating information, fact-checking, and understanding the biases that may be inherent in online content. With the proliferation of fake news, deepfakes, and misinformation campaigns, individuals must cultivate a sense of media literacy to navigate the digital landscape responsibly. By staying informed about media manipulation techniques and actively seeking diverse perspectives, readers can contribute to a more informed and resilient society.

The encouragement to stay informed is not limited to individual efforts but extends to advocating for digital literacy in broader educational contexts. As technology becomes increasingly intertwined with education, there is a collective responsibility to ensure that students are equipped with the skills to navigate the digital world responsibly. This involves integrating digital literacy into educational curricula, fostering critical thinking skills, and promoting ethical considerations in the use of technology. By actively supporting initiatives that prioritize digital literacy in education, readers contribute to the empowerment of future generations in navigating the evolving landscape of computing.

The evolving computing landscape also brings ethical considerations to the forefront, requiring individuals to reflect on the societal impact of technology. Readers are encouraged to engage in ethical discussions surrounding topics such as data privacy, algorithmic bias, and the ethical implications of artificial intelligence. This involves staying informed about emerging ethical frameworks, participating in conversations about responsible technology use, and advocating for policies that prioritize ethical considerations in the development and deployment of technologies. By actively engaging in ethical discussions, readers contribute to shaping a tech landscape that aligns with values of fairness, accountability, and inclusivity.

Furthermore, the encouragement to stay informed involves an awareness of the environmental impact of technology and the need for sustainable computing practices. Readers are urged to consider the ecological footprint of their digital activities, from the energy consumption of data centers to the lifecycle of electronic devices. Exploring eco-friendly computing practices, supporting initiatives for sustainable technology development, and advocating for responsible e-waste management are crucial components of staying informed about the environmental implications of computing. By incorporating sustainability considerations into their technological choices, readers play a role in promoting a more environmentally conscious computing landscape.

In conclusion, the encouragement for readers to stay informed and adapt to the evolving landscape of computing is a call to action that goes beyond individual benefits to encompass societal well-being. It involves developing a multifaceted understanding of emerging technologies, cultivating adaptability in the face of change, actively participating in tech communities, and engaging with ethical and environmental considerations. In a world where the impact of technology extends into every aspect of our lives, staying informed is not just a choice but a responsibility—one that empowers individuals to navigate the complexities of the digital age with resilience, critical thinking, and a commitment to positive societal impact.